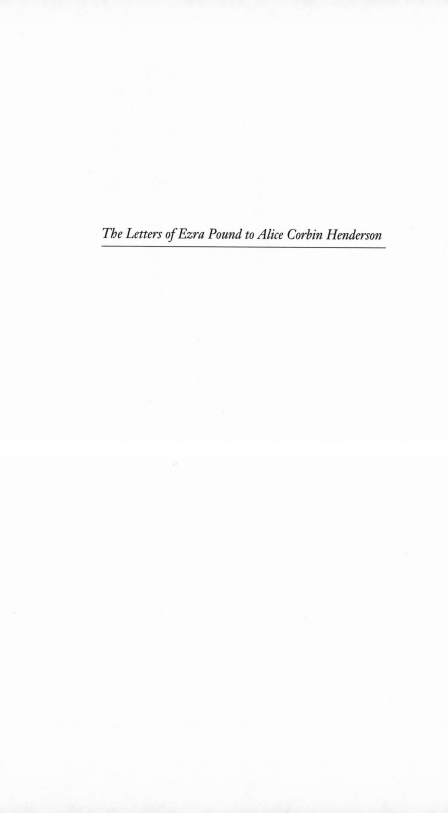

The Letters of Ezra Pound to Alice Corbin Henderson

Yaas 'm'
Dank you —
can't read names of
yr witnesses but
wd be glad know
who are
_____
Sarasate ? which
gd' son or wdT.
ef you'd print 'em
like yr address.
Hally daze yr 2 EZ

11 Ap '49
ezra pound
S. Liz
D.C.

J'AYME DONC JE SUIS

Letter from Ezra Pound to Alice Corbin Henderson, 11 April 1949 (Letter 78).

The Letters of
EZRA POUND
to Alice Corbin Henderson

Edited by Ira B. Nadel

*Published in cooperation with the
Harry Ransom Humanities Research Center,
University of Texas at Austin*

 University of Texas Press, Austin

First edition, 1993

⊗ The paper used in this publication meets the minimum requirements
of American National Standard for Information Sciences—Permanence
of Paper for Printed Library Materials, ANSI Z39.48-1984.

Library of Congress Cataloging-in-Publication Data

Pound, Ezra, 1885–1972.
    [Correspondence. Selections]
    The letters of Ezra Pound to Alice Corbin Henderson / edited by
Ira B. Nadel. — 1st ed.
        p.   cm.
    Comprises 69 letters from Pound to Henderson and 9 from
Henderson to Pound, written between 1912 and 1949.
    "Published in cooperation with the Harry Ransom Humanities
Research Center, University of Texas at Austin."
    Includes bibliographical references and index.
    ISBN 0-292-71134-4 (alk. paper)
    1. Pound, Ezra, 1885–1972—Correspondence. 2. Henderson,
Alice Corbin, 1881–1949—Correspondence. 3. Poets, American—
20th century—Correspondence. 4. Editors—United States—
Correspondence. I. Henderson, Alice Corbin, 1881–1949. II.
Nadel, Ira Bruce. III. Title.
    PS3531.O82Z4873   1993
    811'.52—dc20
    [B]   93-9162

For Pamela

Contents

Abbreviations

EP/DS	*Ezra Pound and Dorothy Shakespear: Their Letters, 1909-1914*, ed. Omar Pound and A. Walton Litz. New York: New Directions, 1984.
EP/JQ	*The Selected Letters of Ezra Pound to John Quinn*, ed. Timothy Materer. Durham, NC: Duke University Press, 1991.
EP/LR	*Pound/The Little Review*, ed. Thomas L. Scott, et al. New York: New Directions, 1988.
EP/MC	*Ezra Pound and Margaret Cravens: A Tragic Friendship, 1910-1912*, ed. Omar Pound and Robert Spoo. Durham, NC : Duke University Press, 1988.
EP/WL	*Pound/Lewis: The Letters of Ezra Pound and Wyndham Lewis*, ed. Timothy Materer. New York: New Directions, 1985.
G	Donald Gallup. *Ezra Pound: A Bibliography*. Charlottesville: University Press of Virginia, 1983.
LE	Ezra Pound.*The Literary Essays of Ezra Pound*, ed. T. S. Eliot. New York: New Directions, 1968.
'Noh'	———. *'Noh' or Accomplishment*. London: Macmillan, 1916.
P	———. *Personae: The Shorter Poems*, revised edition, ed. Lea Baechler & A. Walton Litz. New York: New Directions, 1990.
SL	———. *Selected Letters of Ezra Pound, 1907-1941*, ed. D. D. Paige. 1950. New York: New Directions, 1971.
SR	———. *The Spirit of Romance*. 1910. New York: New Directions, 1968.

Acknowledgments

This edition could not have been possible without the assistance of many, beginning with Cathy Henderson, Research Librarian at the Harry Ransom Humanities Research Center, The University of Texas at Austin. Her enthusiasm and knowledge of the Alice Corbin Henderson Collection has made work on these letters as pleasurable as it has been stimulating. Thomas F. Staley, Director of the Harry Ransom Humanities Research Center, has not only made research there efficient and productive but through his support and friendship has provided the catalyst for the completion of this volume. Similarly, Ralph Franklin and the staff at the Beinecke, especially Patricia Willis, were also helpful in satisfying an impatient visitor's requests, while curators at the Harriet Monroe Poetry Collection of the Regenstein Library at the University of Chicago and at the Lilly Library of Indiana University supplied important information and assistance.

A legion of "Poundians" has provided direction, encouragement, and help. Hugh Kenner was an early supporter of the edition, while A. Walton Litz has been a continual source of guidance and direction. Terry Terrell allowed me the opportunity to present my earliest ideas on the value of the Pound/Henderson correspondence at a 1990 Yeats/Pound conference and, subsequently, in print. Tim Redman has been a constant companion down Poundian corridors, while Lawrence Rainey and Ron Bush shared with me their wide knowledge of Pound's cultural and textual sources. Donald Gallup has remained a reliable and generous source of Poundian bibliographic details, and his bibliography has been a persistent and welcomed sourcebook for much of my work. Mary de Rachewiltz has encouraged this project as she has so many other recent efforts in Pound scholarship, while Richard Taylor has been a remarkable source of textual and other details. Charles Bolding, my research assistant, not only remained in good spirits in the face of various delays and detours but contributed much important information that advanced the completion of the edition. Frankie Westbrook has been both a patient and practical editor, while Robin Bradford, Randolph Lewis, Will Goodwin, and David Oliphant—all at the Ransom Center—provided various assistance with the production of the book. My colleague W. E. Fredeman once again located important information when it was most needed, while my children Ryan and Dara became able students of Pound through their excursion to Brunnenburg, encounter with the crow, and constant queries as to the progress of these letters.

Thanks are due to the following libraries for permission to use materials in their possession: the Harry Ransom Humanities Research Center at The University of Texas at Austin; the Beinecke Rare Book and Manuscript Library, Yale University; the Lilly Library, Indiana University; and Special Collections, Regenstein Library, University of Chicago.

I would finally like to thank the Ezra Pound Literary Property Trust for permission to quote from the unpublished letters of Ezra Pound and the estate of Alice Henderson Colquitt for permission to quote from the letters of Alice Corbin Henderson. In addition, thanks are due to *Paideuma* for allowing me to include portions of an essay dealing with the collection published in Volume 20 (1991): 187-192, and to the estate of Harriet Monroe for permission to quote from several of her letters. Finally, I wish to acknowledge the valuable support from the University of British Columbia's Social Science and Humanities Research Council committee which enhanced the completion of the edition.

Introduction

Ezra Pound corresponded with Alice Corbin Henderson, Associate Editor of *Poetry*, from the start of his alliance with the magazine. Harriet Monroe's preoccupation with finances, editorial policy, and contributors prevented her from nurturing the volatile American expatriate; Alice Corbin Henderson, however, quickly sensed that Pound was an important link to the new poetry and tolerated his often outrageous demands while welcoming his literary candor. In Pound she also found someone who shared her own thoughtfulness about writing and intolerance of sentiment and cant. Furthermore, she saw beyond the shores of the United States and realized that for *Poetry* to flourish it must include the most recent and important writing from England and Europe. A question Pound asked of Harriet Monroe expresses his response to this enthusiasm: "besides yourself and Mrs. Henderson, whom do you know who takes the Art of poetry seriously?" (*SL* 15).

Others who dealt with Alice Corbin Henderson equally admired her critical acumen, energetic mind, and challenging perceptiveness. Wallace Stevens, Carl Sandburg, Yeats, and, after she moved to Santa Fe, Witter Bynner and D. H. Lawrence, all found in her a keen sensitivity to literary matters which did not sacrifice standards in the process of encouraging the new. When she left Chicago for New Mexico with her artist husband and daughter in March 1916 because of tuberculosis, *Poetry* seemed to have lost its edge, and Pound felt her absence. In 1917 he wrote to Harriet Monroe: "Since Alice went to New Mexico I have been wholly, or almost wholly cut off" from *Poetry* (*SL* 111); that same year he complained to John Quinn that besides his

father and William Carlos Williams, there is "no one else whom
I can trust to buy a two cent postage stamp (Save Alice
Henderson, stuck in a consumptive hospital in New Mexico)"
(*EP/JQ* 118).

Ten years later from Rapallo, at the end of a lengthy letter,
Pound again asked Monroe, "what has become of A.C.H.?" (*SL*
206). And in the midst of a December 1931 letter, he interrupted
a paragraph with this thought: "I spose Alice is still vigorously
tubercular?" (*SL* 238). After years of not writing, Alice Corbin
Henderson spontaneously contacted Pound at St. Elizabeths
when Witter Bynner reported on a recent visit. Candidly, she
wrote, "I have always cherished our real friendship—this is just a
little gesture of our continuing affection—in spite of the hub-
bub" (Letter 77, 24 August 1948). And after her death in July
1949, Carl Sandburg wrote an elegy expressing his attachment to
her through the images of her adopted Southwest and its culture.[1]

Although she never achieved the reputation of her contemporaries, Alice Corbin Henderson, whom Harriet Monroe in her
autobiography ungenerously referred to as "blond and little," and
"ruthless," played a critical role in the evolution of *Poetry*—
contributing eighty-five reviews of such works as Pound's *Des
Imagistes* anthology, Masters' *Spoon River Anthology*, and Joyce's
Chamber Music, plus a score of editorials on subjects ranging
from the nature of *vers libre* to the value of European movements
and the originality of Yeats' *At the Hawk's Well*.[2] In addition,
Henderson promoted a series of writers including Sandburg (it
was she who had his *Chicago Poems* published by Holt), Masters,
and Pound, who at one point encouraged her to make an anthology of *his* work for publication (Letter 49). To Witter Bynner,
Pound confided that "Alice [Corbin Henderson] was [the] only
intelligent element (in that frying pan) 1911-12 or whenever—
only means of getting an idea into dear ole 'Arriet's hickory
block. In short Alice my only comfort during that struggle." To
John Quinn he revealed that she "will always buy my books but I
dont believe she can afford it."[3] Henderson's view of Pound was
equally sympathetic and direct. Recognizing their shared impa-
tience with sentiment and idealization, she stated to him in May
1916 that "I think *we* can be frank with one another without

being disloyal" (Letter 50). The letters in this collection confirm
her view.

Alice Corbin Henderson (1881-1949) was a poet, editor,
anthologist, and publisher. As poet, she authored two well-
received books: *The Spinning Woman of the Sky: Poems* (1912) and
Red Earth: Poems of New Mexico (1920). English, French, and
Italian anthologies soon reprinted her work and André Spire
translated a group of her poems for *Le Monde Nouveau*. Pound
included her poetry in *Catholic Anthology, 1914-1915* (1915) and
Profile (1932). As editor, she maintained a high level of modern
American and European verse in *Poetry* during her years as
Associate Editor, 1912-1922, with her most active involvement
between 1912-1916. In Chicago, she mingled with Tagore,
Yeats, and other literary visitors. When she resigned in October
1922, a resignation which coincided with the tenth anniversary of
Poetry, she printed a two-page statement in the magazine noting
that she originally thought residence in New Mexico would be
temporary but that she became "as firmly rooted as a pinyon
tree." She also recorded her admiration for the "tenacity and zeal
and high purpose" of Harriet Monroe and the success of *Poetry*
in creating a greater public appreciation of poetry. An imper-
sonal editorial note by Harriet Monroe, recognizing
Henderson's contribution and devotion, supplements the
statement.[4]

Henderson, however, did discover a number of important
writers for *Poetry* including Carl Sandburg, Sherwood Anderson,
and Edgar Lee Masters. Her relationship with Sandburg was
especially valuable and he proved to be a strong ally who supported her editorial focus and celebrated her poetry. "Coiled
inside the graphite of my pencil . . . is a disquisition on your
poetry and your personal urge for the brief and poignant," he
told her in December 1915. He also proudly acknowledged her
discovery of his *Chicago Poems*, as well as her choice of its title
and publisher. In March 1916 he began to write to Henderson in
Santa Fe, providing news and knowledge of the Chicago literary
scene, while recommending new works and sharing his praise for
Pound. Reiterating his desire to promote her work, Sandburg in
a 1920 letter told her that "sometimes I think how in the
afterworld you and Wallace Stevens, writing better poetry than

the mass of the listed, printing and performing poetry, will have your laugh."[5] On three occasions Sandburg visited Alice Corbin Henderson in New Mexico.

Another admirer of Henderson was the Arkansas-born expatriate poet and imagist, celebrated for a time by Pound, John Gould Fletcher. Recalling an early meeting with Henderson in Chicago, Fletcher writes that she, like himself, was

> a southerner, with all the easy-going individualism that is so natural to the southerner, and with none of the angularity which was manifest in such notable middle-westerners as Miss Monroe and Masters. . . . [W]ithout her influence Miss Monroe's paper might have been, I felt, narrower in its scope and less epoch-making in its effect.

Her influence on *Poetry*, Fletcher concludes, was "decisive."[6]

As anthologist, Henderson edited a distinguished collection of Southwest poetry, *The Turquoise Trail* (1928), having earlier assisted Harriet Monroe with *The New Poetry* (1917), a book of critical as well as commercial success. Widely reviewed, *The Turquoise Trail* did no less than establish New Mexico "as a physical and cultural entity, through the responses of the poets who lived there" according to James Rorty in *The Nation*.[7] In addition to such residents as Mary Austin, Yvor Winters, Witter Bynner, and Arthur Ficke, visitors like D. H. Lawrence, Willa Cather, Edgar Lee Masters, Alfred Kreymborg, and Sandburg were included. As a publisher, she founded Writers Editions, Ltd., a specialized publishing house in Santa Fe which concentrated on limited editions of promising and established writers. This both cultivated and confirmed the importance of Southwestern writers, providing them with a vehicle for their distinctive native and regional writing.

Born in 1881 in St. Louis, Missouri, Alice Corbin grew up in Virginia and Chicago and attended the University of Chicago. She met and in 1905 married William Penhallow Henderson (1877-1943), a painter, architect, and designer. The birth of a daughter, Alice Olive, in 1907 did not interrupt her writing or

travelling, and in 1910-1911 she visited Europe where she met
Margaret Cravens at Bidart and learned of Pound firsthand,
although she was already familiar with his work.[8] In August 1912,
Harriet Monroe visited Henderson at her studio-home in the
Chicago suburb of Lake Bluff, having earlier been introduced to
her. A month later Henderson joined Monroe in setting up
Poetry: A Magazine of Verse, where she began as Associate Editor,
remaining active in that post until illness forced her to move to
Santa Fe, New Mexico, in the spring of 1916. Nevertheless,
Henderson continued to contribute reviews and essays to *Poetry*
up to 1933, although she resigned as Associate Editor in 1922.

Alice Corbin Henderson's first year in Santa Fe was difficult.
Bed-ridden with tuberculosis, she was constantly watched by the
staff at Sunmount sanatorium. But Witter Bynner, hospitalized
with influenza in the same sanatorium, later reported that as her
health improved, coffee, cigarettes, and one or two glasses of
"Taos Lightning," local corn whiskey, would be consumed in her
room over convivial exchanges on poetry and Southwest art.[9]
This talent for organizing a circle of artists and writers continued
when Henderson moved to her adobe home on Camino del
Monte Sol on the *loma* south of town which soon became a
popular residential area for Santa Fe artists. Her study/studio
built behind the house in a sloping field just before the moun-
tains became a weekly meeting place for poetry readings, discussions, and the exchange of ideas between Henderson, Bynner,
Spud Johnson, Lynn Riggs, and Haniel Long.

Henderson and her husband, nicknamed "Whippy," became
keen supporters of New Mexican art and history, helping to
organize the Spanish Colonial Arts Fund and participating in the
New Mexico Association on Indian Affairs. William Penhallow
Henderson designed the Museum for Navajo Ceremonial Arts,
while Alice Corbin Henderson, who had been studying Indian
folklore and translating verse from Spanish, composed texts for
the legends expressed in Navajo sand paintings. It was
Henderson who suggested the famous "Poets' Round Up" as a
popular yearly fund-raiser in Santa Fe for the New Mexico
Association of Indian Affairs. This poetry reading in the form of
a rodeo with the poets as horses, charging out of pens and

declaiming their verse, drew many visitors. Henderson undertook the selection of writers, the shape of the program, and the
elimination of confusion.

Not surprisingly, Henderson became the center of a group
of Santa Fe writers and artists that included Mary Austin, Witter
Bynner, Haniel Long, Willard Nash, Arthur Ficke, and Yvor
Winters. When D. H. Lawrence visited Santa Fe in the fall of
1922, Henderson became his part-time assistant, at one point
acting as his typist. In December 1922, her daughter married the
son of Mabel Dodge Luhan (John Evans) with Witter Bynner as
the best man. Other Santa Fe visitors with whom Henderson had
contact include the composer Ernest Bloch, who came to work
on his American Symphony, and Willa Cather who was checking
material for *Death Comes for the Archbishop*. At the age of sixty-
eight, Henderson was celebrated as one of the two earliest
interpreters of "New Mexico life in American Literature" (the
other was Mary Austin) and honored with a special section
devoted to her work in a 1949 issue of the *New Mexico Quarterly
Review*.[10]

Pound admired Henderson's poetry and independent critical
judgment. He found her poetry incisive and direct, unlike the
work of the many "Chicago poets" who appeared in *Poetry*.
Experimenting with meter and quantity while employing the
techniques of *vers libre*, Henderson's writing was proof to Pound
that an American poet could incorporate an international
aesthetic, although he did not hesitate to offer criticism: "not
quite right yet" he pencilled next to a box he drew around the
three concluding lines of her poem "Four O'Clock" in a January
1917 letter to her (Letter 61). The lines read

> Space — volume — silence —
> Nothing but life on the desert,
> Intense life.

Henderson, however, chose not to change these lines when she
printed the poem in *The Red Earth: Poems of New Mexico* (1920).

Henderson's independent critical judgment, valued by
Pound, found expression in her many editorials and reviews. Her

critique of John Masefield in "The Daffodil Fields: John Masefield," *Poetry* II (May 1913): 76, contradicted the usual praise of the popular poet, while her remarks on editors and poets displays a self criticism that may have had special resonance for Pound: "All the poet in me hates the editor. The editor in me swears that I am a very bad poet; the poet knows the editor is a fool. And neither one is entirely wrong!" (*Poetry* VIII [September 1916]: 308). Her essay "Don'ts for Critics" in the *Little Review* 3 (1916): 12-14, echoing Pound's "A Few Don'ts by an Imagist," exhibits the confident critical intelligence Pound appreciated. In 1917 Pound wrote to Margaret Anderson of the *Little Review*, "I think . . . [Henderson's] criticism has been the best American criticism in *Poetry*" (*EP/LR* 100). Not surprisingly, Pound sent Henderson copies of his latest work and her library, now at the Harry Ransom Humanities Research Center, contains a presentation copy of *Cathay*, plus one of his *Canzoni* inscribed to her by Margaret Cravens. Other Pound volumes in her collection include *Exultations, Provença, Lustra, Quia Pauper Amavi, Instigations*, and *Poems, 1918-1921*.

Once in Santa Fe, Henderson turned to Indian myths and folklore, her subject matter altering her form to more conventional narrative supported by intense, natural imagery. Her belief that "the folk-spirit is a necessary sub-soil for any fine national flowering" supported her concentration on American Indian culture and explained her fascination with this life in her poetry from 1915, when she introduced Marion F. Washburn's *Indian Legends*, until her death.[11] Her "New Mexico Folk-Songs" (*Poetry* XVI [August 1920]: 254-263) confirmed her commitment to Southwest art, also indirectly incorporating Pound's influences. Analyzing the importance of the folk traditions, she wrote: "as Ernest Fenollosa has pointed out, it has never been sufficiently realized how much the alien is at the root of the national" ("Folk Poetry," 268). Reviewing *The Red Earth: Poems of New Mexico* in *Poetry* XVIII (June 1921), Carl Sandburg explained that Henderson's poetry is as "clean and aloof as the high deliberate table-lands where it was written" (157). Her last book, entitled *Brothers of Light: The Penitentes of the Southwest* (1937) and illustrated by her husband, narrates the Holy Week rites of a secret lay order derived from the Franciscans in a New Mexican village; the account includes an actual crucifixion. During the last sixteen years of her life, however, she published no poetry.

The present collection comprises 78 letters, 69 from Pound to Henderson and 9 from Henderson to Pound. All of the Pound letters are from the Harry Ransom Humanities Research Center; seven of the Henderson letters are from the Beinecke Rare Book and Manuscript Library at Yale, and the two remaining are from the Lilly Library at Indiana University and the HRHRC. Three additional published letters from Pound to Henderson can be found in D. D. Paige's 1950 edition of *Selected Letters of Ezra Pound* (*SL* Nos. 12, 25, and 121), while a published letter from Henderson to Pound appears in *Ezra Pound and Margaret Cravens* (1988).

The correspondence in this collection begins in 1912 and ends in 1949, although 88 percent of the letters are dated between December 1912 and February 1918, coinciding with a crucial period in Pound's career: the establishment of Imagism, his association with the sculptor Henri Gaudier-Brzeska, his absorption with the work of Orientalist Ernest Fenollosa, his residence with W. B. Yeats at Stone Cottage, his early conception of *The Cantos*, and his constant effort to publish and support Eliot, Lewis, and Joyce. The later correspondence, dating from 1921, 1922, 1931, 1933, 1934, 1939, 1948, and 1949, comments on Rapallo, the formation of the *Active Anthology*, a concert by Olga Rudge, and the possibility of Pound and Henderson meeting one day, although this would not occur.

One fascinating set of documents in the letters consists of a twenty-page section of poems returned by Pound to Henderson after he corrected, revised, and analyzed them. Contained in a letter dated 23 January 1917 (Letter 61), the poems illustrate Pound as editor, although he adds this *caveat*: "I have chalked up this lot considerable, and perhaps too hastily." Bluntly, he tells her the Provençal-styled "Song," beginning with the stanza "I know you beautiful and fair / Beyond delight, / I know our bodies bare / In love unite, / Yet weep for passion's flight" is "the best," although on the typescript of the poem he writes "keep this / good / despite inversions." "Old Houses" also receives

Pound's measured approval, although penciled on the typescript is the criticism "too long / too many prose phrases." He also commends a poem entitled "Here in the Desert," possibly because Henderson concludes with a favorite Poundian image, Venice:

> Here in the desert,
>   under the cottonwoods
> That keep up a monotonous
>   wind-murmur of leaves,
>
> I can hear the water dripping
>   through the canals in Venice
> From the oar of the gondola
> Hugging the old palaces,
> Beautiful old houses
> Sinking quietly into decay. . . .

Pound's marginal note is a bold "O.K."

Other manuscript comments by Pound refer to matters of cadence, diction, and sound. Of the poem "Four O'Clock," he remarks at the end of the two-page typescript, "something in it," but then asks "can you make it more compact[?]" As a final comment, he scrawls diagonally across the bottom of the page "I think Eliot in *Blast* did almost the same thing as part of this with more grip and tenseness," referring to Eliot's "Preludes I-IV" and "Rhapsody of a Windy Night," *BLAST* 2 (July 1915): 48-51. Forthright and direct, Pound's criticisms are, nevertheless, received sceptically by Henderson, who responds with "Some I accept at once, and I'll ponder the others. I'm not *sure* but you chop your cadence off too short at times ??? for the full value of a mood and sound too ????" (Letter 63). Three of Henderson's poems, with Pound's comments, are reproduced in full with Letter 61.

In the letter containing the corrected typescripts, Pound remarks that a week or ten days earlier he had sent to Henderson in Santa Fe "the three cantos" which "are my virtuous deeds. I am paying the rent with the translation of a libretto. Strange are the uses" (Letter 61). His decision to send "Three Cantos" to

Henderson, rather than Monroe, confirms his affinity with her critical sensibility and appreciation of his efforts in writing a long poem. In one of the few extant replies to Pound by Henderson, dated 17 February 1917, she offers what is likely one of the earliest written responses to the "ur-Cantos." Appropriately, it begins with an eleven-line poem summarizing the text followed by a paragraph of criticism concluding with "You've explored worlds beyond worlds, and it's a pleasure to follow you. *Bueno, Bueno!*" (Letter 63). Her note to Harriet Monroe when she forwarded the poem to Chicago accompanies the letter; two unpublished letters from Harriet Monroe, in response, register the unsympathetic reading of the editor. The first contains this unintentionally comic opening: "I read two or three pages of Ezra's Cantos and then took sick—no doubt that was the cause. Since then I haven't had brains enough to tackle it. . . ." (Letter 63, note 2).

Pound's reaction to Henderson's praise of "Three Cantos," dated 3 March 1917, acknowledges her "metric outburst" but complains that "it seems very difficult to get any CRITICISM." Eliot, he reports, "said it was worth doing and after standing over him with a club I got some very valuable objections to various details." But in anticipation of later textual cruxes in *The Cantos*, Pound adds "I can't remember whether I've included the emendations in the mss. I sent you. Don't delay publication in trying to find out, the changes were all very minute and dont matter for a first publication." But he stresses that he cannot produce cantos like a machine: "The form of the bloody whole has got to begin to commence to inchoho sometime or other. Also there is a great deal to be left out" (Letter 64).

Other discoveries also exist in this collection of letters, perhaps the most important the publication for the first time of a Noh play, "Takasago," translated by Ernest Fenollosa and edited by Pound. This is an important find because in his earliest correspondence with Monroe concerning the plan of "Three Cantos," Pound cites this work as an essential prototype of his long poem. In an undated letter, he tells her that his theme for *The Cantos* is "roughly the theme of 'Takasago,' which story I hope to incorporate more explicitly in a later part of the poem."

Pound also refers to the play on pages 11 and 45-46 of *'Noh' or Accomplishment* (1916) but until now one of the most crucial Noh dramas for Pound has remained unavailable.[12]

"Takasago," by the Japanese dramatist Motokiyo, was among the manuscripts translated by Ernest Fenollosa which Pound edited and sent with two other works—"Genjo" by Kongo and "Chorio" by Nobumitsu—in a letter to Henderson postmarked 7 July 1915 (Letter 41). The latter two works were published in *'Noh' or Accomplishment*, but the more important "Takasago" was not, nor was it published in any periodical, having apparently been mislaid among the papers sent to Henderson in Chicago which she was to forward to the journal *Drama* if *Poetry* could not use it. (A number of Noh dramas, part of Pound's "The Classical Stage of Japan," were published in the May 1915 issue.) However, none of the three plays sent to Henderson appeared until Macmillan published *'Noh' or Accomplishment* in January 1917 (the two that did were presumably included because Pound had copies; he evidently did not keep one of "Takasago").

According to Pound, "Takasago" "might be called the very core of the 'Noh'" because of its "flawless structure." It is considered "*Shin no issei*" or "the Most Correct," and other Noh plays are "held to vary from it as from a norm." Its form is the "*Shugen*," works used at the beginning or end of a full Noh program, and this "very ending on the opening note is a sort of symbol of perpetuity," Pound adds. The value of "Takasago" is that it "expresses a sense of past time in the present" ("Introductory Note," "Takasago," Letter 41). In the "Introduction" to *'Noh' or Accomplishment*, Pound remarks that the pine tree—the central image of the play—is a "symbol of the unchanging" while he later notes that it is "a congratulatory symbol of unchanging green and strength" (*'Noh'* 19, 59).

Hugh Kenner recognized the importance of "Takasago" in *The Pound Era* when he explained that "Takasago" meant "twin pines, to whose spirits distance is no barrier; people metamorphosing into trees; trees emblematizing the proposition that all things speak, all things are poems, and the diligent quester may behold a tree become a dancing god" (Kenner 284). This Japanese version of the Baucis and Philemon myth expressed

what Yeats termed "the rhythm of metaphor," an organizing
principle for the early cantos (Yeats, "Introduction," *Certain
Noble Plays of Japan*).

Pound thought of using the Takasago story in a later Canto,
although a good deal of *Rock-Drill* is, to quote Kenner, a "hymn
to vegetal powers" (284). However, one allusion to the play exists
in *The Cantos*:

> The pine at Takasago
> grows with the pine of Isé!
> (Canto 4/15)

A gloss on the passage notes the reference to the Noh play
named after the legendary pine tree that grows on the shore of
Takasago Bay in Southern Honshu (Terrell 13). The play itself
dramatizes the love of an aging couple symbolized by two
separated pine trees, one at Takasago and the other at Sumiyoshi
in Settsu Province, although, as the playwright emphasizes,
"though the mountain and river lie between us, we are near in
the ways of love." This identity and union beyond space and time
emerges as a central theme in the early as well as late cantos. To
build *The Cantos* around the legend of the twin pines of Takasago
and Sumiyoshi, displaying a union between places and people
remote from each other, appealed to Pound as a structure as well
as a theme for the poem which is constantly uniting unlike
cultures and figures which vary from China and America to
Jefferson and Mussolini.

Pound favored Motokiyo, including two additional works by
him in *'Noh' or Accomplishment*: "Nishikigi" and "Kagekiyo." But
"Takasago" was forgotten, despite its importance and unique-
ness, which he explained through ironic understatement to Alice
Corbin Henderson: it "is so full of poetry that Harriet might like
it" (Letter 41). Both Henderson and Pound overlooked it,
however, until it surfaced in their correspondence which had for
some seventy-two years resided silently in Santa Fe.[13]

Additional new material in this collection includes two short
poems and a poetic fragment by Pound, plus eleven satiric poems
on American poets by Henderson. Pound calls his two brief
poems in Letter 49 "impermanent petals," while the fragment in

Letter 11 offers a critique of American complacency.
Henderson's satires on American writers (Letter 60) display her
versatility, although they, too, have remained unpublished
largely because they were too frank for 1917. An additional new
item is a letter from Homer L. Pound to Henderson,
complimenting her for a poem about a bobcat that appeared in
Poetry for August 1917. The directness in the prose of the son is
evident in that of the father who wonders, when the magazine
begins for another year, "whether it will be short of one. *E.P.* or
is the 'Giantess' = willing to keep him on the staff = ?" And
reflecting what his son has no doubt emphasized, he adds "I
know that *E.P.* - thinks *A-C-H* = about his *fir*mest friend" (Letter
69, enclosure).

Pound and Henderson did not, however, always agree. She
often acted as *Poetry*'s diplomat, smoothing out difficulties
between Pound and Monroe, balancing her own desire for
aggressive and original poetry with Monroe's more conservative
and even restrictive sense of verse. Henderson was particularly
disturbed by Pound's acceptance of the post of Foreign Editor
for the *Little Review* and vented her anger to Monroe over his
shabby treatment of *Poetry*, although to Pound she more carefully presented her objections. Pound, in turn, offered *his*
complaints: the appearance of weak and often minor poets in the
journal (although he realized this was largely insisted upon by
Harriet Monroe); the selection of his work printed in *The New
Poetry* anthology, work he would have rather left forgotten; and
what he calls "the most serious critical error you have made . . .
not liking Joyce." "You did lose your head over that ass [John]
Masefield," he tells her, "but this is worse, being a negation"
(Letter 67).

Throughout the correspondence, Pound's prose is vigorous
and precise. He begins a letter of 29 March 1915 (Letter 35) with
the declaration that "rest for the iracible is limited to a
minimim"; on 5 May 1916 (Letter 48) he tells Henderson that
"the plain damn unvarnished fact is that Harriet is a fool. A
noble, sincere, long strugglin impeccable fool. [But] that is
infinitely better than being Amy-just-selling-the-goods. . . ." At
the end of a particularly lengthy letter, he comically concludes
with "*There*. I guess I've been as disagreeable as I've got time to

be" (Letter 2). But while discussing such crucial subjects as the suicide of Margaret Cravens, the death of Gaudier-Brzeska, the inadequacies of *Poetry*, or the development of Yeats' style, Pound writes with unflagging intensity and strength. Not only do the letters register the formulation of his most important work, but they define the nature of his evolving relation with American and European writers as he tested and created his own form of prose expression.

The value of these letters is clear. Those concerned with Pound's career will find his accounts of the 1912-1917 period essential; those with an interest in *Poetry* will find his ideas for and relationship with the journal surprising; and those with an interest in the emergence of Pound's modernism will find the letters absorbing. They also underscore the importance of Alice Corbin Henderson as an American critic promoting an international style and a catalytic agent who discovered in Pound a vibrant imagination eager for her news and at times guidance (one could never provide direction for Pound). Whether it was trying to place his "Essay on the Chinese Written Character" or preparing a selection of his poems, Alice Corbin Henderson remained an important ingredient in the formation and publication of Pound's work in America, providing a sympathetic eye but always a resiliant voice.

A coda to their closeness is a poignant statement concerning Henderson's illness written by Pound on 24 April 1917. Harriet, he writes,

> says you are reported to be better. I hope it is so,
> and that we can both be in Paris in the spring. Some
> spring or other, one need not specify which. Or
> perhaps I shall be dragged back to New Mexico to
> drill. as a conscript.

Some twenty-eight years later Pound *was* dragged back, not to New Mexico but to Washington. Fittingly, the final letter in the Pound-Henderson correspondence is from St. Elizabeths dated 11 April 1949, three months before Henderson died. In it Pound thanks her for sending a copy of a festschrift honoring her life and work, ending with the ironic phrase "Happy Daze / Yrz / EZ."

1. Sandburg's twelve-line poem, "Alice Corbin is Gone," appeared in *Poetry* XCV (January 1960): 201. Although apparently written shortly after her death on 18 July 1949, the poem was not published until it appeared in *Poetry* to coincide with its printing in Sandburg's *Wind Song* (New York: Harcourt Brace, 1960), 30.

2. Harriet Monroe, *A Poet's Life* (New York: Macmillan, 1938), 323-324. Monroe appears to have had an ambivalent relationship with Henderson, welcoming her sharp mind and help when the magazine began in 1912 but growing restless with her as she supported Pound and the experimentalists from Europe and America at the expense of the younger and more regionally focused American poets Monroe grew to favor. However, Monroe recalled that "during those first years Alice Corbin was not only a well-nigh indispensible member of *Poetry*'s staff, but also one of the gayest and most brilliant slingers of repartee in the groups which soon began to gather in the *Poetry* office" (319). At first "a fine poet and intelligent critic," Henderson later became something of a thorn in Monroe's side through her constant criticism of the journal, offered in the spirit of improving its contents (284). Indeed, a later disagreement over copyright and royalties regarding republication of *The New Poetry* anthology they edited in 1917 led to further alienation between the two. Nevertheless, Henderson was the "first reader" of the material submitted to *Poetry* and, writes Monroe, "I could trust her to detect the keen note, the original style" (286).

3. EP to Witter Bynner in *The Works of Witter Bynner: Prose Pieces*, ed. James Kraft (New York: Farrar Straus Giroux, 1979), 137; *EP/JQ* 108.

4. Alice Corbin Henderson, "A Word from Mrs. Henderson," *Poetry* XXI (October 1922): 55-56. Monroe's note appears on p. 56.

5. Carl Sandburg, *The Letters of Carl Sandburg*, ed. Herbert Mitgang (New York: Harcourt, Brace & World, 1968), 177. Other references are to pages 104, 114, 123, 124.

6. John Gould Fletcher, *The Autobiography of John Gould Fletcher*, ed. Lucas Carpenter, introd. by Ben Kimpel (Fayetteville, AR: University of Arkansas Press, 1988), 197; originally published as *Life is My Song* in 1937.

7. James Rorty, "Southwestern Poetry," *The Nation* 127 (26 September 1928): 298.

8. Margaret Cravens (1881-1912), the American music student from Indiana in Paris to study with Ravel, admired Pound and provided him with financial assistance. Cravens visited ACH and her family who were vacationing in Bidart, France in 1911. From Cravens, ACH learned firsthand details of EP who was invited to visit but declined (*EP/MC* 132-133).

9. Witter Bynner, "Alice and I," *New Mexico Quarterly Review* 19 (1949): 37.

10. John Gould Fletcher, "Alice Corbin and Imagism," ibid., 49. For the full account of her work and life see "Alice Corbin: An Appreciation," ed. Witter Bynner and Oliver La Farge, ibid., 33-79. Also see Letter 78, note 1.

11. Alice Corbin Henderson, "The Folk Poetry of These States," *Poetry* XVI (August 1920): 269. The essay is one of the earliest and important analyses of American Indian Poetry and its place in the American literary canon.

12. Cited in Myles Slatin, "A History of Pound's Cantos I-XVI, 1915-1925," *American Literature* XXXV (1963/1964): 186.

Among EP/Fenollosa papers recently acquired by Princeton University is a 7-page ribbon typescript of "Takasago" heavily corrected in pencil by EP. The copy in the EP/ACH correspondence contains no corrections and only minor insertions. See Earl L. Miner, "Pound and Fenollosa Papers Relating to No," *Princeton University Library Chronicle* LII (Autumn 1991): 12-17. For a clear statement of the value of Noh drama and its use of an image as the source of its dramatic structure, see the formerly unpublished essay by Pound, "Affirmations VI: The 'Image' and the Japanese Classical Stage," ibid., 17-22.

As an aside, the title of Pound's study of Noh derives from Frank Brinkley's *Japan: Its History, Arts and Literature* (Boston: J. B. Millet Co., 1901), read by Pound during his stay at Stone Cottage in December 1913 and shortly after he received the Fenollosa manuscripts from Fenollosa's widow. In his book, Brinkley translates "Noh" as "accomplishment."

13. The Pound-Henderson correspondence did not come to light until 1987 when it was acquired by the Harry Ransom Humanities Research Center. Between 1949 and 1987 it had remained in Santa Fe. Few of ACH's letters to EP survive, however, probably because EP mislaid them during his various moves at this early stage of his career.

The absence of information concerning the relationship of Pound to Henderson has meant little commentary on or critical study of their association. See, however, T. M. Pearce's brief monograph, *Alice Corbin Henderson* (Austin: Steck-Vaughn, 1969); Ellen Williams, *Harriet Monroe and the Poetry Renaissance* (Urbana: University of Illinois Press, 1977), passim; and, more recently, Shari and Bernard Benstock, "The Role of Little Magazines in the Emergence of Modernism," *The Library Chronicle of The University of Texas at Austin* 20, no. 4 (1991): 72-75, 79.

Editorial Note

The following editorial procedures and devices have been employed. All transcriptions have been collated against the originals, which, for the most part, are typescripts, although Alice Corbin Henderson's letters are largely in manuscript. All letters are reproduced in their entirety and are part of the Alice Corbin Henderson collection at the Harry Ransom Humanities Research Center, The University of Texas at Austin, unless otherwise noted. With the exception of one or two carbons (so indicated), all letters are originals.

Angled brackets < > indicate substantive manuscript insertions by either Pound or Henderson. Square brackets [ ] indicate an editorial insertion. When canceled material is relevant, it is transcribed and struck through. At the beginning of each letter are an identification number, description of the text, date, number of leaves, and, if warranted, textual comment and originating address. A number of enclosures accompany various letters and have been indicated in the headnotes. They also follow the body of the letter. Textual abbreviations in the volume include:

ALS   Autograph letter, signed
TLS   Typed letter, signed
TS   Typescript, unsigned
APC   Autograph postcard

Most letters have been dated by Pound or Henderson, but where a text is undated, I have provided a date, presented in brackets but with a question mark if doubtful; the date has usually been determined by postmark, internal evidence or other evidence. When misspellings have seemed trivial or were obvious typographical inversions, they have been corrected; however, when they seem intentional, significant, and characteristic of Pound, they have remained in the text. The titles of journals and books have been italicized for ease of identification and the spelling of proper names has been regularized.

Pound's punctuation at this period of his career had not yet become erratic, although it is frequently irregular. To convey the character of his prose, it is reproduced as it appears in his correspondence, although for clarity and ease of expression, I have silently added closing quotation marks and end stops as the context requires. However, when Pound corrected his punctuation, the original punctuation has not been recorded. Foreign expressions appear as Pound wrote them.

The Letters of Ezra Pound to Alice Corbin Henderson

Previously unpublished photograph of Ezra Pound, possibly taken in a Paris garden in 1912, sent to Alice Corbin Henderson by Margaret Cravens with a copy of Pound's Canzoni. *See Letter 2.*

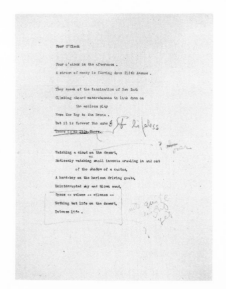

Two-page typescript of Alice Corbin Henderson's poem "Four O'Clock" with Pound's corrections. See Letter 61.

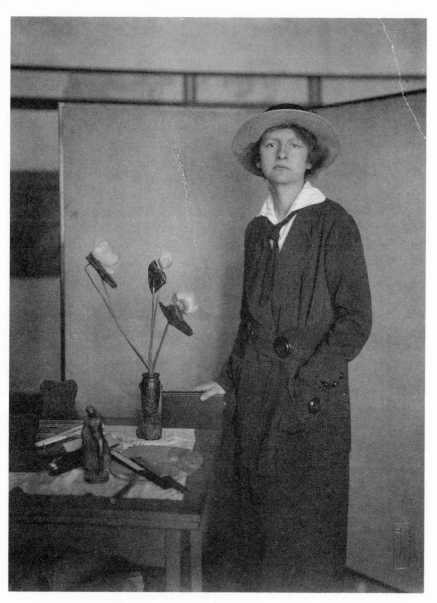

Alice Corbin Henderson, n.d., unidentified photographer (E.B.).

Dear A.C.H.

Rest for the iracible is limited to a minimim .
Having got my anthology on the way , or out of the way

or off my mind , there remain at least two more campaigns
for Poetry or the Dial . A. will either you or Lucian
Cary get me a copy of the present law for the tariff
on books imported into America. B. a list of the members
of the American Academy of Art and Letters , and of the
~~peeeee~~ lesser or rather more numerous penumbra of associates
or the Institute , or whatever its called .
. The first law is iniquitous and forms the excuse for
a lot of swindling and a restriction on the circulation
of contemporary and even modern books , especially of the
non-commercial sort . etc. vide my attack not yet written .

The second affair , is with dead wood , but that
rag bag Current Opinion has taken on my letter in the Dial
and your editorial , etc. And perhaps I can issue some
sort challenge that will even move part of that dead skunk
the Am. Acad . It ought to be made to get up or get
under . Also it should take the part of literature against
the old magazines . At present it is only a lot of
rusting and idle machinery .

So long as the campaigns are set under way I dont
care who does it , but I may as well have an oar in ,
I can be a shade more insulting than any one else who
is likely to take on the job . If Poetry , The Dial and
the Mirror can all be started , we may be able to get
something done .

I shan t vent my indignation here , but will save
it for my articles . You might get a copy of the Am.
Copyright law also , though I care less about that . Merely
I dont want to make misstatements . A la guerre .

Poetry is by now a public institution & there are
jobs for it to take on .

yours ever

Ezra Pound

Letter from Pound to Henderson, 29 March 1915 (Letter 35).

Alice Corbin Henderson, 1915.

Cover of Pound's Catholic Anthology, 1914–1915 *(1915),*
designed by Dorothy Shakespeare.

Alice Corbin Henderson, 1917.

VOL. X   NO. IV

Poetry
A Magazine of Verse

Edited by Harriet Monroe

JULY 1917

543 CASS STREET, CHICAGO

$1.50 PER YEAR   SINGLE NUMBERS, 15 CENTS

Published monthly by Ralph Fletcher Seymour, 1025 Fine Arts Building, Chicago
Entered as second-class matter at Postoffice, Chicago

Cover of Poetry X *(July 1917) listing contributions by Alice Corbin (Henderson) and William Carlos Williams as well as the second of Pound's "Three Cantos."*

Alice Corbin Henderson, Santa Fe, NM, n.d.

Alice Corbin Henderson in New Mexico, n.d. Photograph by Albert Fenn.

I

EP to ACH   TLS n.d. [Fall 1912?] 2 ll.

10 Church Walk, Kensington W.

My Dear Lady, you take me all a travers.
I dont advocate subsidizing mediocre sculptors.
BUT.

I have divers pictures on my wall here many of which I suspect of being inferior to Durer, whose originals I am unlikely ever to possess. These pictures cheer an otherwise not over beautiful apartment.[1] They do not waste my eyesight. They do not keep me away from the National Gallery. There are bits of colour which rest my eyes from the London greyness.

Now a volume of mediocre verse does none of these things. <It isn't even an improvement on faded wall paper.> There is no time when I can not get the best poetry.

Let us say if you like. "There are places (e.g. 10 Church Walk. etc) where minor painting is reasonably free from the competition of the great masters. There is no corner where the mediocre poet <need be> free from the competition of the greatest."
<E.P.>

[on verso:]
<No! I never said it was easier to paint than to write. jamais.>

---

1. Pound moved into his small, bed-sitting room at the front of the top floor of 10 Church Walk, Kensington, W. London, in August 1909 and lived there until he departed for America in June 1910. He returned to his flat in November 1911, remaining until the end of February 1914 when he left for larger quarters at 5, Holland Place Chambers because of his impending marriage to Dorothy Shakespear. The "divers paintings" on his walls were watercolors by William Henry Hunt (1790-1864) on loan to Pound from Violet Hunt, the artist's daughter and an early friend of Pound's. She was also the mistress of Ford Madox Ford.

2

10 Church Walk
Kensington
London. W.

Dear Mrs. Henderson:

There is no use my trying to answer the first part of your letter. She went like the god in a mystery.[1]

A nos moutons.

No, for heaven's sake make your own exchanges direct with the English periodicals.

I pray daily that the edtr & owners of the Eng. Rev. die of the pip. viendra.[2]

The Edtr. of the Poet. Rev. is an imbecele. I never meant that the 25 copies should be sent to me. Of course I can "put 'em about".[3]

10 will be enough I think. or 20 for Dec. if it has Tagore. H.D. & Yeats.[4] The only two exchanges I want sent to me here, are the "Mercure" and "L'Effort Libre." (more anon.)

So please send 'Poetry' direct to

1. Henry B. Davray. 25 rue Servandorie.

Paris.

(I've sent that address once.)

& to. =

2. *L'Effort Libre*. Poitiers. France

I suppressed the Oct. number. because I thought it would do more harm than good *here*—Tho' thats between ourselves.

I'd have the *adv.* dept. try. Dent.,—"Mathews",—"Lane"—, "Metheuen"—"Martin Secker, Adelphi",—"Fisher Unwin"—

"Oxford Press"—"Longmans", *etc.*
"Heineman".

Tagore is published by the India Society. I don't think there is any of the 1ˢᵗ edtn. left. and the swine haven't sent me mine yet. I'm doing the best I can for you in sending a set of mutilated proof-sheets by the same mail.

I don't quite understand what "Seymour" wants with the short story or how short? etc.—does he publish *one* short story in a booklet or ??

He'd better write to Frederic Manning, Edenham, Bourne Lincolnshire. Eng. and see if it would be possible to use one of the series of "Scenes & Portraits".[5]
I don't know how, the rights are arranged with 'Murray'.
In the mene time I'll look about.
? Does he want a *new* tale or does he want to reprint some contemporary thing that has a chance of living? I've got a damn rotten prose thing. neither fish nor feather, a walk in the troubadour country, with notes on the troubadour lives. etc —awful hash. "Herzreise" with Heine left out. sort of muddle.[6] I dont know that it would do him any good to print it, even if he were fool enough to want to do so. ? What can the estimable gentleman pay? Prose has a commercial value, increasing according to its worseness.
"Poor Mathews." he can't afford it, i.e. standard of excellence, one should judge him by the very few books which he prints at his own expense.

Your phrase on N.Y. "sophistication without knowledge" hits the mark.

I must send you my scheme for a "college of the arts". I'll have it printed in the *N.A.* sometime or other.[7]
N<ew> A<ge> is deplorable in some ways. but it has its points. Its about the only place where the convictions of the writers are *not* for sale.

We agree about Yeats. only we disagree as to the sense of the word *negative*. It is perhaps ill chosen.
Still he has purged out faults he has taught the few intelligent writers what *not* to do.

He now sees that his *manner* is played out and he is himself setting about to get rid of it. That is clumsily said but it would be a mornings work to get the precice expression.

His work has been to cut away, and cut away, and cut away from the bosh and blurr of English sloppiness.

Now: a word about Imagism.
I seem to do nothing but object. I refrained from defining Imagism, because I think it bad for a school to put out a lot of formulae before there is any large body of work whereon to apply them.
The note in *Poetry* is very incorrect.[8]
Imagism is concerned solely with *language and presentation*.

Hellenism & vers libre have nothing to do with it. It is not a matter of subject. The imagiste is as much at liberty to admire Villon as Sappho.

One might say that Sappho, Villon & Gautier were our parents.—There is Imagism in all the *best* poetry of the past. <This does not include Milton who is perdù.>

For the moment we owe more to the *metres* of the melic poets than to France.[9]
=

But the poor word "Hellenist" is so frightfully at a discount that one hates to see a new school damned with it.

Pleasant note from Henri de Regnier two days ago. Says he will be glad to collaborate and will let me know as soon as he has anything ready.[10]
Miss Widdemer is about the best America has done for the November *no.* & Mrs. Van Rensselaer about the worst.[11]
And the change in my review 2 words or perhaps it was only 1, and the other my own oversight, is very distressing.[12] Don't bother Miss Monroe with it, she is probably rushed to death.

Miss Widdemer has mettle. The few faults are only matters of minutae. The "Long" person is infected with the unutterably silly note of American magazitis. vid. J. P. Peabody when she isn't doing childrens song. E. W. Wilcox, et *cie.*[13]
There. I guess I've been as disagreeable as I've got time to be.

I was very glad to get your letter. I'll go on answering it as I get time. — And perhaps you too will keep on writing. I hope so.
                    Yours
                    Ezra Pound

1. EP appears to be writing in answer to ACH's letter to him of 6 November 1912 printed in *EP/MC* 132-133.

Margaret Cravens had committed suicide in Paris in June 1912. In her 6 November 1912 letter, ACH describes "the flame-like enthusiasm of Margaret Cravens" who was "delighted that I knew your first book and liked it" (*EP/MC* 132). Although ACH knew Cravens for only two months, she admired the American pianist and her literary taste. ACH's letter concludes with this paragraph:

> I haven't told you yet that I like your poems. I don't need to. I think Margaret Cravens must have. I am waiting for Ripostes which I ordered as soon as I saw it announced in your Guido. Margaret Cravens gave me your Canzoni, with a little kodak picture of the author . . . (*EP/MC* 133).

The photograph of Pound is reproduced elsewhere in this volume.

2. In 1908 Joseph Conrad, Edward Garnett, and Ford Madox Ford founded the *English Review*, sponsored by the wealthy industrialist Sir Alfred Mond. The first issue included work by Conrad, Hardy, James, Wells, W. H. Hudson, Tolstoy (a translation of "The Raid") and Galsworthy. Later contributors included Yeats, D. H. Lawrence, Lewis, Forster, Moore, and Pound. Ford edited the journal the first year; Austin Harrison became editor in 1912. "Mond killed the English Review / and Ford went to Paris (an interval)," EP wrote in Canto 104/758. Douglas Goldring, Ford's sub-editor on the review, has left the memoir *South Lodge: Reminiscences of Violet Hunt, Ford Madox Ford and the English Review* (1943). See Letter 7, note 4.

3. Harold Monro (1879-1932), poet, anthologist, publisher, and founding editor of *The Poetry Review* from January to December 1912 (succeeded by Stephen Phillips), published from his Poetry Bookshop in Bloomsbury, a center for poets and writers.

4. *Poetry* I (December 1912) contained work by Yeats, Alice Corbin, and Rabindranath Tagore in addition to EP's essay "Tagore's Poems." Three poems by H. D. appeared in the next issue of *Poetry* (January 1913) where Pound had her sign herself as "H. D., / 'Imagiste.'" (122).

5. *Scenes and Portraits* (1909) is a series of imaginary conversations by the Australian writer Frederic Manning (1882-1935) who emigrated to England with Rev. Arthur Galton in 1897; he met Pound in 1909 and remained a friend until his death in 1935. Praised by Beerbohm and E. M. Forster, *Scenes and Portraits* was an important volume for Pound, who placed it alongside *Dubliners, Portrait of the Artist as a Young Man,* and *Tarr* as one of the key texts of the early modern period (*LE* 14). In November 1909, Pound had visited Manning at the Lincolnshire home of Galton; that same month Pound sent a copy of Manning's "Korè" for publication in the *English Review*. After its appearance, EP published a poetic response: "Canzon: The Yearly Slain," *English Review* IV (January 1910): 193-194. EP later cited Manning, along with Bridges and Hewlett, as one of the few writers concerned with "overhauling the metric" (*LE* 12). EP reviewed

Manning's first book, *The Vigil of Brunhild* (1907) in the *Book News Monthly* XXVII (April 1909): 620-621. Manning introduced EP to Eva Fowler, and through them EP met Olivia Shakespear and her daughter Dorothy. Manning also introduced EP to Laurence Binyon and would be part of the 18 January 1914 entourage to Wilfrid Scawen Blunt, which included Yeats, Aldington, Flint, and EP.

6. "Gironde," EP's 1912 walking tour of France which deals with the troubadour poets; edited by Richard Sieburth and published for the first time by New Directions (New York, 1992) as *A Walking Tour in Southern France*. The manuscript was the source of EP's "Near Perigord," *Lustra* (1916). The reference is to Heine's poem "Die Harzreise." Pound included translations from Heine in *Canzoni* (London: Mathews, 1911). The seventh section, headed "Song from 'Die Harzreise'," was preceded by the following note:

TRANSLATOR to TRANSLATED

> O Harry Heine, curses be,
> I live too late to sup with thee!
> Who can demolish at such polished ease
> Philistia's pomp and Art's pomposities!

(41)

For EP's positive view of Heine see *SL* 67 and Letter 20, note 9.

7. EP's plan for a "College of Arts" appeared in the *New Age* XIII (29 May 1913): 115-116.

8. *Poetry* I (November 1912): 65 contains an editorial note on Richard Aldington which reads:

> Mr. Aldington is a young English poet, one of the "Imagistes," a group of ardent Hellenists who are pursuing interesting experiments in *vers libre*; trying to attain in English certain subtleties of cadence of the kind which Mallarmé and his followers have studied in French. Mr. Aldington has published little as yet, and nothing in America.

As a result of Pound's letter, an editorial footnote appeared attached to a subsequent article by F. S. Flint entitled "Imagisme," *Poetry* I (March 1913): 198. It reads:

> in response to many requests for information regarding *Imagism* and *Imagistes*, we publish this note by Mr. Flint, supplementing it with further exemplification by Mr. Pound. It will be seen from these that *Imagism* is not necessarily associated with Hellenic subjects, or with *vers libre* as a prescribed form.

9. Melic poetry is Ancient Greek lyric verse meant to be sung or danced to. In *How to Read* (1931) and *ABC of Reading* (1934), Pound explained melic poetry in detail. *Melopoeia*, he writes, is one of "three kinds of poetry . . . wherein the words are charged, over and above their plain meaning, with some musical property, which directs the bearing or trend of that meaning." See *How to Read* (London: Desmond Harmsworth, 1931), 25.

10. Henri de Régnier (1864-1936), French poet and novelist who employed elements of *vers libre* in his work.

11. Margaret Widdemer (1884-1978) was the wife of the poet Robert H. Schauffler. EP praised two of her poems which appeared in the second number of *Poetry* I (November 1912): 51-53. In 1918 she would share the Pulitzer Prize with Carl Sandburg for her book *The Old Road to Paradise*.

Mrs. Schulyer Van Rensselaer's three-page poem "Under Two Windows" appeared on pp. 44-46 of *Poetry* I (November 1912).

12. "Bohemian Poetry," *Poetry* I (November 1912): 57-59. The change EP refers to is not clear.

13. Lily A. Long who appeared in *Poetry* I (November 1912): 47-49; Josephine Preston Peabody (1874-1922), American poet (see Letter 7, note 8); Ella Wheeler Wilcox (1855-1919), author of the infamous lines "Laugh and the world laughs with you, / Weep and you weep alone" (see Letter 7, note 19).

3

10 Church Walk
Kensington
London. W.

Dear Mrs Henderson:

I have just written a violent epistle to Miss Monroe, on the sins of American poetasters. =

I entrust the negotiations to your care.—Do tell me when she gets really tired of tirades.

I don't suppose I can write to you about Margaret, at all. She wanted a beauty that is more than the beauty of this world and she went toward it. She left very wonderful letters.—saying that she affirmed this life even as she was going from it.

And now her people seem inclined to think her unbalanced—which is a very stupid point of view.

I began a longish letter to you a week ago, but can't find it.

The general scheme of it was, that I was interested in what you said of Chicago. and that what Chicago really needed was *me* in some chair or other at the University or the Art Institute.

See that you get some more things from Miss Widdemer.

And make her stop using the word "pulsed" all your rotten contributers "pulse" at least once to each page.

Also she must shake loose from "-ants" at least from some of 'em. "vibrant", "palpitant" rum forms those.
The verb "to voice =" also is in bad odour, on this side of the ditch.[1]

I wonder will Miss Monroe stand or welcome any more criticism of individual poems from yr. hmbl. svt.?

Vale.

E. Pound

Salute *il pittore* also with our most excellent salutating[2]

---

1. EP's reference to "pulsed" is to two lines in Margaret Widdemer's poem "The Jester," *Poetry* I (November 1912). The lines read, "Where white magnolia and tuberose hauntingly / Pulsed their regretful sweets along the air —" (51). His additional comments refer to "The Beggars" (52-53).

2. William Penhallow Henderson (1877-1943), artist husband of Alice Corbin whom she married in 1905. In 1913, the year Tagore won the Nobel Prize for Literature, Henderson painted his portrait; about that time he was also invited by Frank Lloyd Wright to contribute several murals to the Midway Gardens project in Chicago. Following the family move to Santa Fe in 1916 after ACH developed tuberculosis, he focused on the art and culture of the Southwest, especially architecture, restoring many buildings around the historic Sena Plaza and designing the Museum of Navajo Ceremonial Art which won a design award in 1938. A memoir of him by Ruth Laughlin, a Santa Fe journalist and historian, recalls a good-humored, tall figure in cowboy boots with "eyes twinkling under his big sombrero, small moustache widened in a grin." ("Santa Fe in the Twenties," *New Mexico Quarterly Review* 19 [1949]: 59). His work is in the Art Institute of Chicago and the Art Museum of New Mexico.

4

■■■■■■■ **EP to ACH**   TLS [December 1912/January 1913?] 2 ll.

10 Church Walk, Kensington W.

Dear A.C.H. :

Knew I'd forgotten something. Am sending the "Arnaut" along anyhow. I dont suppose Seymour will have the indecency to neglect the opportunity.[1] It is, after all, a land mark in the study of Provençal matters. and polyphonic rime is a thing so obvious and so obviously difficult, that *them as wot* can't hear it can at least see it when it's in print.

Beside[s] Arnaut *Was the best* troubadour and from him Dante learned a deal of his trade. And some of the canzoni are beautiful, and *mirabile dictu*. almost readable. even in my translation. Besides I am giving him very civil terms.

Enc. list of books recd. for "Poetry".

<Yours ever
E.P.>

Books Received.

Paris

Alexandre Mercereau, "Paroles devant le Vie" E. Figuière & Cie., 7, Rue Corneille.

          francs 3.50

Jean Metzinger "Alexandre Mercereau"

          Figuière, fr 1.

Florian-Parmentier "Anthologie-Critique" Gastein-Serge, 17 rue Fintaine, fr 4.

PERIODICALS

Mercure de France, 26 rue de Condé, (etranger 1fr 50)
L'Effort Libre, Galerie Vildrac, 11 rue de Seine
                     fifty centimes
Les Poètes, E. Basset, 3 rue Dante,
                     etranger fr 2.50
This number devoted to poems selected from *the* work of Nicolas
BEAUDUIN. "Paroxyste"
L'Ile Sonnante, 21 rue Rousselet, sixty centimes.

1. Pound began his translation and edition of the canzoni of Arnaut Daniel in Paris in February 1911, completing twelve of the fifteen cantos by May, although partial translations of four canzoni had appeared in his chapter on Arnaut Daniel in *The Spirit of Romance* (1910). By 13 October 1912 Pound could refer to "*The Canzoni of Arnaut Daniel* (now in publisher's hands)" (*SL* 11). Ralph Fletcher Seymour of Chicago had agreed to publish the manuscript, printing a Prospectus the next year; however, a lack of public interest in the project led to its cancellation. For details see Letter 7, note 17 and *G* E6a. For a copy of the Prospectus, see *EP/DS* 199.

Ralph Fletcher Seymour (1876-1966) was a Chicago artist, designer, and publisher who studied art in the Midwest and Europe. Beginning as a newspaper artist, he became a publisher in 1899, issuing and designing various fine editions and privately printed books. From 1907 to 1915 he taught at the Art Institute of Chicago where his etchings are in the permanent collections as well as those of the Sorbonne. In 1913 his publishing company became incorporated as Seymour, Daughaday and Company but the partnership dissolved by 1915. Nevertheless, he continued on his own, publishing, among other things, *Poetry* magazine. His autobiography entitled *Some Went This Way*, largely about Chicago artists and expatriates in France, appeared in 1945. In 1950 Seymour published Pound's *Patria Mia*, originally sent to him for publication in 1913.

5

EP to ACH   TS [January 1913?] 2 ll.

10 Church Walk.

Kensington, W

Dear A.C.H.

Its angelic of you to bother with my rotten old mssssss. Surely
PART of it is legible and part IS printed, and the furrin langwidge IS
in typing (very odd typing, but then).[1]

And NO *nice* people will ever be able to buy the edtn. de luxe,
and this printing of cheap books which you and I approve of, is the
ruin of both author and publisher, and c'est un metier du chien. And
if I ever see the mssss. OR proofs of this wretched opus <again> I shall
throw a foamish fit and "pass on".

Bless you my children. Seriously, only its too early in the day to be
serious over anything, besides I've been typing steadily for eight days.

Yes, I like the idea. Only we'll all be ruined and nobody will buy
the book except the sanctified Emil Levy of Freiburg to whom I have
promised a copy.[2]

This impounding of the poor guarantors is a quaint piratical idea,
still I don't see why they shouldn't give up a night at the opera for
Arnaut's funeral expenses.

Do send a wad of blanks to H.L. Pound, U.S. Mint Philadelphia.
<(not that he can afford jeweled bindings)>

Comfort the good Seymour. I'll try to send on the reproductions
of the music and there wont be any trouble about the printing, just
photograph blocks or whatever the usual stunt is.[3]

I've just written him within the week and there seems nothing
especial to answer in his last.

Yours ever

<E.P.>

1. EP's ms. of "The Canzoni of Arnaut Daniel." Presumably, the Provençal section was printed, the translation by EP a typescript. See Letter 4, note 1.

2. In the summer of 1911, EP visited the Provençal scholar Professor Emil Lévy (1855-1918) in Freiburg with transcriptions of Arnaut's notations made in Milan. See his Canto 20/89. Lévy compiled the eight-volume *Provençal supplement dictionnaire* (1892-1925).

3. Original music by Walter Morse Rommel (1887-1953) was to accompany "The Canzoni of Arnaut Daniel." See *EP/MC* 151-158 for a biographical note. EP recalls Rommel at the opening of Canto 80/507.

6

<16/1/13>
Church Walk, Kensington, W.

Dear Mrs. Henderson:

Dont know the Ashnur Galerie. By all means let him be a depot for distribution, but for heavens sake dont let him collect poems if he has managed to get impressed by the Autumn Salon. The boss of the Autumn Salon <and> his friends have been deluging me with books and letters which I mostly don't want and haven't time to read.[1] *AND* *warning* me against the pretensions of the men who write better than they do.

I'm sending a thing of Vildrac's. I think him really important, sorry we cant use a long poem.[2] Note his end sounds, however. and the 2 lines

Et il vit son regard s'eteindre
Des qu'il fut un peu loin des autres.

that took intelligence.
I wish we had had the Visite which does really matter, still we couldn't do better in our presentation of france than to begin with him.
Sorry I havent time to retype my note about him, but I'm damned with this nuisance of gathering food, such a fag . .

Send Vildrac's cash to him
             12 Rue de Seine. Paris.

Thanks for the clipping. Glad someone has refrained from swallowing the "Lyric Year".[3] Glad of the Boston "Poetry Journal"[.][4] it will drain a lot of bad stuff out of our mail box, and Sterling <with it> I HOPE.[5] what a morass of bad adjectives he is.
Sorry <to learn that> Braithwaite is a nigger. I have taken the trouble to be more contemptuous to him than I should have ever thought of being to any one but a man of equal race. And now that I know his affliction I shall have to stop saying what I think of him. A Boston coon!! that explains a lot. Still his brand of intelligence is quite indistinguishable from that of most of his pale-face confreres. Poor devil! Please destroy this <last> sheet.

<etc. etc I've got to get out of this.>

<Yours ever,
E.P.>

[Enclosure: 2 neatly typed single-spaced pages in French of Charles Vildrac's poem "Gloire" in fifteen stanzas.]

1. The *Salon d'Automne* began in Paris in 1902 to showcase new work by innovative artists in the visual arts; by 1912 it included a literature section and announced its intention to publish an anthology of works from the *salon*. "The boss" may refer to Roger Allard, in charge of the poetry section.

2. Charles Vildrac, pseudonym of Charles Messager (1882-1971), French essayist, critic, dramatist and poet. He began his literary career with an essay entitled "*Verslibrisme*" in 1901. His *Poems* appeared in 1905 and *Images et mirages* in 1908. "Gloire" appeared in French in *Poetry* II (August 1913): 168-170 with the following editorial note on p. 189:

> Mr Charles Vildrac, of Paris is, says Mr. Pound, "one of the little band who are really set to the revival of poetry as an efficient art." He has achieved one masterpiece of narration, *Visite*, "which is distinctly his own and like nothing else. . . ."

3. *The Lyric Year*, a 1912 poetry annual published by Mitchell Kennerley and edited by Ferdinand Phinney Earle, contained one hundred poems out of some 10,000 submitted. The contest was designed to provide an "Annual Exhibition or Salon of American Poetry" with a first-prize award of $500. Controversy erupted when Edna St. Vincent Millay's "Renascence" was passed over for a lesser work. The book was criticized by Harriet Monroe in a long review in *Poetry* I (January 1913): 128-131 (see Williams 25-26).

4. Published in Boston and edited by W. S. Braithwaite (1878-1962), American black poet and anthologist, *The Poetry Journal* was critical of new developments in modern poetry, although it published work by Conrad Aiken, Louis Untermeyer, John Gould Fletcher, Alfred Kreymborg, Amy Lowell, Witter Bynner, Richard Aldington, and William Carlos Williams. The August 1912 circular announcing its October commencement threatened Harriet Monroe whose own plans for *Poetry* were well along. The first issue of *The Poetry Journal*, however, did not appear until two months after the initial publication of *Poetry*. Pound believed the journal embodied the worst in American poetic sensibility and production and constantly castigated the periodical and its editor.

5. George Sterling (1869-1926), American poet centered in San Francisco. Three of his poems appeared in *Poetry* I (December 1912): 75-77, including "At the Grand Canyon" containing this passage: "Lo! the abyss wherein great Satan's wings / Might gender tempests, and his dragons' breath / Fume up in pestilence" (76).

7

10 Church Walk, Kensington, W.
Jan. 20

Dear Mrs. Henderson:-

Thanks for the letter, at last, and for the book and the pretty picture.[1] Let me take things categorically.

Criticism - etc. see DONTS for beginners, here adjoined.[2] As for foreigners in the U.S. and their *langwidge*, I'm saying a little to England in *New Age*, if that's any relief.[3] Beginning with the remark that their Lion. B-ritish lion is stuffed with cotton wool. There are fools everywhere, more in London than elsewhere because of the greater population. Only you can't exhort the suburbs to improve their d.d minds by telling them that the metropolitans are as stupid as they are.

As for the *English Review*, remember that F. M. H<ueffer> made it and went broke and it was bought on the understanding that he should stay at the throttle as long as he liked. And they promptly put him out. The present edtr. is what I can't name, no not even <I> can't name to a madame even if she is a poet.[4] I had a brush with him not long since and I said I'd write to his employers, and he said I better had. And I did write to his employers and he went to bed with the jaundice. But alas he did not die of it. I daily pray that the concern may go to smash. There are sparks of hope. In the <mean> time we'd better print a note warning the U.S. that the critical position of the *Eng. Rev.* is a standing joke in London and that the *Rev.* now sells in Edinburgh.

ABsolutely, comme j'ai dit. There just IS nothing alive here except W.B.Y. and Les Imagistes. God knows I dont want to hide any body from deserved honours. BUTTTTTTTTTTT.!!!!!!!!!

It'd be so much easier to love Hewlett's work.[5] I like him so much. And I see him so often and he is so really pleased when he has given one a jolly evening. And then there's Newbolt ready to pray over any christening, delightful man. buttt since "Drake's Drum," what ?????[6] And De la Mare, with a wife and four kids.[7] I shall simply have to send in some of his work, but he is no better than Mrs Peabody Marks, whose child verses are really charming. and whose Piper is atrocious except where it is child verse.[8] (Another pleasant acquaintance ruined for I told he[r] so) more gently but quite firmly.

All that poetry shop crowd are SO dull. As for Masefield, Yeats likes the man personally, but he was saying the other evening "How easy it would be to do one of these things (we were discussing "slices" of life) but how frightfully bored one would be before one got to the end of doing it.[9]

Oh no!! you are quite right in citing Enoch Arden.[10]

There's no use criticising the *bad*. one's criticism should be constructive where possible. Besides I'd have to read so much bilge. I want to find traces of virtue and praise them. vid. my note on Vildrac. which is sheer propaganda.[11]

I've asked Flint to write you a note on Imagisme. I can't very well do it myself. and he is getting known for his knowledge of contemporary work in France so I thought him the best person to describe the school here.[12]

Dont worry about the other poetry journal. There is no other. WE *Are*. the "Boston Bucket" will do for our leavings.[13]

Lyric Year?[14] fine illustration of all that I've said about the pittiful condition of American poetry, A mine of invaluable examples.

But ME criticize that slush <!>. I'm not Scarmiglione or an under devil watching over the more dingy and remote cubicles of the inferno !!!!.[15]

Kennerley is a block head, John Lane's ex-office boy, he will take anything I do provided its in immitation of the nineties.[16]

Seymour is Welcome to my *"Arnaut Daniel"* if he wants it. That's all I have ready to send at the moment.. No money in it. Provençal text.

16 canzoni. music to two of them. in fac simile and translated into
modern notation by Rummel.[17] translation into the original verse
form<s> and rime schemes. This is the first troubadour to appear in
English complete. (ie, all his important work) text<,> translation
<into forms,> music,. *all* the extant music. There's a long introduc-
tion, which is what I am most anxious to have set up ..
Print in paper @ 60 cents. . I dont think he'd loose on it. I'd take 50
copies as advance on Royalties @ 10% counted as $30. . . <N>ot a
great deal for nine months solid work. but one is not competing with
the new york stock exchange in <the cash> line. He can leave me the
copyright but I won't take the book from him until I want to use it
in "Collected Works" and he can even then keep the right to print it
separately, though I will not grant him power to sell or transfer such
right with my permission specially. given.

       Now I must get on. to that Ars Poetica. I advise you to print it
in *Poetry*. not the number with my stuff in it. and then to have
50000000000 copies of it separately printed on thin paper and insert
one in each returned msss. for the next decade.[18]
              yours ever
                    <Ezra>

PPPPPP SSSSSSS
Memento.
       We cant support all the versifiers in christendom. We can
however make a living for all the good ones. I have no modesty
<about> my belief in our usefullness. We can become so authorita-
tive that *no* periodical will be able to refuse the work of a man whom
we praise. Thus we will turn a vastly larger sum than our $5000 per
year toward the artists who are seriously working for the
risorgimento of "poesy".
       With this in mind. (and its d .. d high stakes) we can afford the
utmost strictness. we can and must take risks. and we can quite well
afford to insult any one we like. Beginning with the "Atlantic
<Monthly>," "Harpers" and the whole east cost coast.
...
I have begun on my own. Dr. Lewis whoever he may be, has advised
Tagore to have his stuff printed in some of the other magaxzines .
I've written to both Dr. L. and <to> Rabindranath ..

Of course for the sake of his <Tagore's> sales and for the school <which he supports> at Bhopal or wherever it is. It would be only fair to Tagore to have the poems printed in other magazines as well as in ours. It will also advertise the fact that _WE_ had him first

I'v<e> accordingly writ to the *Atlantic*. Telling them that "we" or rather I expect to blow them off the map, and calling the edtr. an antediluvian for his soul[']s good. and sayin<g> that he was dam'd lucky to get the poem.

I can't expect H.M. to assume quite this attitude in "our columns" but one may I think move toward it gradually.

<T>here simply is no one in America (or here either), who writes, and who has made anything like the study of the laws of the art. the fundamental eternal etc. in ten languages that I have.. I set out 12 years ago determined that whatever I might eventually be able to DO <compose> — (<creation> would depend on inspiration on any number of things outside my controll.) this at least I could do and it would be my own fault and no one else's if I didn't. i.e. know more about poetry of every time and place. than any man living. Not conventions, but laws, like the laws of physics and chemistry,
                resistance, light pressure, the logical
magic.

                e.g. nine months on Arnaut for polyphonic rime. which is not an isolated case of how I've gone at things. <6 months on Sapphics. 400 sonnets destroyed.> DDDD ---n it <I> can speak, not merely give a fuzzy impression of whether a poem pleases me or not, but I can speak with something vaguely resembling authority.

And this critical position can s*tand*<,> *entirely apart from* anybodys like or dislike of what I happen to produce<,> in the way of original composition.

Forgive this braggadoccio. but I want you and H.M. to feel secure. in the moderately certain knowledge that I can annihilate anyone who gets in front of us. Simply I've got the artillery. You may — being on the spot — be able to arrange the position better, *much better* than I can from here, but in your campaigns and diplomacy, you can take a certain assurance.

There are probably, any number of greater poets in the U.S. — mute, inglorious, etc. — but in a matter of dialectic. I can take on the lot. and I jolly well know it.

I admit it ill becomes me to say so.

And you can be quite sure of one more thing. to wit that I wont
leave our galleon in mid-ocean. Not even if you print more Sterling.
not even if you print a number devoted to Woodbury, van Dyke and
e.w. Wilcox (who was left with a widowed mother to support and for
whom there is *ergo* some excuse)[.][19]

P.S.. Some more.

    Is there any writer in America (or here) whom you want to have
"with us" and who hasn't already sent in something.

    I wrote to Bronner and he promises to boost all he can.[20]

P.S. still further.

    If your own poems have any flaws which I have ommitted to
mention in the following article, let me know and I'll apply some
special pleading.

    From hurried inspection, and re/those in Dec. number. I should
say RHYTHM, watch the rhythm. dissect good lyrics. cut out Yeats'
limited vocabulary.

"And an old man appeared in the dusk" etc.
note the special effort of voice required to begin every line.
Dissect Yeats.
"The Danan children laugh". note how rarely he is uniform. in the
feet. iambs. anapests, quantitative feet alternating with stressed. . I
think its probably nothing but his wonderful ear for really long
syllables that does <much of> his trick for him. You must make your
own studies and dissections. I haven't yet had time, to go over all the
book perhaps my notes following will answer your questions.
<Dear lady, your *script is* so hard to read. . The enclosed has taken
me all day. since breakfast. I'll go on to the rest of your letter *later*.
Yes. do go on writing. — only *do* type it, it saves me so much time.
                  E.>
more p.s.ss on rereading your letter.
Re Lady Gregory's attitude . .
THINK of what they'd say if they didnt get such jolly comfortable
receptions .!!!!! The things W.B.Y. forbid me to repeat because he
HAD accepted hospitality, and because he already had 904 enemies
to the square inch !!!!! oh lá lá [.]

    Poor dears they DO want to be nice to us. And what virtues we have are mostly those which they cant understand never having met em before ..

For "Victorian" in my anathemas, read "Borston and easytish."[21]

NO there simply IS nothing here that I've not mentioned and there is this new School in france.

                                            not quite
so vigorous as imagism but very much alive and very sound. vid. notes already sent. re Jouve and Vildrac. <Buttt>. that dont excuse a large and healthy nation like the U.S.
Of course I want to get home. but gosh darn it il faut vivre, show me a salary <or a pension — I have no pride — what's Carnegie's hero fund for. if not for fools that will persist in writing poetry. Asquith gives one to Yeats.> and I'll treck.

    <No. I wouldn't call any one 'dead' if he worked in XVI Jap. or in Greek 400 B.C. = or any great *period*. only when they work in a style just about 20, 30 or 40 yrs old. = all the tricks & turns cata-logued. = orig. work. *real* work *never* comes in this kind of following of a so called "tradition," i.e. in *Atlantic Monthly* manner. = HOW did H.M. get her "Hotel" into that gallery???>[22]

---

1. EP refers to Alice Corbin, *The Spinning Woman of the Sky: Poems* (Chicago: R. F. Seymour, 1912) which ACH sent to him in early January 1913. The inscription reads "To Ezra Pound — / from Alice Corbin — / Jan. 3. 1913." *The Chicago Daily Tribune* for 5 April 1913 reviewed the *Spinning Woman of the Sky* on page 8, commenting on the frontispiece of Alice Corbin drawn by William Penhallow Henderson and noting that the "poems have that lyric charm mounting now and then to genuine passion." The anonymous reviewer stressed the potential but as yet unrealized power of Alice Corbin as a poet.

2. "A Few Don'ts by an Imagiste," sent to Henderson, appeared in *Poetry* I (March 1913): 200-207, and contains EP's basic statement on imagism, as well as his definition of an image: "that which presents an intellectual and emotional complex in an instant of time" (200). It also expresses his manifesto for writing poetry of precision calling for the direct treatment of the subject, the use of only essential words, and the need to use a sequence of musical phrasing to compose language and rhythm. Accompanying EP's essay is a note on "Imagisme" signed by the poet and translator F. S. Flint (*Poetry* I [March 1913]: 198-200), actually drafted by EP. For a reprint of both works see HM, *A Poet's Life*, 297-301. The

version of "A Few Don'ts" in *Pavannes and Divisions* (1918), 96-101, differs slightly from the orginal with three extra paragraphs added at the end; this version also appears in *LE* 4-8.

3. Most likely "Through Alien Eyes," *New Age* XII (16 January 1913): 252, the first of a four-part series that concluded on 6 February 1913.

4. Sir Alfred Mond, a wealthy politician, purchased the *English Review* after Hueffer's original backer bowed out because of Hueffer's disastrous management of the magazine; Mond installed Austin Harrison as editor.

5. Maurice Hewlett (1861-1923), popular novelist and poet who wrote an historical novel set in Provence which naturally interested Pound. Called to the bar, Hewlett never practiced, choosing to write fiction and later poetry, his most famous work being *The Song of the Plow* (1916). In 1909 Hewlett praised *A Quinzane for This Yule*; EP, in turn, read one of Hewlett's books in proof, most likely *Artemisian: Idylls and Songs* (London: Mathews, 1909) (Stock, 60-61). EP proudly reported to William Carlos Williams in 1909 that his publishing terms from Elkin Mathews for *Personae* compared favorably with those of Hewlett. Christmas 1911 was spent with Hewlett at the Old Rectory, Salisbury, and, possibly, while still with Hewlett, EP wrote his "Prolegomena" containing his "Credo" for Harold Monro's *Poetry Review*. In it, EP cited Hewlett's prediction that the poetry of the future would be "harder and saner . . . what Mr. Hewlett calls 'nearer the bone'" (*LE* 12). EP expressed genuine admiration for Hewlett (as well as Bridges and Manning) in the essay because he was "seriously concerned with overhauling the metric, in testing the language and its adaptability to certain modes" (*LE* 12). Four years later, in a letter to his father, EP expressed further approval of Hewlett, noting that at a dinner Hewlett and Tagore were both "mildly amusing." He particularly praised Hewlett's *Love of Persephone*, although he candidly admitted to his father that he hadn't yet read it (*SL* 7, 21). By 1917, however, EP objected to Hewlett's opinions and literary taste (*EP/JQ* 131).

Canto 74/447 refers to "Maurice who wrote historical novels"; Canto 80/529 recalls the 1911 Christmas visit, while in Canto 92/633 EP recalls a line from Hewlett's poem "Leto's Child."

6. Sir Henry Newbolt (1862-1937), poet and author of *Admirals All and Other Verses* (13th ed., 1910), which included "Drake's Drum." A founder of the Poets' Club started in 1908, Newbolt, along with Gosse, was considered by Pound and his circle to be the *éminence grise* of the Edwardian period.

7. Walter de la Mare (1873-1956), one of the newer poets of 1912, associated with Harold Monro's Poetry Bookshop in London. De la Mare often wrote verse about children, hence the comparison to Mrs. Peabody Marks. De la Mare also published a hostile, unsigned review of *Canzoni* in the *Westminster Gazette* in 1911, although Pound later submitted some of his work to *Poetry*. Pound originally met de la Mare at the Square Club, a literary gathering founded by G. K. Chesterton.

8. EP has the name slightly confused. He means the American Josephine Preston Peabody (1874-1922), married to Professor Lionel Marks of Harvard,

prolific poet, dramatist, and writer of children's verses. A friend of Amy Lowell's, Josephine Peabody provided her with a letter of introduction to Thomas Hardy when Lowell made her 1914 visit to England.

9. John Masefield (1878-1967), a member of the Square Club in London and author of the controversial long poem "The Everlasting Mercy" which appeared in the *English Review* in 1911. Masefield was to join Pound, Yeats, Aldington, and Sturge Moore in the pilgrimage to Wilfred Scawen Blunt on 18 January 1914 to mark his 75th birthday. However, at the last moment Masefield was unable to attend. Masefield's *Salt-Water Ballads* was spoofed by Pound in a letter to May Sinclair, 19 March 1920. From 1930 to 1967 he was Poet Laureate.

10. "Enoch Arden," Tennyson's sentimental poem of 911 lines published in 1864 and celebrated by Matthew Arnold as "perhaps the best thing Tennyson has done," is a brooding, sacrificial narrative of a hero's return after ten years to discover his wife married to another because she believed her husband died at sea. The hero nobly decides not to intrude on her new life and shortly after dies, believing that to present himself would be to "shatter all the happiness of the hearth" (l. 766). A Victorian best-seller, the poem soon came to embody Victorian sentimentality at its worst. Although he read Tennyson early in his career, EP later parodied him in his Alf Venison series and was generally critical of the diction and style of Tennyson's verse. See *LE* 276 and Canto 80/522. On EP and Tennyson see Ira B. Nadel, "Ezra Pound: Two Poems," *Journal of Modern Literature* 5 (1988): 141-145.

11. Accompanying the publication of Charles Vildrac's "Gloire," *Poetry* II (August 1913): 168-70, is a brief note by Pound which declares that Vildrac is "one of the little band who are really set to the revival of poetry as an efficient art" (ibid. 189).

12. Despite Pound's remark that he couldn't very well do it himself, he drafted and corrected Flint's essay entitled "Imagisme," *Poetry* I (March 1913): 198-200, a purported interview with an imagist poet, actually Pound. Immediately following Flint's essay was Pound's "A Few Don'ts by an Imagiste" (200-206).

13. A reference to W. S. Braithwaite's *Poetry Journal* published in Boston.

14. Contributors to *The Lyric Year* (1912) included elder statesmen like Bliss Carmen, Richard Le Gallienne, Madison Cawein, and George Edward Woodberry, as well as newer poets: Millay, Sara Teasdale, and Vachel Lindsay. See William Carlos Williams' poem "On First Opening *The Lyric Year*," *Poetry* II (June 1913): 114 and Letter 6, note 3.

15. Scarmiglione appears in *Inferno* XXI: 105 as one of a squadron of demons who plague Dante and Virgil on the sixth embankment.

16. Mitchell Kennerley (1878-1932), manager of the New York branch of John Lane and later publisher of *The Forum*, 1910-1916; promoter of the anthology *Spectra* (1916) which sustained the hoax of a "Spectric school" of poetry supported by three poets (Witter Bynner, A. D. Ficke, and Marjorie Allen Seiffert) who published under pseudonyms in the anthology. In her editorial of June 1918 in *Poetry* XI: 169-171, ACH congratulated *Poetry* for not being

deceived by the "Spectrist School," while admonishing those critics unable to distinguish between the faux poetry of free verse and the true (170). Readers could easily be misled, she believed, especially when "in the presence of the 'new poetry' or 'new art'" (170).

17. The text incorporates the work Pound did for Walter Morse Rummell which appeared in *Hesternae Rosae, Serta, II. Neuf Chansons des Troubadours des XIIième et XIIIième Siècles* (London: Augener, Ltd., 1913) and material later to be included under the heading "Arnaut Daniel" in *Instigations* (New York: Boni & Liveright, 1920). Pound began publishing on Arnaut Daniel as early as 1910. See Ch. II of *The Spirit of Romance* (London: J. M. Dent, 1910). Ralph Fletcher Seymour initially agreed to publish *The Canzoni of Arnaut Daniel*, preparing approximately 300 prospectuses describing a book of 180 pages, 8 x 11 inches in an edition of 300 copies at between $4-$5 each with 10 copies on Japanese vellum at $15.00 each (*EP/DS* 199). Seymour advertised the book in the *New Freewoman* for the fall of 1913. Little public interest, however, resulted in his cancelling the project. By late 1917 EP could write he was "profoundly glad" the book did not appear in 1913. Early in 1918 he revised the ms. and sent it to a publisher in Cleveland but it was apparently lost and never published. See *G* E6a and Letter 4, note 1.

18. Most likely EP's "Tradition," *Poetry* III (January 1914): 137-141 in which he comments on prosody as well as aesthetics.

19. George Edward Woodberry (1885-1930), critic, biographer, and minor American poet whose book *Kingdom of All Souls* was reviewed by ACH in *Poetry* III (November 1913): 69-72.

Henry Van Dyke (1852-1933), popular American poet, minister and writer on outdoor life, who also composed short stories and romances. See Letter 48, note 3.

Ella Wheeler Wilcox (1855-1919), successful American "magazine" poet who in September 1913 wrote to Harriet Monroe in response to a stinging criticism of her work in the May 1913 issue of *Poetry*. See Letter 2, note 13.

20. Milton Bronner, a journalist on the *Kentucky Post* when he began to correspond with Pound in 1913. He later moved to Brooklyn where he continued to write and edit. See *EP/JQ* 60.

21. Perhaps "Boston and easternish," referring to Braithwaite and the *Poetry Journal*.

22. Harriet Monroe published her long prose poem "The Hotel" in the *Atlantic Monthly* in March 1909. Her 1914 volume *You and I* (New York: Macmillan) began with "The Hotel," a poem she described as "free verse" and "an adventurous departure in modern poetry" in her autobiography, *A Poet's Life* (New York: Macmillan, 1938), 190.

8

EP to ACH   TS [January 1913] 2 ll + 1 Enclosure.

10 Church Walk, Kensington W.

There's novelty with a vengeance . .
He's sent me a one page section of a "long" poem to see if I like the flavour.

What is our subscription list. and the gross sales<??> I haven't been had time to do much in that line. enc<losed> one more.
I'd like five more Nov. nos. if there to spare.[1] We'll get a bit out of back numbers. you know, and our bound vols. needn't be considered as sheer loss, IF we're good enough . .

In two years we'll expand the critical section into what the *Mercure* thinks its "revue de quinzaine" is, only we'll be really effi-cient, and we'll all be drawing fat salaries from a paying concern.[2] Je rêve? Mais non. Ca va venir . . But never any more poetry per month. Higher rates yes. but there'll never be more good poetry made per month than ~~what~~ the amount that we're now printing. I'll get on to your book as soon as this jaw grind. (vid. card) is over. and another yawp at Oxford.[3]

Luck to the pittore and his immoral show.[4] Hope he has paved the way for my strictly proper if slightly orgaic verses. The nude in paint is one thing. but poetry. strictly hygenic, and nude without the Swinburnian slither and without the preraphaelitic confusion of the soul with the solar plexus . . ehem. and I've no particular committee to <prevent> the mayor of Chicago (or whoever should prevent such outbursts) from object<ing>.

Ai!hem. I'm too tired to stay even as coherent as this for much longer.

Hasta Luego.

<E.P.>

[Enclosure: Card announcing the three lectures Pound was to give at Mrs. Fowler's, 26 Gilbert Street, Mayfair, on 21, 23, 28 January 1913. Reprinted in *EP/DS* 179.]

1. "Long poem" presumably refers to a passage from Yeats' 121-line poem, "The Grey Rock," which appeared in *Poetry* II (April 1913): 17–21 and won the *Poetry* award for the best poem published in the first year of the magazine. Alice Corbin and EP were among the jurors (*Poetry* III [November 1913]: 72–73). Yeats, however, kept only $50 of the prize, suggesting the balance be given to a younger poet. He nominated Pound, who bought two sculptures from Gaudier-Brzeska and a typewriter with the money. See *Poetry* III (January 1914): 149–150; *SL* 27–28. The November 1912 issue of *Poetry* contained poems by Richard Aldington and Harriet Monroe, as well as EP's review of *An Anthology of Bohemian Poetry* trans. P. Selver (57–59). The "Notes" section to the volume reports that EP "has consented to act as foreign correspondent of POETRY, keeping its readers informed of the present interests of the art in England, France and elsewhere" (64).

2. Edited by Alfred Vallette, the bi-monthly *Mercure de France* contained a "Revue de la Quinzaine," or fortnightly review, comprising short reviews of recently published works divided into genres with literature from other countries making up nearly half of each issue. A listing of new publications plus an editorial section headed "Echos" containing letters, announcements, news, and opinions also appeared.

3. Corbin, *The Spinning Woman of the Sky*. The enclosure was a card announcing that "EZRA POUND will give THREE LECTURES at 26 Gilbert Street, Mayfair" on the 21st, 23rd, and 28th of January, 1913. This three-part series was given by Pound at the behest of Mrs. Alfred Fowler for society ladies at which Pound mostly read from the manuscript of *The Spirit of Romance*. The money he earned assisted him in surviving in London. The invitation listed the three lectures as "The Normal Opportunity of the Provençal Troubadour," "Rabindranath Tagore" and "'Vers Libre and Systems of Metric,' with readings from the Lecturer's own work." Several years later at Mrs. Fowler's he met Mrs. Olivia Shakespear who invited him to tea at her home where he was soon to meet her daughter Dorothy. For a reproduction of the invitation see *EP/DS* 179. Additionally, Pound was invited to speak to the St. John's College Essay Society at Oxford on 2 February 1913; he spoke on Cavalcanti and later recounted his experience of dining in the college and discussing literature in his *Patria Mia* (Chicago: Seymour, 1950), 90-91.

4. Pound's reference may be to William Penhallow Henderson's role in sponsoring the impending visit to Chicago of the New York Armory Show with its controversial "Nude Descending a Staircase" by Marcel Duchamp. The show was exhibited at the Art Institute of Chicago 24 March-16 April 1913. An indication of the debate swirling about the exhibition is Harriet Monroe's column of 16 March 1913 for the *Chicago Sunday Tribune* entitled "International Art Show to Open at the Institute on March 24" (II.8). A later article entitled "Nude Descending Staircase," *Chicago Daily Tribune* (23 March 1913): 5, has as its subhead: "Here She Is: White Outline Shows Nude Descending Staircase, Gives Direction for Seeing It." The next day, however, the following article appeared: "Cubist Art Baffles Crowd, Diagram No Aid to Seeing Nude Descending Staircase," *Chicago Daily Tribune* (25 March 1913): 7.

9

EP to ACH   TS (unsigned) 21 January 1913 | l.
10 Church Walk, Kensington, W.

<10 C. Walk

21/1/13>

Dear A.C.H.

Have been writing all .a.m., lecturing p.m. and dinner looming.[1]
As to your letter. the written part: yes you [are] right. Craig is really
outside our scope, we're under no necessity of booming him. If I
remember, I sent that note at the very beginning before I was sure of
having too much news, and when Craig was actually the only thing
going on in the immediate village.[2] Don't for heavens sake feel that I
want all my despatches printed, I'll send on what I see and you must
decide which doses are fittest for "Chi".

I must get some formally polite slips printed in french explaining that "our format does not permit us to print the truly amazing
production of Auguste Swallou, John Doe et alliorum.["]

No !! mediocrity is not confined even to New York.

Lo the proud denoument in the two final words of this line.

Et l'âme par les plis de son manteau, la chair.

1. EP gave the first of his three lectures at Mrs. Fowler's, "The Normal
Opportunity of the Provençal Troubadour" on 21 January 1913. See Letter 8,
note 3.

2. Edward Gordon Craig (1872-1966), dramatist, stage designer, and
theoretician of the theatre who in 1910 produced a revolutionary production of
Hamlet in Moscow and in 1913 attempted to establish an experimental theatre
school in Florence. His English committee, chaired by Sir William Rothenstein,
included Yeats, EP, and John Cournos; it met first at the Leicester Gallery and
then at the school's office, No. 7 John Street, Adelphi. Late in 1913 Craig
successfully opened the School for the Art of the Theatre in the Arena Goldoni
in Florence but the outbreak of WWI in 1914 forced it to close.

10

■■■■■■■ **EP to ACH**   TS 4 February 1913 4 ll.

10 Church Walk

4/2/'12[1]

Dear Mrs. Henderson: —

I've been going through your book again.[2] It is really very hard
to criticize. You say you have made 'em, off and on, for your own
amusement and that you know most of their faults. Quant a moi, I
have no scales and balances for work done in this way. If you'd made
'em out of blood and sweat and were set to do this one thing or
nothing, I might be invoked to some purpose. I know a little of how
to weigh the offering<s> to the implacable.

Your most obvious superficial fault is that you invert, and in
various ways disturb the natural prose order of the words. Every
alteration of this sort, that is not made for definite and worthy
reason weakens the impact . .

Then again, your wording is in places, obviously derivative . .

<Y>our best lines are

"While Tahitian girls

Weave coral poppies <in their cloudy hair>"[3]

And I like "To the rulers" and think "Dim Arcadian Pastures" about
the <best> complete poem freer from faults. Trust the *Century* for
the negative scale of criticism![4]

Of course you haven't a language of your own. That's the work
of a life time, I suppose.

Yes, your two <Tahitian> lines are O.K. A master would have used
perhaps one adjective with 'music' in the next one. I'm not sure that
"unknown" isn't quite the right one, and it would probably convey
the image quite well without the two trailers.

Of course this thing is miles above the Arcadian matter. and so
perhaps is the "Grey Woods" if .... Oh well, we all write our peck of

Yeats at one time or another . . It takes a certain actual bulk of output to rid one of the immitative part of ones work. The immitation is good training and no loss. When one's grasp on the tools becomes firmer the knowledge of the method we once immitated stays with us, only we are at once conscious of what effects seem immitative and are more careful to alter them just enough to make our own. (Or else to bow and leave them as it were in inverted commas.)

As for America, you are quite right. I don't know of anyone there who can tell you anything you don't already know. Cela, ce n'est pas assez. There are the great dead and the very high gods their taste is finniky and they are very difficult to please and nothing else is worth while . . As to audience, The bloomin bird of Avon is sounder on that point than Mr Whitman, tho' there's no use in saying so to the prospective subscriber.
E basta.

.Yours sincerely
<E.P.>

<P.S.>
Of course, it is only in the capital that one can get the atmosphere where the best men sit about bewailing the rottenness of their early work <&> the imperfection of everything they've ever printed. And where they mourn together seeking some minute advance . .
How in heaven's name anything ever gets done anywhere else I dont know. And if one looks at history one sees it seldom was done.

---

1. EP has typed '12 for '13. Date confirmed by reference to ACH's *The Spinning Woman of the Sky: Poems* published in December 1912 and the inscription to EP on the copy sent to him dated 3 January 1913. Furthermore, EP did not begin corresponding with either Harriet Monroe or ACH before [18] August 1912. See *SL* 9.

2. *The Spinning Woman of the Sky: Poems*.

3. The lines are from the closing section of "Modernity," *The Spinning Woman* (1912), 50. It is the only passage marked in EP's copy of the book held at the HRHRC.

4. ACH, "What Dim Arcadian Pastures," appeared in the *Century* 81 (December 1910): 224.

11

 EP to ACH   TLS 10? February [1913] 6 ll. The letter ends with an unpublished poetic fragment by EP.

<Feb. 10 ??
answer to one lett*er*>
10 Church Walk, Kensington, W

Dear A.C.H. :-

I am not responsible for the vagaries of the Celtic theatre. I like your "Flees the second" and shall present it to W.B.Y. (Anonymously, be calm).[1] But if you think he was "Easily led astray" I think you are wrong. He and Lady G. had a frightful row about something. I suppose it was the pea green lighting or whatever it is, and he arrived in London with his insides ALL out of order from emotions and he sits around even now drinking Vichey water while the rest of us guzzle his new wine. He's spent most of his pension on Bacchus, partly for his friends' sake and partly because an old and rascally publisher has turned wine merchant and imports wines with strange names and tells W.B.Y. romances about the vintages.

The second of the Harvard twins (nice thought that!) has just a trace of something bearable in his stuff.[2] As for neo-classics I still prefer "The silent children of the pure" as a phrase to his fine frenzy anent the "Picene melodies which the veritable ikthi squirt up against the lunar vibrations["]. I still feel, ut ante dictum, that he does not die daily on the crucifix of the arts but we can not all have names chosen from scripture, I dare say if I'd been called Twitter I should have come to nothing better my self.

Why I should have been pushed out of the March number to make way for Noyes, I do not know.[3] The presence of Noyes in the magazine at all seems an indignity which might have been spared us.

We'll have poor Mrs. E.W. Wilcox herself NEXT.[4]

[Marginal insertion commenting on the following paragraph which has two wavy lines drawn across it:]

<you now say you understand it so this is unnecessary>

As to Yeats Aoife.[5] It means I believe that there was once a man who [was] conquered by the help of his Goddess lover who gave him the gift of invisibility. And being taunted with this and wishing open glory in the sight of men he broke the charm and was killed, and the goddess curses and bids the gods "Come out and dig for a dead man" and then they when they get tired of her noise souse her with. wine of forgetfulness. And that passage is I think quite wonderful. The interspersed passages are the allegory of "The nineties" of a few men who didn't sell out. Who were content with the almost invisible glory of artistic creation.

Yes. I berated Lewis, and if he didn't put young Tagore up to wanting me to get stuff of R.T[agore']s into the magazines then someone else did and he can save my firey fury and pass it on to its due destinatio<n>. Any<how,> he KNOWS NOW what I think of the american periodicals, which may do him good, he has <also> a poor opinion of my manners and carriage, but that will do neither of us very much harm.

I dont see how, in honesty to Tagore, I can print all his stuff in "Poetry" if the other magazines will take it. We haven't the standing of the *Atlantic* or even of *Harpers* and at the present rate of speed we wont get it and I dont see how we can expect Mr Tagore to take part in a faction fight. It is one thing for me to boycot all other magazines or even for Yeats to do so, supposing he would, but Tagore is a different proposition and in so far as I am entrusted with his interest I've got to consider that interest quite apart from mine [or] 'ours'.

Many of T's things seem to me unsuited for serial publication. We might however print one of the plays if Scribner won't. Frankly I cant see that we are even better than the *Forum*.[6] ??? what IS our circulation[?] I've got to judge this Tagore matter on that ground also. Our quality simply IS NOT any better than that of the other magazines and we dont seem to be making much of a stand for criticism.

If we dont use precisely what the other magazines wont, what good are we !!!! Noyes !!! Oh my god ! O Montreal !!

Ehem ! I may come over on a lecturing tour next autumn, if one

G.A. Shaw, 12 Charles St. N.Y. succeeds in getting me a reasonable number of engagements which seems unlikely.

No, No, your last sheet was very comforting. Quant a Ficke, he should take a kindergarten course in crocheting or in something equally suited to his temper and capacities.

Indifference! re/your defence of my "dolts", indifference is what one expects, its these dam charlatans who go about professing to be artists that draw forth one's bile . . Their indifference if you like, their indifference to the excellence of the art, that is the disgusting phenomenon, as to the public one knows they're a set of asses and one expects 'em to behave accordingly. My "dolts" was leveled more at the pseudo-artists than at that helpless stupid cow the bloomin' vulgus.

The public, voila folk poetry, dont WANT good stuff any more than they want bad, but they are tolerent of it, je crois, they have no natural preference for either the bad or the good. It is <the> apes that annoy one.

Quant a moi, I think I might well learn French despite the Basilikon Doron, and take to composing in that tongue.[7]

> I hear America a singing,
> Fat, sleek, contented, with emotions well
> below the far expanded diaphram,
> And children rotting in her factories
> and art as lazy and as stupid as
> The boasted ass of Balaam ever was
> That unique ass, as Mr Whistler says
> In whom the voice of angels ever riz.
>
> Bid William P.H. draw an Uncle Sam
> To show the Nation what it really am,
> And put therein his very best intentions
> to show that <critter> in <its> new dimension.
> <end of the *Pliocene fragment.*>

Feb. 16.
P.S., some more in continuation of the first section.
!!!

Two navvys have sprung upon the breathless world of letters. one
"The Kipling of the moment" and the other hovering between Keats
and Swinburne. I'm to meet him this week and pursuade him that
Keats is the safer. Also to pursuade him Not to rime Night with
Aphrodite. I'll send a note on them soon as they have both "some-
thing in them".

M.S. has discovered a female Masefield supposed to have the
come-over on poor John.[8] As I do not yet know all my Villon by
heart these events do not greatly disturb me.
"Quand mort sera vous lui ferez chandeaux"[9]
I spent yesterday trying to put the Goodly Fere into french as I
could think of nothing less likely to come off.[10] The result does
NOT resemble F.V[illon]. Helas !! et Helas !!!! Nor yet Mallarme.

More anon.
    Yours ever

                    <E.P.>

_____

1. A reference to ACH's "Nodes," *Poetry* I (December 1912): 83.

2. Arthur Davison Ficke (1883-1945), who like Frost, went to Harvard.
They are most likely the "Harvard twins" Pound refers to. The line Pound
quotes—or fabricates—alludes to Ficke's elegy "Swinburne," *Poetry* I (February
1913): 137-144, especially stanzas IV and V. Three years later Ficke, with Witter
Bynner, would publish a volume entitled *Spectra*, supposedly the work of a new
group of imagists. Some critics took the hoax seriously and in the June 1916 issue
of the *Forum*, Bynner and Ficke explained the Spectricist aesthetic. Ficke would
later become part of ACH's circle in Santa Fe following her move there in 1916.
See Letter 7, note 16.

3. Alfred Noyes (1880-1959) whose poem "The Hill-Flowers" appeared in
Poetry I (March 1913): 192-194. The issue did contain, however, EP's "A Few
Don'ts by an Imagiste," 200-206.

4. E.W. Wilcox; see Letter 7, note 19.

5. Pound refers to Yeats' "The Grey Rock," to appear in *Poetry* II (April
1913): 17-21. Aoife is a woman, the mother of Cuchulain's son and the subject of
the gods' lament in the poem which became the opening work of *Responsibilities*
(1914). Doused with the wine of forgetfulness by the gods following her lament
of betrayal by her mortal lover, Aoife rises freed from her despair. The poem won
Poetry's $250 prize for the best work published in its first year. Yeats kept only
$50, suggesting that the balance be given to a younger poet; he nominated
Pound. See *Poetry* III (January 1914): 149-150.

6. The *Forum*, a monthly New York (later Philadelphia) magazine devoted to literary, political, and intellectual issues published by Mitchell Kennerley in which EP printed several poems in 1910 and 1911 plus what he called a "vitriolic essay," "The Wisdom of Poetry," *Forum* 47 (April 1912): 497. See *EP/MC* 55. Other contributors included H. G. Wells, Allen Upward, and Frederic Manning.

7. "Kingly or Royal Doron," possibly George H. Doran (1869-1956), successful Canadian-born American publisher who began with religious books but later became a popular trade publisher and the exclusive American publisher of Arnold Bennett. Doran's frequent trips to London, where he held "court" at the Savoy, were widely publicized among writers and agents. A moralist, Doran opposed the nihilism and frankness of many post-World War I writers, although he did publish Michael Arlen, W. Somerset Maugham, and Aldous Huxley. However, he also admitted to censoring passages in Dos Passos' *Three Soldiers* (1921) and rejecting the work of D. H. Lawrence, Hemingway, and Dreiser. In 1927 Doran merged with Doubleday, Page and Co. to become the largest trade publisher in the United States.

8. May Sinclair (1865?-1946), English novelist and essayist, close friend of Olivia Shakespear and participant in various women's movements. Elkin Mathews arranged a meeting between EP and Sinclair in 1909 and she, in turn, introduced him to her circle of friends including Ford Madox Hueffer. She later defended EP's work in her 1912 book *Feminism*, and in a 1920 essay, "The Reputation of Ezra Pound," *North American Review* CCXI (May 1920): 658-668. Sinclair also became a friend and supporter of H. D. See Hilda Doolittle, *End to Torment* (New York: New Directions, 1979), *passim*.

9. EP has quoted a line from Villon's "Epître à ses amis," forgetting a comma and mistyping the final word. The corrected line reads, "Quand mort sera, vous lui ferez chaudeaux!"

10. "Ballad of the Goodly Fere" first appeared in the *English Review* III (October 1909): 382-384, reprinted in *Exultations* (London: Mathews, 1909).

12

■■■■■■■ **EP to ACH**   TS unsigned 16 February [1913] 2 ll.

<answer to yr. note of Feb. 6>
10 Church Walk. Feb. 16

Dear A.C.H. —

The "letter at home" must have missed the boat for only the one from the office has yet arrived

About Yeats, he is constitutionally incapable of attending to his own affairs and he feels that if Paget acts as his agent he must give him a certain amount of work.[1] Besides, in this case Paget was recommended to send the stuff to us unless there was some good reason not to. I think we can almost make a "Corner" in W.B.Y. ... And as you know he is the only person whom I think worth cornering.

Quant a Noyes. you can see the scraps of the enclosed note which has been lying about this room for several days.

I DONT think we ought to follow booms. We ought to start 'em. We OUGHT to make a market for the good stuff and the stuff of "Promise" (much abused word) that other magazines wont print.

However, I'll bone Masefield for a LYRIC when I see him.

A.E. is a rank amateur.[2] Anyhow I dont think he has written anything for years. Good character god yes. but that only confuses the issue. Tagore likes him because he dilutes the oriental teachings.

As to the last number. Bynner isnt wholly bad.[3] He has some intention of telling the truth and working directly. But he is damd irritating, that floppy personality !!! So pleasant and etc.. . . . . .

■■■■■■■

1. R. Harold Paget, New York publisher who printed Yeats' *The Green Helmet and Other Poems* in January 1911.

2. A.E., the Ulster-born Irish poet, dramatist, and essayist George Russell (1867-1935), was a friend of Yeats. Given to Swedenborgian visions, he later became an economist, journalist, and editor.

3. Witter Bynner (1881-1968), American poet who arranged for EP's first publisher in America, Small, Maynard and Company of Boston. At first valued by EP, Bynner soon epitomized the transparency of American writers. See *SL* 15-16. Many years later in Santa Fe, Bynner became a close friend of ACH and was best man at her daughter's wedding. Pound refers to seven poems by Bynner that were printed in *Poetry* I (February 1913): 150-159. Also see Letter 77, note 1.

1 3

ACH to EP   TLS 2 April 1913 1 1 + 3 Enclosures: TS 2 ll + ALS
EP to ACH [? April 1913] on verso.

Dear E. P. : — We do feel a little troubled sometime for fear that
we may be returning masterpieces. Look at these. There aren't
many that have their unconscious charm!

A.C.H.

April 2, 1913.

<They're from Kalamazoo, *Mich.*>

[Enclosures:]

Sonnet

TAKING THE OLD PIANO AWAY TO WHICH MOTHER IS ATTACHED

O thou of years gone down into the Past
When Future's way stretched far beyond my view, -
How many happy hours I've passed with you!
The mem'ry of that time will ever last;
Now just because you have grown old they cast
You off; but, like an old friends tried and true
You're dearer to my heart than others, new,
And so I have clung to you to the last.
What hallowed scenes again come to my mind
As I stand by your side! Again I hear
A voice, — now of the choir unseen, — and blind
Become my eyes with tears; you bring her near.
Farewell then only tie that now does bind
Me to the Past! Farewell forever, dear.

FOR WHAT HE WAS

John Henry's really growing old,
He shambles so, and feels the cold;
He spills his food upon his shirt
And always has a pain or hurt;
Though once erect as nature meant,
Like sapling in the wind he's bent.

So softly has the hand of Time
Rung in the years on silver chime
He scarcely knows that he is old
And if I told him he might scold;
For now he's peevish, — strong of will;
But even so, I love him still;
In spite of change or what he does
I LOVE HIM NOW FOR WHAT HE WAS.

▬▬▬▬▬▬ [ALS by EP apparently written from Sirmione on the reverse of the
poems sent to him by ACH:]

Holy. Holy HOLY
Lord Gord Orlmighty!

No. I didn't know it was quite as bad.

I suppose you do get a lot of cute ideas sentimentaly expressed.
One might do an editorial under that heading.

Still you (the official "you") did object to Richard & H.D. &
would object to me if I weren't "established".[1] Of course the poor
gentleman on the reverse of this. ought to stay in the village choir

His work is simple, without ambiguity. It is written in the
"speech of the people" which we are always having recommended to
us as the one language for art.

Poor dear, he may be a "she". The village soprano. They (the
verses) do open ones eyes to vistas of life unheeded. Your "gent":
(term used specifically) in the *Newark Times* is the other sort of
american pest.

Damns Matisse, Marinetti & Manet in one breath & exhorts the
plebs to consider the sole manners i.e. of Messonier or Bougareau.

Ehem. I met Holly on my way thru Paris, by accident. His

gallery is next to "my" restaurant. He is pleasant. Also I fell in with the younger energies, Romains, Vildrac, Duhamel etc. And came thence to my lake & sun.[2] It is still cold from the Alps but I managed to breakfast in the giardino this morning. And I hope to gaud no one will say ART to me for the next six weeks.

I am glad about the Tagore. & I suppose the Chines[e] number.[3]

yours ever,
Ezra Pound

1. HM and ACH were not keen at first to support the work of Aldington and H. D. See Williams 40-42.

2. Sirmione on Lago di Garda. EP travelled to Italy via Paris in late March 1913 where he met Jules Romains, Charles Vildrac, Georges Duhamel, and others. By the middle of April he arrived at Sirmione and his favored Hotel Eden. In Venice he planned to meet H. D. travelling with Richard Aldington but settled for her unhappy parents, although H. D. and Aldington later appeared. At the same time, Dorothy Shakespear was travelling in Italy with her mother and relative, Georgie Hyde Lees, later to marry Yeats. After another stop in Paris where he met Skipwith Cannell and John Gould Fletcher, EP returned to London in mid-May.

3. EP is anticipating *Poetry* II (June 1913): 81-91 with fourteen poems by Tagore (see his letter to HM, in *SL* 19). The "Chinese number" would become *Poetry* II (September 1913): 191-199 which featured Allen Upward's "Scented Leaves from a Chinese Jar."

14

10 Church Walk.

Dear A.C.H.

Dont go and get discouraged now, just when the magazine appears to be looking up and when even I begin to believe that it may have a chance to amount to something.

Naturally W.R., with whom the magazine is NOT "identified", is sore.[1] HE hasn't come off and he dislikes to see H.M. doing so.

As to editing, considering that our honoured chief has been writing for newspapers for ten years she does d. . d well.

I cant be bothered replying to the small fry tho' I was on the point of asking Prof. Alden to please explain why he thought my stuff would appeal to "the frankly licentious" rather than to those who were licentious without being frank about it.[2]

There were various mino<r> flaws in the reviews but dont bother. As a rule dont trouble to review anything that isnt interesting. You dont need to read ALL a book to find out that the author is weak minded.

Seymour is ALL right.

I'm just back and have hay mows of truck to attend to.[3] Dont buy <too> many October nos. I am returning some. ten or 15. I think.

This is just a scrawl to tell you not to lie down and die, immediately.

yours.

<E.P.>

___

1. William Marion Reedy (1862-1920) of St. Louis, editor of *Reedy's Mirror* from 1913-1920. In an 8 July 1913 article, "A Boom in Poetry," Reedy celebrated

the appearance of "half a dozen periodicals devoted exclusively to poetry . . . and an improvement in the economic conditions of the poets themselves. . . . [all] recent phenomena that indicate a 'boom in poetry'" (9). Also see Letter 36, note 3, and Letter 63, note 13.

2. Raymond M. Alden, reviewer who criticized EP's "Contemporania," *Poetry* II (April 1913): 1-12, in the *Nation* as indecent and appealing to the "frankly lascivious." See "The New Poetry," *Nation* XCVI (17 April 1913): 386-387. HM and ACH replied to Alden in *Poetry* II (May 1913): 67-72.

3. See Letter 13, note 2 on EP's trip to Italy.

15

10 Church Walk. Kensington, W.

Dear A.C.H.

Prose is the devil. ALL prose is the devil, except perhaps a little of Flaubert and De Maupassant.

I dont see that we can do anything except be as condensed as possible, and then cut out everything (in proof, if need be) that isn't absolutely pertinent to POETRY.

For instance the grumble that a certain book was printed with caps. at head of each strophe, was trivial. We're not "Printer's Art."[1] What difference does it make who prints how?.

2. I dont think it is worth while saying that a book is bad. If a vol. isn't worth praising we should ignore it.

I dont think it does much good to argue with fools.
All argument is a sort of machine.
We dogmatize. that's our job. Then let the dam reporters scratch each other out with the discussion. Our "replies" should consist in a new formulation of facts.

I'm sending you Vildrac and Duhamel, on "L'art poetique." "Vers Libre" is various things. there's "Vers Libre". And "our vers libre" and "their vers libre".

I'm not called on to defend it. As for "Imagisme" you'll find information re/rhythmic construction in the March no.[2]

Certainly "vers libre" has nothing to do with things being rimed or unrimed. It refers to the rhythmic construction. Some mean merely "spontaneous writing". some mean ditto and hope that it corresponds to an emotion. vid. Guido Cavalcanti, by me.[3] Some mean a very complicated system of combining rhythmic units. God save all our souls.

About F.G.[4] I suppose she did get born. its a hard job. I should only attempt to treat maternity from the point of view of the unfortunate offspring. My only addend<um>, not much of an addendum at that, is that a cat has the sense to stop being a mother when the kit is able to shift for itself. I dislike adhesions.

Can our august edetrix use another half no. of me in Sept. ?. Yeats says he is in the Oct.

   NEXT MORNING.
From what I have written you will easily see that I was mentally and thoroughly exhausted last evening. A nos moutons. I've read your rev. of Masefield.[5] I think it's well enough written. It goes a bit further than I should have cared to go myself, but no matter . . I haven't much fault to find with the way the prose is written. The only criticism I would make of some of the earlier prose is that there might be more pith per page. That'll come. Dont worry.

As for controversy. I dont mean by what I wrote last night that I want to shun my share of it. I dont see the attacks. If you think any of them are important enough to reply to. Send 'em on to me and I'll bring up the batteries. Attacks on me, be hanged. I can stand 'em. Mis-statements as to fact. I think it O.K. to correct.

I think I may as well do a few brief essays on "Good Writing", Rhythm, etc. The "Don'ts" seem to have reached the *Tribune*.[6] I liked that paragraph on Literzarism. Also it would seem (as I said,) that the excessive attack begets defenders, in that case on the very paper that did the attacking.

When I reply I think I may as well take a dozen or so attackers at once, as illustrations of provincial ignorance.

Also the little essays may answer some of the questions in your letter that I havent gone into very fully.

I am still in a state of fuddle from the rush I've been in since I got back.[7]

more anon.   <E.P.>

1. EP has created a fictitious journal, possibly thinking of *Printer's Ink*, a trade publication started in New York in 1888.

2. EP refers to F. S. Flint, "Imagisme," *Poetry* I (March 1913): 198-200 and his own "A Few Don'ts by an Imagiste," ibid., 200-206. Three years later ACH was to write "Don'ts for Critics (*Apropos* of Recent Criticism of Imagism, Vers Libre and Modern Poetry Generally)," *Little Review* 3 (March 1916): 12-14 echoing EP's essay.

3. *Sonnets and Ballate of Guido Cavalcanti*, tr. Ezra Pound (Boston: Small, Maynard and Company, 1912).

4. Frances Gregg (1884-1941), a minor but at one time promising poet and close girlhood friend of H. D. and EP who often called her "the Egg." In *End to Torment* (ed. N. H. Pearson and M. King; NY: New Directions, 1979), H. D. wrote that Frances Gregg "filled the gap in my Philadelphia life after Ezra was gone, after our 'engagement' was broken. Maybe the loss of Ezra left a vacuum; anyway, Frances filled it like a blue flame" (8-9).

Gregg and her mother accompanied H. D. on her first trip to Europe in 1911. In 1912 she married the Englishman Louis Wilkinson, partly to return to England and H. D. In 1923, however, Gregg divorced him. EP opposed Gregg's interference with H. D.'s life and is likely criticizing this tendency when he tells ACH that he dislikes "adhesions." H. D. dedicated her 1927 novel, published in 1981, *HERmione*, to Gregg, who appears as "Fayne Rabb" in the text; EP is "George Lowndes."

5. ACH reviewed Masefield's *The Daffodil Fields* in *Poetry* II (May 1913): 76-78.

6. Between 17-22 April 1913, the column "A Line-O'-Type or Two" which appeared on the editorial page of the *Chicago Daily Tribune*, frequently cited Pound. His reference to "A Few Don'ts" may be to a passage in the column for 17 April 1913 where, after a satiric poem entitled "Spring in State Street" in the manner of the "Contemporania" series (*Poetry* II [April 1913]: 1-12), the following appears: "GET it straight. Ezra Pound is a poet and much of his stuff contrasts refreshingly with the conventional compa-compa. Formal rhymes and rhythms are not necessary to poetry. On the complemental hand, a 'new beauty' is not to be achieved merely by chopping lines into irregular lengths. A line is

poetic or it isn't" (p. 6). According to Ellen Williams, the parodist was Wallace Rice (49).

Two days later a debate occurred in the column over the issue of formal rhythms identifying poetry or not and the importance of content in poetry, both ideas allied with Pound. In the "Our Village" portion of the column that day (19 April 1913), the following also appeared: "Ralph Seymour has been traipsing around London with Ezray Pound, the former poet, and he writes that Ezray is contemplating locating in Our Village and joining the art uplift here. Come along, Ezray, the uplifting is fine" (6).

A 20 April 1913 editorial entitled "Hard on the Classics" appears to draw from Pound, complaining that it is impossible to obtain good editions of the classics: "in the U.S. we seem to publish books more for display than for use" it declares (4). Finally, on 22 April 1913, EP was subject to another satire, a poem in Latin entitled "Horace to Ezra Pound" (6). It begins:

> *Q.II.F. suo cato sed dementi Ezrae libras salutem*
> QUO USQUE TANDEM
> ABUTERE. MI EZRA PATIENTIA NOSTRA?

and ends with:

> O EZRA. QUO MODO HOC POTES?
> DESILI, DESINE;
> NOS FESSOS REDDIS;
> SATIS HABUIMUS.
> CARMIA MEA MM ANORUM VIXERUNT:
> NUCAE ISTIUSMODI TAMEN,
> CONSIMILES CULICUM,
> CRAS MORIENTUR.
>   P.S.W.

7. See Letter 13, note 2.

16

---

10 Church Walk.

Re/The review of Yeats' "Cutting of an Agate" in the *Post* for May 9th.[1]

Yes, I think it a good review. I wish we could get "Ellen FitzGerald" \<to\> do some of "our" prose for us. (Unless she happens to be doing it already, under an alias.)

yrs. hastily
<E.P.>

1. Ellen FitzGerald, "The Life of Art, W. B. Yeats, *The Cutting of an Agate* (NY: Macmillan, 1912)," *Chicago Evening Post* (9 May 1913): 9.

FitzGerald's double-column review, appearing in the "Friday Literary Review" of the *Post*, edited by Floyd Dell with Lucian Cary as associate editor, praises Yeats' prose volume, declaring that the poet is a prophet whose vision is of "living shapes and fantasies, and of a world whose substance is of other worlds" (9). Objecting to George Moore's charge that Yeats is anti-intellectual, FitzGerald argues that Yeats "knows the why of his dream" and that "life and art are one" for him. He constantly "measures one by the other." The faith of Yeats is in beauty, she asserts, while his criticism is "creative" because "it enriches our own being." She concludes by quoting the final eight lines of Yeats' poem, "The Grey Rock," published in *Poetry* II (April 1913): 21. EP's "Contemporania" series and Harriet Moore's "Mother Earth" also appeared in that issue. Also see Letter 18, note 9.

10 Ch. Wlk.

July 1st [1913]

Dear A.C.H.

Thanks plentitudinously for the pictures.

The 'Tagore' is very good & the "you" looks decorative and well painted.[1] Tho' I can't be expected to know about the likeness & its hard to make the face quite fit with your letters. Presumably its another dimension, anyhow I don't yet know you. Voila. So I put you on the wall for a time, to see what I can learn. You look less "worn't" across the room. also one makes out the "paint" rather better.

I guess W.H. is all right (*Don't* rage) some day i shall see the splendour unveiled & then i shall *know* & adore.[2] I've writ 19 letters to H.M. since I last heard *anything* — not that it matters. I suppose I acknowledged my last cheque.

Peace. mercy & hope rest upon you.

Yours ever

Ezra Pound

1. ACH sent photographs of two paintings done by her husband, William Penhallow Henderson: the first was of Tagore, painted in 1913, the year he won the Nobel Prize; the second, of herself, probably done in 1911. Both were exhibited at the Art Institute of Chicago.

2. William Penhallow Henderson, ACH's husband.

18

EP to ACH   TLS [July/August ? 1913] 3 ll. Letter included with one dated 8-9 August 1913 in an envelope postmarked "Kensington W. 2.15pm 18 Nov. 1912." However, internal evidence confirms summer 1913 date.

10 Church Walk.
Kensington.

Dear A.C.H. .

I've just time to jab down a few answers.

NO. <H>elston knows me and his backers can just as well send his stuff and him to me for consultation.[1] I like the navvy personally but he has the rottenest crowd in London booming him. Also he hasn't half learne[d] his trade. He may do something if he works. <Dont boom what the *Eng. Rev.* does — it's usually wrong.>

I will start an account for you so that you can order direct from CURTIs and Davison, booksellers.[2] As that part of your letter is labeled JUNE I will let you order what ever books you havent yet received.

Yes, I thought two of Williams' things looked well. And even Flint better than I expected.[3]

Cannell may do something.[4] "The Dance" was done after I put the "fear-er-Gord" into him. I think he is worth watching.

Yes. I knew Johnson has left.[5] Thank God that detestable sheet the *Century* hasnt made a cent during the last five years. Thats something to cheer the heart.

I believe the *Yale Review* is in the hands of the Stand-pat-ers.

About the french stuff.[6] What I said was "Send back ALL my french notes and I'll recast 'em." I'm jolly glad the one you sent back did not get into print. . I'll send you a new article.[7] Dont bother to send back anything more. Just burn whatever happens to be lying about.

I'mm glad about Johns.[8] dilectus filius, $\underline{if}$ he cares to own the
paternity . .

Yes. get the FitzGerald woman onto our staff.[9]

I'm more or less taking on the "NEW Freewoman;" as the official
organ of Imagism etc. plans and treaties not yet fully ratified . . Will
arrange exchange . .[10]

I have refused to appear in the Rittenhouse coop. That is I put such
conditions as I dont think she can accept.[11]

Cannell is worth starting. dont worry about it. Fletcher has more
guts. Will send him along later. Also a Frost narrative . . . which
will probably bore everyone to tears.[12]

Dell dont so much matter.[13] Right-o

More anon.

　　　　　　　　yours ever
　　　　　　　　　　<E.P.>

------

1. John Helston (1877-1928?), a turner and fitter who visited EP at Church
Walk, was best known for *Aphrodite and Other Poems* (1913) which HM reviewed
in *Poetry* IV (May 1914): 69-71.

2. Curtis and Davison, London booksellers at 11a Church Street,
Kensington W., London.

3. Pound refers here to two of four poems by Williams which appeared in
Poetry II (June 1913): 93-96, his first appearance in the journal. F. S. Flint
published "Four Poems in Unrhymed Cadence" in *Poetry* II (July 1913): 136-139.

4. Skipwith Cannell (1887-1957), an American expatriate poet from
Philadelphia, whom Pound first met in Paris in the spring of 1913. Cannell and
his wife later moved to London and stayed in a room Pound found for them at 10
Church Walk. He sent several of Cannell's poems to Harriet Monroe; they
appeared in *Poetry* II (August 1913): 171-176. Pound also included a work by
Cannell in his 1914 anthology, *Des Imagistes* (1914).

5. Johnson is the unidentified editor of *Century, A Popular Quarterly* (1870-
1930) published in New York which Pound saw as representative of conservative
and moribund literary values. However, the magazine included a color reproduction of a painting by Edmund Dulac in October 1913.

6. Pound may be referring to his review of *Presences* by P. Jouve, *Poetry* I (February 1913): 165-166 and *Odes et prières* by Jules Romains, *Poetry* II (August 1913): 187-189 plus "Paris," *Poetry* III (October 1913): 26-30. The last summarizes his conclusions outlined in his series entitled "The Approach to Paris," which ran in the *New Age* from 4 September 1913 to 16 October 1913.

7. The new article may have been "Paris," *Poetry* III (October 1913): 26-30 which summarizes EP's conclusions from his seven part series "The Approach to Paris" which started in *New Age* XIII (4 September 1913): 551-552.

8. Orrick Johns (1887-1946) American poet and journalist from St. Louis whose "Songs of Deliverance" appeared in *Poetry* III (February 1914): 172-178. See Williams 55 and *EP/JQ passim*.

9. Ellen FitzGerald contributed "The Modern Epic of War," *Poetry* V (March 1915): 288-293 but did not join the editorial staff of the journal.

10. Pound began to publish in the *New Freewoman* on 15 October 1913 with a three-part series entitled "The Serious Artist."

11. *The Little Book of Modern American Verse*, ed. Jessie B. Rittenhouse (Boston: Houghton Mifflin, 1913) which sold over 100,000 copies was reviewed by HM in *Poetry* III (January 1914): 144-145. Rittenhouse was also the founder of the Poetry Society of America which was formed in 1910 and later included Witter Bynner among its members.

12. John Gould Fletcher (1886-1950), from Arkansas, arrived in London in 1908 via Harvard; in April 1913 he met Pound in Paris who convinced him to lend financial support to *The Egoist*. Fletcher soon became a disciple of Pound's *vers libre* technique; his first poem in *Poetry*, entitled "Irradiations," appeared in Volume III (December 1913): 85-91.

The "Frost narrative" probably refers to Frost's "The Code - Heroics" which appeared in *Poetry* III (February 1914): 167-171.

13. Floyd Dell, writer for the *Chicago Evening Post*, who praised *Provença* (Boston: Small, Maynard and Co., 1910) in his column the "Friday Literary Review" (6 April 1911). The first book of Pound's poetry published in America, the volume was a selection from *Personae* and *Exultations*. Dell later edited the literary section of the paper, also called the "Friday Literary Review," and subsequently became co-editor, with Max Eastman, of *The Masses* (1912-1917).

19

EP to ACH   TLS 8 & 9 August 1913 4 ll.

10 Church Walk, Kensington, W.

<8 & 9/8/'13>

Dear Alice Henderson

Fer Gorrds sake dont compare the infant Richard, dilectus fillius etc. in the year one of his age to F.M.H. an artist mature, accomplished. perhaps the most accomplished writer in England.[1] Almost a Great man, one is constantly trying to find why one can not apply just that word to the most intelligent of ones friends.

No. I dare say what you say about Richard is O.K., I'm not so stuck on this lot, I only think it is better than what we have been getting, or are likely to get from others.

H.Ds 1/2 two ought to have gone in.[2] It is to be noted that R. and I have squabbled over this lot of his for about six months, I pray you have me excused.

As for Cannell, when I found him I gave thanks to God that I had found at last an American resolved on perfection. I thought it worth while pushing. I still think so. He has got to be printed.

Fletcher will probably cheer yo<u> a lot more tho' he looks like a flint-stone quarry and sounds like a bolodoly circus.

I've taken on "THE New Freewoman" a fortnightly, as our, or at least my organ on this side the drink, and shall controll its literchure.[3]

I will shove your criticism into R., having exhausted myself in reproofs and exhortations.

Also. H.M. may as well use some of him, cela n'impeche (or however it spells itself) pas.

Bes[i]des the "Argyria" Is charming. I picked that out of an old wad of mss in a book Brigit had returned <or> in some forgotten cranny.[4]

We're printing a translation of DeGourmonts *Chevaux de Diomedes* in the *Freewoman*.

I've started a bookseller to look after you.

To return. Le pauvre petit is of an age when <one's> stuff is usually only fit for the ash heap . .

Also I am trying to do you a perfectly dammmmmdd <article> on the TREDITION, without doing a whole text book and history, and without beccoming wholly totally and utterly incoherent . . Oh! OHG! its musicianly, MEWsicianly my use of prose is !!!![5]

To return to R/. I should have said, meaning about what you do, that the things lacked emotion. There must be intense emotion before language simplifies itself to the point of Imagism.

The austerity or economy of the speech represents that intense emotion, and if <the emotion, the fusing. arranging. unifying force> it aren't there then the stuff goes to pieces.

In the "Caesar's Plate," however I think the fault is not in the swift turn at the end but in his failure to make the image before it. i.e. where he used the vague "through it all" without their being any possible thing, veil, or other "all" for anything to be "through".[6]

About Hueffer, he is still playing about, but he has it in him to be the most important prose author in England, before he shuffles off, after James and Hardy have departed etc.

He and Yeats are the two intelligent men in London. F.M.H. will do too much, and people havent yet sifted out his serious stuff from the rest sufficiently to realize how seriously he must "be taken".

etc etc. I've a pile of ten letters heaped and waiting.

The gods avail you.

Salaams to W.P.H.[7]

yours sincerely,

<E.P.>

---

1. Richard Aldington (1892-1962), admirer and supporter of Pound, whom Pound promoted. Aldington's first appearance in *Poetry* occurred in Volume I

(November 1912): 39-43. Pound argued that he and Aldington and H. D. invented "Imagism." In the fall of 1913, as a result of Pound's manipulations, Aldington became sub-editor of *The Egoist*, formerly the *New Freewoman*. F. M. H. is Ford Madox Hueffer.

2. Pound most likely refers to H. D.'s poems which appeared under the title of "Verses, Translations, and Reflections from 'The Anthology'," *Poetry* I (January 1913): 118-122. The last of the set, "Epigram," is signed "H. D., / 'Imagiste'" (122). The contributor's note on H. D. enigmatically reads "'H. D. *Imagiste*,' is an American lady resident abroad, whose identity is unknown to the editor. Her sketches from the Greek are not offered as exact translations, or as in any sense finalities, but as experiments in delicate and elusive cadences, which attain sometimes a haunting beauty" (135).

3. EP became literary editor of *The New Freewoman*, later *The Egoist*, in June 1913. Harriet Shaw Weaver supported the magazine edited by her companion Dora Marsden (*NF*, June-December 1913; *Egoist*, January-June 1914) and which she later edited herself (July 1914-1919).

4. "Argyria" by Aldington appeared in *Poetry* III (January 1914): 134. The fourteen-line poem opens with "O you, / O you most fair, / Swayer of reeds, whisperer / Among the flowering rushes" and ends with the more controlled, "White limbs, white song, / Pan mourns for you" (134). Immediately following is EP's essay on "The Tradition," 137-141, then HM's review of *The Little Book of Modern Verse*, ed. Jessie B. Rittenhouse, and ACH's review of two volumes by Madison Cawein (144-148). Completing the issue are two letters by Yeats (149-150). The issue began with eight poems by D. H. Lawrence (115-125).

Brigit Patmore (1882-1965), born in Dublin as Elizabeth Morrison-Scott, married the grandson of Coventry Patmore, John Deighton Patmore, in London in 1907. She soon became a good friend of Violet Hunt who knew the Patmores through her father William Hunt, brother of Holman Hunt. Patmore was often at South Lodge on Campden Hill, London, where Hunt and Ford Madox Ford frequently entertained writers, novelists, poets, and "fashionable people who liked a dash of ink with their tea or to pick a bright brain for dinner" (Brigit Patmore, *My Friends When Young*, ed. Derek Patmore [London: Heinemann, 1968], 51). EP called her "one of the most charming people on this planet" (Patmore 1) and dedicated *Lustra* to her under the Provençal name he had given her, "V[ail de] L[encour]." Ford fell in love with her but she rejected him after a brief affair; nevertheless, she may have inspired *The Good Soldier* and the character Nancy Rufford. She also brought Richard Aldington to EP's attention.

5. EP's essay "The Tradition," emphasizing the great lyric traditions of Greece and Provence, was published in *Poetry* III (January 1914): 137-141; rpt. in *LE* 91-93.

6. Pound refers to the final stanza of Aldington's "Lesbia," *Poetry* III (January 1914): 134, which reads, "And through it all I see your pale Greek face; / Tenderness / Makes me eager as a little child to love you, / You morsel left half cold on Caesar's plate."

7. ACH's husband, William Penhallow Henderson.

20

EP to ACH   TLS 14 October 1913 4 ll (8 pp: TS on both sides of each leaf).

<14 Oct. 1913>
10 Church Walk, Kensington, W

Dear A.C.H.

Thanks for your note. I'm not going to quit till I'm asked, but I do get mildly annoyed.[1]

Of course my position is extreme. I do not think the art of anything is ever assisted by the assistance of mediocrity. Videlicet the [P]oetry Journal of Boston.[2]

Of course if you print only the best or at least all of the best <you can get> you'll be accused of running a clique. But all advances in the art that have not been made specifically by ONE person have been made by cliques. or rather clique is a misnomer when applied to a groupe that is selected purely on account of ability.

I think that *Poetry* should print all the Yeats and all the me it can get, and when it gets us. I think it should fill in <with> people whom I can take seriously, or who are at least trying to do honest work.

En effet W.B.Y. and myself seem to have been shove<d> in with a lot of shisters and amateurs. at least that's the general effect. and provincial shisters at that.

At no time have there been many passable poets on this planet, she can't expect a galaxy of a hundred major planets.

Mediocrity is anathema, and modernity does not consist in rehashing labour disputes and rhetorizing about aeroplani. Shakespear didn't write "lines on the discovery of the Laocoon" in order to catch the spirit of his times and be "really Elizabethan."

As to prose, I think my suggestion for more space and an enlargement of format is sound. My French stuff in The N.A. [*New*

Age] ought to have appeared in *Poetry*. likewise my "Serious Artist" about to appear in the N.F. . .[3]

I think appearance in the *Poetry Journal* ought to disbar anyone from appearing in us. Obviously anyone who gets into that thing does not need the courtesy [of] our pages to display his triumphs.

I dont care a hang about the *Smart Set*, or about getting 25 cents more per line.[4] I'm perfectly willing to go to 2000 readers instead of 75 000, but if I'm left about on the shelf while H.M. prints Buzzle et cie., it isnt good enough to preserve a monopoly on my stuff.

You do not advance the arts in the U.S. by tolerating rot, but you might do some good by holding up a passable standard.

She cant possibly think all these little fry are going to interest anyone. (Even Johns hasnt appeared yet.[5])

About the last trio. Frost is certainly dull. and I'm not wild over <C>annell, and Fletcher is a disconnected volcano, but they are all trying in one way or another and they are all utterly incapable of getting into the ordinary magazines,[6] God knows they aren't ensconsed in the temple of apollo, but they've each one got at least a trace of character.

... re/other paragraphs in your letter.
I liked Miniver Cheevy, but BUT BBUUTTTTTTTT some of the other stuff in his vol !!!!!![7]

I think we might have him, but I strongly suspect he has written himself out, and it is to be noted that he NEVER *got* a serious effect in the whole book.

America, undiluted, rises to Bret Hearte and Riley.[8] that's about their speed, the <N>ational TONE etc.

2. I wish Seymour would get on with my books.
3. Fletcher IS precisely a centipede, mostly *pedes*
4. Of course Frost isnt quintessence, it is honest homespun, dull and virtuous. and he is as pig headed as any <N>ew <H>ampshire hecker that eve<r> put punkin seed into a granite field with a shot-gun. He'd gain a lot if he could mobilize, but he can't and one has to put up with it. Wordsworth is equally stolid. (and THAT is NO excuse,

for either of 'em.) There was once a poet named Villon, and once
another called Guido Cavalcanti, and once there was a little hunched
back jew. H.H.[9] And God dammmm most of the rest of 'em.

5. Thanks for the clipping, I'll pass it on to W.B.Y.

6. The *N. Age*, I only write in occasionally, *The Freewoman* I'm more
or less running, I don't mean all of it. (Thank god *not* E. Carpenter
et cie. and all that bilge) but I'm somewhat a guiding star and I
choose about a third, sometimes more sometimes less of the
contents. Loosely, for we haven't a red cent to pay authors. It is just
run *pour effarer le mouffle*, and to keep ourselves from being utterly
idle.

I had 15 pounds to spend on my poets but that's gone and
heaven knows when I'll get any more.

Re/poetry, How HOW HHOOWW can I be expected to carry my
high hand here, if the home office accepts rot.

E.G. Hewlett tells me a good outline of a narrative.[10] I ask him
to do it. The result is such that my conscience forces me to refuse it
over his own dinner table. C'est bien difficile. (Actually it wasn't AT
table, but it *was* smoking after dinner.) Qu' est ce qu'on peut faire?

And then we Kind Kerry Kow.

My feeling is that we should give certain people a show and then
drop 'em.

H.M. has gathered rosebuds in every fie[l]d for a full year.

I now think the bac[k] bone of paper, and the bulk of the stuff
should be ch[o]sen from the following people.

1. Yeats, Hueffer and myself.

2. Under rather strict surveillance, (or on the rare occasions when
they do write)

Colum (who has done nothing at all for a year)

Richard/. H.D./Lawrence (whom I dislike)

Upward (only he probably will never do anything more)

W.C. Williams (very severly chosen) A. Lowell (ditto)

Flint (now and again).

Translations, three or four times a year.

<? is that beastly Bezruc coming out?>[11]

And that dull beast Frost, whom I continue to believe in. <(O, more
or less)>

That lot would make an interesting review.

scratch everyone who appears in the *[P]oetry Journal*, and almost
anyone who appears in *Poetry and Drama*[12]
Also as I've suggested, we could pay half present rate for prose and
print double the ammount and that would give us space for respect-
able essays, Chosen by yr. hmbl. svt.

Precisement. MY idea, the sort of periodical I an<d> my circle
(not merely my intimates who write) could be interested in.

I've named twelve people. five of 'em americans.

Colum, Hueffer and Upward, hardly write any verse. that leaves
Yeats, Flint and Lawrence, and Richard, as the "english" staff.

A list of contents like the last two <numbers> bar Yeats and
Upward, and one simpl<y> STOPS reading the thing.

An old fashioned thing like Yeats['s] "Two Kings" ought to
have been ballanced with something like John's "Whoop of deliverance" and my modern things could carry such embalmed bodies as
Cawein and Stringer.[13]

Etc. I must go out and rescue Ford from a bore that he's <got> to
lunch and who wont go unless something intervenes.

yours ever.

Ezra>

Best of luck to W. P. H. and his show.

<pardon misprints.>

---

1. Pound was having difficulty with Harriet Monroe because of her
objections to "Prufrock" and her censoring of various texts (*SL* 44-45); the
following month he asked Ford Madox Hueffer to take over his role as Foreign
Editor. Hueffer declined but acted as a catalyst to reconcile, temporarily, Pound
to Monroe. In a letter to Amy Lowell, Pound laconically summarized and
prophesied his situation: "Yes, I resigned from Poetry in accumulated disgust,
and they axed me back. And I consented to return 'on condition of general
improvement of the magazine'—which won't happen—so I shall be compelled to
resign permanently some time or other" (SL 29).

2. *The Poetry Journal*, published in Boston and edited by W. S. Braithwaite.
See Letter 7, note 4.

3. Pound's three-part series "The Serious Artist" appeared in the *New Freewoman* on 15 October, 1 November, and 15 November 1913. He republished the series in *Pavannes and Divisions* (New York: Knopf, 1918), 219-242.

4. H. L. Mencken edited *Smart Set* and favorably reviewed *Provença*. As early as May 1912, Pound's poetry began to appear in the New York journal, including "Portrait d'une Femme." In January 1916 his last piece in the magazine appeared, an unsigned poem attributed to Pound:

> I know that what Nietzsche said is true,
> And yet —
> I saw the face of a little child in the street,
> And it was beautiful.

5. Orrick Johns, whose poem "Songs of Deliverance" was sent by Harriet Monroe to Pound for comment. On 13 June 1913, Pound wrote to Monroe that Johns was "about the best you've found on your side of the wet" (Williams 55).

6. Notice of Frost first occurred in *Poetry* in May 1913 when Pound reviewed *A Boy's Will* (London: David Nutt, 1913), which EP characterized as "a little raw" with "a number of infelicities," although underneath them "it has the tang of the New Hampshire woods and it has just this utter sincerity." "This man," EP continued, "has the good sense to speak naturally and to paint the thing, the thing as he sees it" (*Poetry* II: 72-73). EP later called Frost's work "parochial," but nonetheless admired it because it was written in "the natural spoken speech" of New England. "His stuff sticks in your head—not his words, nor his phrases, nor his cadences, but his subject matter" (*Poetry* V [December 1914]: 127, 128, 130). EP continued to be critical of Frost but supportive, "booming" him to H. L. Mencken, although by August 1915 he complained to the *Boston Transcript* that it misrepresented Frost as being the only writer of his generation to win the acceptance of an English publisher. "What about me?" he asked, as he summarized what he did to get Frost known (*SL* 51, 62-3). By 1918, however, he believed that Frost was sinking under his own weight (*SL* 135). Ironically, Frost was one of the earliest readers of "Three Cantos," being given the work by Harriet Monroe in March 1917 when it arrived in Chicago from Santa Fe; see Letter 63, note 2.

Frost became similarly chary of EP, actually resenting the 1913 *Poetry* review of *A Boy's Will* because of its indelicacies and criticism of American editors which Frost believed would jeopardize his chances of finding an American publisher. Furthermore, he became jealous of EP's attentions to H. D. and Richard Aldington rather than to himself. A parody written by Frost and sent to F. S. Flint records these feelings (Thompson I: 420). When he left England in 1915, Frost carefully avoided seeing EP, although he wrote a farewell note to which EP kindly responded (Thompson II: 533). Many years later, Frost extended his dislike of EP through his private outrage over EP's winning the Bollingen Prize for *The Pisan Cantos* (Thompson III: 176). However, by 1954 his attitude softened having re-read EP's 1914 review of *North of Boston* (*Poetry* V [December 1914]: 127-130); and by 1957 Frost assisted Archibald MacLeish in gaining EP's freedom from St. Elizabeths, first by joining T. S. Eliot and

Hemingway in signing a 1957 letter to the Attorney General requesting EP's release, then by playing a decisive role through meetings with Acting U.S. Attorney General William P. Rodgers, and later President Eisenhower in February 1958. A statement written by Frost was actually read at the hearing on 18 April 1958 to dismiss the treason indictment and release EP. The Department of Justice did not oppose the motion for dismissal and EP was free. Neglecting (or perhaps unaware of) the behind-the-scenes role of MacLeish, the *New York Times* the next day reported that Frost was the individual most responsible for the release of EP (Thompson III: 258).

Skipwith Cannell, the American expatriate, published infrequently in *Poetry*, although Pound felt his "Poems in Prose and Verse" (*Poetry* II [August 1913]: 171-176) were the literary find of 1913.

John Gould Fletcher was reviewed by Pound in *Poetry* for December 1913 (III: 111-113), and praised for two titles: *Fire and Wine* and *The Dominant City*. In that same issue appeared Fletcher's poetic series entitled "Irradiations," originally sent to HM by EP in August 1913; revisions and Fletcher's generally mediocre work, however, led to a flareup between EP and HM, delaying its publication.

7. Edwin Arlington Robinson's "Miniver Cheevy" appeared in *The Town Down the River* (NY: Scribner's, 1910), a volume dedicated to Theodore Roosevelt. Unlike the frustrated idealism and irony of "Cheevy," however, the other poems in the book celebrate various heroes such as Abraham Lincoln in the opening poem, "The Master," or Theodore Roosevelt in "The Revealer." Dramatic monologues imitative of Browning vie with Tennysonian lines such as these from the opening of "Leonora": "They have made for Leonora this low dwelling in the ground, / And with cedar they have woven the four walls round." EP would have, of course, objected to such poetry, as well as to the sentimental religiosity of the poem "But for the Grace of God." The poet James Dickey has noted that Robinson's best work and his worst "are remarkably alike." "Introduction," *Selected Poetry of E.A. Robinson*, ed. Morton Dauwen Zabel (NY: Macmillan, 1965), xix. Also see *SL* 58.

8. Francis Bret Harte (1836-1902), American western journalist, short story writer, and poet, is best known for his stories of the gold country like "The Outcasts of Poker Flat." Despite the use of local dialect and landscape by Harte—who actually lived in London from 1885 until his death—EP found his work "facetious" and facile (*SL* 55). Nevertheless, EP included Harte's popular 1870 comic ballad about a wily Chinese gambler who outwits two deceptive card sharks, "Plain Language from Truthful James," in his anthology *Confucius to Cummings* (1964), 274-276.

James Whitcomb Riley (1849-1916), the Indiana journalist and poet, was an early interest of EP's; Stock suggests he was a "household name" for the youthful EP because of his poems of rural America and attempts at dialect (11). In a positive review of Richard Middleton's emotional *Poems and Songs*, EP declared "lovers of Riley will go mad over him" (*Poetry* III [October 1913]: 34). EP cited Riley in his 1914 essay "The Renaissance" as an artist who might benefit from an endowment to escape from the commercial pressures of publication (*LE* 224), while in *The Pisan Cantos* Pound wondered: "wd / Whitcomb Riley be still found in highbrow anthology?" (80/524). EP partly answers the question by including Riley's dialect poem, "Good-By. Er Howdy-Do," in *Confucius to Cummings*, 276-277.

9. Heinrich Heine (1797-1856), satirist as well as poet and journalist. EP published his four-line poem "Translator to the Translated" (see Letter 2, note 6). EP praised Heine's work as a poet of detail and concreteness in "A Retrospect" and "The Renaissance" and celebrated his satire in "How to Read" (*LE* 17, 216, 30, 33). In a letter of 21 January 1916 to HM, EP cited Heine as a source for Imagism (*SL* 67). For background, see Walter Baumann, "Ezra Pound and Heinrich Heine," *PAI* 18 (1989): 59-75.

10. See Letter 7, note 5.

11. Petr Bezruc (1867-1958), pseudonym of popular Czech poet Vladimir Vasek, known for his "Silesian Songs" (1903, 1937) which EP praised in "Bohemian Poetry," *Poetry* I (November 1912): 58-59.

12. *Poetry and Drama*, edited by Harold Monro in London, published from March 1913 to December 1914 and, despite EP's criticism, printed his work as well as contributions from Frost, D. H. Lawrence, Fletcher, Aldington, and Amy Lowell.

13. Yeats, "The Two Kings," *Poetry* III (October 1913): [1]-10. In his review of *Responsibilities* (*Poetry* IV [May 1914]: 64-69), EP continued to criticize the outdated quality of "The Two Kings," although he praised the "new note" in Yeats' poetry as seen in a "greater hardness of outline" and demonstrated by the opening of "The Magi" (66, 67).

Orrick Johns, "Songs of Deliverance," would appear in *Poetry* III (February 1914): 172-178.

Madison Cawein (1865-1914) born in Kentucky, was known for his nature poetry and published "Waste Land" and "My Lady of the Beeches" in *Poetry* I (January 1913): 104-107. However, his traditional syntax, metre, and imagery, more Georgian than Romantic, disturbed EP. Cawein's "The Old Home" appeared in the same issue as Yeats' "The Two Kings" and contains such awkward lines as: "The shrubs, which snowed their blossoms on / The walks wide-stretching from its doors / Like friendly arms, are dead and gone, / And over all a grand house soars," *Poetry* III (October 1913): 17-19.

Arthur Stringer (1874-1950), American poet who moved to Canada; his "A Woman at Dusk" opened *Poetry* II (August 1913): [153]-158. More syntactically adventurous than Cawein, Stringer sought a new drama in his verse that in some ways evoked Swinburne as in these lines from "A Woman at Dusk": "My lips seek out your lips of mortal rose, / And tremulous you yield, and from the pain / Of utter sacrifice still garner joy" (158). HM reviewed his *Open Water* in *Poetry* V (February 1915): 243-245.

2 1

■■■■■■■■■ **EP to ACH**   TLS 22 October 1913 1 1.

10 Church Walk, W.

Dear A.C.H.

When are you going to India? The reason I ask is this, Rebecca West talks of going to America. For what reason Gord only knows, save that she hath an insatiable and bizarre curiosity. H.M. would have a hard time to find a better, or at least a more intelligent assistant editor.[1]

R[ebecca].W[est]. is favorably disposed toward "Poetry". You always write as if you were either un- or under-paid. *ma che!*

Anyhow, there's the fact. R.W. may emigrate (at least for a year or so) and you may be (or are) departing or about to depart. I dont know whether this [is] a solution. R.W. was asst. on the *Freewoman* until she fit and resigned about three days ago (re/ political creeds etc.) <and I wish to — she hadn't for I am left with a very large edt. office to argue with.> Also she is cou<n>ted one of the ablest journalists here. etc. WHAT the devil do I know about it. (It? i.e. journalism). Anyhow she has SOME sense. And she etc. voila.

<Yours ever

E.P.>

■■■■■■

1. Rebecca West (1892-1983), essayist, critic, and novelist, began her career as a journalist joining the staff of *The Freewoman, A Weekly Feminist Review* (founded and edited by Dora Marsden) in 1911, becoming assistant editor when the journal was renamed the *New Freewoman* with Harriet Shaw Weaver as a backer and, later, editor. She held this post until October 1913 when, frustrated with the politics and management of the journal (as EP suggests in this letter to

ACH), she resigned to be replaced by Richard Aldington. These events coincided with the renewal of her complicated love affair with H. G. Wells which was initiated in 1911 and lasted until 1923.

EP met West through Violet Hunt and Ford Madox Hueffer and it was West who invited him to take the post as literary editor of the *New Freewoman*. West's short story "Indissoluble Matrimony" appeared in the first issue of *Blast* (20 June 1914): 98-117, along with poems by EP, prose by Lewis, and the opening pages of Ford's *The Good Soldier*. However, by 3 August 1917 EP complained in a letter to Margaret Anderson that West "is a journalist, a clever journalist, but not 'of us.' She belongs to Wells and that lot" (*EP/LR* 100).

22

EP to ACH   ALS ? December 1913 I I. 2 pp. Ms. on front and back of leaf.

10 Church Walk, Kensington, W.

Dec. 1913

Dear A.C.H.

Have just written to H.M.

As a first faint sign of grace, you might suggest that she print Aldington.

H.D. (american)

Frost (")

Fletcher (")

and Bezruc

at once.

it would make a fairly decent number.

There will be some *me* in April. & some Yeats in May. & possibly some Sturge-Moore — if America (non-expatriated) can't produce something better. The Lawrence will do for Feb. if it aint in before then. And thereafter what I send over marked definitely to go in. will appear within two months.

Yours

EP.

23

EP to ACH   TLS 27 January 1914 4 ll + 2 Enclosures: a clipping dealing with Tagore from *The Bengalee*, an Indian paper; a 1912 letter from EP to HM reprinted here.

<Jan. 27 - 1914>
10 Church Walk
Kensington, W

Dear A.C.H.

Thanks for your letter and the clippings. I dont know anything about Flint'd guineas (?) or is it "grievance?"[1]

I should judge that H" M" had done quite right in rejecting his stuff. He chose to get enraged at her criticism. at least that was the mumble I heard. As I haven't seen the letter so I cant tell the rights or tacts of it. Dont worry. We can run without him. Anyhow he only does a good thing once in a duck's age and I can easily get it when he does.

Anything that isnt sent by me has been either refused or evaded.

Or in one case (Cannell's) and another Rhys's some time ago. I did tell 'em to send it in.[2] I didnt enthuse and I didn't positively object.

I'll review Bill Williams if you insist, but I'd rather you did it. I've already reviewed him in the *Freewoman*. Also there is the Glebe anthology *Des Imagistes*. You might do the two together.[3] Or I'll do it, if you prefer. But I'd rather you did.

I put the ads into the *Freewoman*. I think you owe the *Egoist* a page on that score. If you insert their adv. I'll see that they keep up the POETRY. Here is a trial adv.

The EGOIST
(Late the New Freewoman)
AN INDIVIDUALIST REVIEW <(fortnightly)>

The only publication in England which recognizes no
tabos (taboos?)
    (you are nearer a dictionary than I am)
Editor Dora Marsden.
Asst. Edt. R. Aldington
Contributors.
Allen Upward. Ford Madox Hueffer, Ezra Pound
Remy de Gourmont, Reginald W Kauffmann
Storm Jameson, Robert Frost, Muriel Ciolkowska
Wyndham Lewis, John Cournos etc. etc.

▬▬▬▬▬▬ [pasted enclosure, printed:]

Terms of Subscription.— Yearly, 14/- (U.S.A.
3 dollars 50 cents); Six Months, 7/- (U.S.A.,
1 dollar 75 cents); ~~Three Months, 3/6 (U.S.A.,
95 cents)~~. Single Copies 7d., post free to any address in the
Postal Union.
~~ADVERTISEMENTS~~
    All orders, ~~letters, & etc., concerning advertise-
ments~~ should be addressed to ~~the Advertisement
Manager,~~ The EGOIST, Oakley House, Bloomsbury Street, London, W.C.

I think I shall send in one of old Fenollosa's Japanese plays instead
of anything of my own for March (or April, it would go very well
with W.B.Y.) <Also W.B.Y. will like it for company, he is very keen
on the stuff [.]>[4]

Yone Noguchi has sent me two bad jobs which I shall return.[5] If he
has anything worse, it may as well come here for rejection.

One or two of the plays are to appear here in the *Quarterly Review.*[6]
The last bulwark of good letters in England.
I have strong doubts about the KABIR being worth printing. It
should go in as prose, if at all but I think the public is too fed up on
Tagore to stand any more India for a decade.

These Nōh plays of Fenollosa's are however a definite find. A new beauty as worth discovering as was Chinese art a few decades ago. The books and translations hitherto printed give nothing, or next to nothing of a notion. If I use "Kinuta" and "Hagoromo" in the *Quarterly*[,] I shall send you a different one.[7]

Do you want a photo of the Blunt presentation as an adornment to the office. It is good of every one except Yeats.?[8]

I am glad Johns is to be in.[9]
Guess that's all at the moment. Good luck.
Hope W.P.H. continues to sell to the municipality.

    <yours ever

        Ezra Pound>

27/1/14

      [Enclosure 1:]
      Clipping of a single page from *The Bengalee*, 26 November 1913, with three articles headlined "Deputation to Mr Rabindranath Tagore," "Meeting at Silchar," and "Messages of Congratulations." The headline of the first article underlined in red by EP.

      [Enclosure 2:]
      EP to Harriet Monroe. ALS 26 October 1912. 4 ll. Postmark 26 October 1912.
          One of two letters in the Alice Corbin Henderson collection at the Harry Ransom Humanities Research Center from EP to HM. In the second (Letter 69), EP concludes by telling HM to pass the letter on to ACH. The appearance of this letter in the EP/ACH correspondence suggests that it, too, was passed on to Henderson at the *Poetry* office.

      10 Church Walk
            Kensington
            London. W.

Dear Miss Monroe:

    Thanks for yr. note. Stationery arrives.

    I've just written to De Gourmont for *one short* poem.

    Told him his future glory depended entirely on its being a good one.

    I don't see why our campaign for an international standard should be confined to the pages of "Poetry."

Is "Neale" <he's circulariz[in]g but I've never heard of him before> of New York, any one reliable? *Je m'en doute.*

But if I could spread myself in a series of articles on French poetry since 1880 [,] I might wake up something.[10]

Do you know any Chicago paper or magazine that would print 'em. —— one a month — articles any length *under* 5000 words. price $100 per slash. or $1000. for series of 12.

En passant my publisher has gone smash & even sooner than I expected.[11] I've got to do something and it may as well be something useful. I'd take.

Gautier (Introduction to series.)

De Gourmont

Verhaeren.

De Regnier.

The americans.: Vide Griffin & Merril

Paul Fort

Tailhade

and other groups to be selected later. (Moreas,. Jammes, (Malarmé, if he's not too well known), Samain, etc. possibly some of *les jeunes.*[)] Tho' they're rather Flint's personal property. and they do seem to run to prefaces rather than to performance.

"Poetry" is and ought to be the place for "poetry", but I think a strong *f*lanking movement in criticism. — printed at some one else's expense might help.

The English & American idea of French "influence" is the "90's" and they dont know anything but Verlaine & the muzzyest of the symbolists.

I believe if I can shift the American eye not from Boston to London — thats past — but from London to Paris it would shake the barnacles off our poetic keel.

"che cantando varca"?[12]

not quite

As for yr. note and "frankness", you'll get the latter O.K. "Euphues" is as dead as old papa Rosencrux.[13]

Yours

E.P.

Will you send the enclosed card with 12 circulars to
   Mrs. J.F. Cross
     136 W. State St
      Trenton, N.J.[14]

Put my name on the outside of
envelope. so that they wont mistake it for
   an "adv."

---

1. F. S. Flint (1885-1960), English poet, translator, and critic prominent in the Imagist movement. See Flint, "Imagisme," *Poetry* I (March 1913): 198-200 partly written by EP who also included five of Flint's poems in *Des Imagistes* (1914).

2. See Cannell's sequence "Poems in Prose and Verse," *Poetry* II (August 1913): 171-176.

Ernest Rhys (1859-1946), Welsh poet, dramatist and editor of the Everyman Library series. His praise to J. M. Dent of Pound's *The Spirit of Romance* led to its publication in June 1910. Pound refers to Rhys' "A Song of Happiness," *Poetry* I (January 1913): 114-116. Pound praised Rhys' work in "Status Rerum," ibid., 127. Rhys also had two poems in *Poetry* II (September 1913): 204-205.

3. Pound reviewed Williams' *The Tempers* in *The New Freewoman* I (1 December 1913): 227.

The February 1914 issue of *Glebe* essentially reprinted *Des Imagistes* published in March 1914 by Boni in New York. The *Glebe* version was Volume I No. 5 of the journal, originally to be published as Volume I No. 1 by the two co-editors, Alfred Kreymborg and Man Ray. However, when Boni took over the journal, they chose to publish the imagist anthology separately, delaying its periodical publication. ACH reviewed the *Glebe* version in *Poetry* V (October 1914): 38-40.

4. Fenollosa's "Nishikigi" appeared in *Poetry* IV (May 1914): [35]-48 with an explanatory note apparently by EP on pp. 71-72. The same issue contained 12 poems by Yeats.

5. The eminent Japanese poet Yoni Noguchi (1875-1947) had sent EP a copy of his collection *The Pilgrimage* from Kamakura and in 1909 Elkin Mathews began to publish his work. (See *EP/MC* 90). Between 1910 and 1915 Mathews produced an elegant edition of *The Pilgrimage: A Book of Poems* admired by EP who corresponded with Noguchi. Invited by Robert Bridges, at one time Noguchi lectured on Japanese poetry at Oxford. At this period, of course, EP was working on the Fenollosa manuscripts and preparing *Cathay* for publication by Mathews in April 1915. ACH cited Noguchi's "The Poet," in "Poetic Prose and

Vers Libre," *Poetry* II (May 1913): 71, and reviewed his *Spirit of Japanese Poetry* in *Poetry* VII (November 1915): 89-95.

6. "Kinuta" and "Hagoromo" appeared in full in "The Classical Drama of Japan," edited by EP from Fenollosa's manuscripts, *Quarterly Review* CCI (October 1914): 450-77. Reprinted and expanded in *'Noh' or Accomplishment* (1916).

7. Pound sent ACH "Nishikigi," printed in *Poetry* IV (May 1914): [35]-48.

8. On 18 January 1914, to celebrate Wilfrid Scawen Blunt's 75th birthday, a group of eight writers visited Blunt in Sussex and posed for a now famous photo. The group consisted of Blunt plus Victor Plarr, Sturge Moore, Yeats, Pound, Aldington, and Flint. Hilaire Belloc and Frederic Manning were not photographed. They presented Blunt with a stone reliquary carved by Henri Gaudier-Brzeska containing within it poetic appreciations by the eight benefactors. See Wilhelm 137 for a reproduction of the photo; page 299 of *EP/DS* reproduces a picture of the reliquary. Canto 81/535-536 concludes with a reference to the Blunt visit.

9. Orrick Johns whose "Songs of Deliverance" Harriet Monroe had sent to Pound for his opinion. He praised the work in a letter to her dated 10 June 1913; the poems appeared in *Poetry* III (February 1914): 172-178.

10. EP published just such a series in his seven-part "The Approach to Paris" in the *New Age* XIII (4 September 1913-16 October 1913). The writers he discussed included de Gourmont, Romains, Vildrac, Tailhade, de Régnier, Jammes, Rimbaud, Fort, and Spire. For *Poetry* EP contributed a summary article, "Paris," *Poetry* III (October 1913): 26-30.

11. Swift and Company of Covent Garden, London, who published *Ripostes* in October 1912, had signed a contract with EP offering him £100 a year for ten years as an advance against royalties for future publications. In turn, Swift was to be his sole British publisher. However, the manager, Charles Granville, absconded to Tangier with most of the funds causing the publisher's collapse. Perhaps more seriously for EP was the suspension of his "engagement" to Dorothy Shakespear whose parents insisted on a secure income for her poet-lover.

12. Will that singing come to pass?

13. John Lyly's prose fiction *Euphues: The Anatomy of Wit* appeared in 1578, his *Euphues and His England* in 1580. The prolix, elaborate, sententious, and exaggerated prose style highlighted the hero and the text.

"Rosencrux" alludes to the repeated refrain in Yeats' "The Mountain Tomb": "Our Father Rosicross is in his tomb," *Poetry* I (December 1912): [67].

14. Mrs. J. F. Cross is the married Mary Moore (1885-1976) of Trenton, N.J., whom EP first met in 1907 and for a while considered his fiancée. She married James F. Cross, Jr., in July 1912; earlier, in April that year, she visited EP in London. EP dedicated *Personae* (1909) to her.

24

<Feb. 26- 1914>
10 Church Walk, Kensington. W.
Note change of address, I am moving to
5 Holland Place Chambers,
Kensington, London. W.

(on Monday so all mail can be sent there from now on)[1]

Dear A.C.H.

Thanks for the hypothetical welcome, but I did not go to America with Mr Yeats.[2]

??2 .

Did you send a wholly unintelligible cable about "KING dark chamber".???

Apparently you or another Alice Henderson wanted "american serial rights for May dramatic quarterly, seventy five dollars. 1000 copies only." (why ???)

There are seventeen minor novelists named King. Is King the author or is it part of the title??? Anyhow I've cabled back for instructions and if you didn't send the message you'll get a very puzzling reply.[3]

Nobody, neither I nor R. nor W.L. George has heard of "King dark chamber". Basil King hasn't answered my note, so I suppose it dont concern him.[4] No, apparently the sender of the cable WILL get the answer,

Anyhow the dark chamber appears untraceable.

I'm to meet the dammm laureate tomorrow.[5] I wonder if it is worth while getting or trying to get a powm from his stodgy pen. I suppose from the vulgar advertising side, I "owe it to the magazine". It might serve to ballance my next consignment.

Thanks for the notice of W.P.H., I cant remember whether or not, I wrote.

<yours ever,

E.P.>

<26-2-'14>

1. Pound moved from 10 Church Walk to 5 Holland Place Chambers at the beginning of March 1914 in anticipation of his marriage to Dorothy Shakespear and the need for larger quarters. He lived there until 1919.

2. Yeats made a lecture tour of the United States in 1914 and *Poetry* held a banquet for him in Chicago on 1 March 1914. For a report of the event see "Poetry's Banquet," *Poetry* IV (April 1914): 25-29. Arthur Davison Ficke introduced Yeats.

3. "The King of the Dark Chamber" was a play by Rabindranath Tagore.

4. R is likely Richard Aldington. W. L. George (1882-1926) is the French-born socialist, early feminist, and novelist whom EP met at an evening held at T. E. Hulme's; author of *The Engines of Social Progress* (1907) and *Woman and To-morrow* (1913), he was included among the "Blasted" in a list published in *BLAST* 2 (July 1915): 2.

Basil King (1859-1928) was an American novelist, short-story writer, and spiritualist best known for *The Inner Shrine* (1909).

5. Despite the harsh attitude expressed toward the poet laureate Robert Bridges (1844-1930) in this letter, Pound had a delightful time when they met the next day in Oxford, later praising Bridges' disarming manner (he apparently referred to his job as laureate as "This Professorship") and appreciating his "flattering familiarity with my works" (*EP/DS* 310). In that same year, EP cited Bridges along with Hewlett and Manning as one who was "seriously concerned with overhauling the metric, in testing the language and its adaptability to certain modes" (*LE* 12). In August 1915, EP praised Bridges' poems to HM (*SL* 62) and positively reviewed Bridges' *Poems Written in the Year MCMXIII* in *Poetry* VIII (October 1915): 40-44, concluding: "the island [England] is to be congratulated

on having at last obtained a laureate who declines to treat himself as an institution" (44). However, Pound later criticized Bridges as the one poet who, after
reading *Personae* and *Exultations*, "(commended every archaism [to my horror],
exclaiming 'We'll git 'em back; we'll git 'em *all* back.' Eheu fugaces!)" (*SL* 179).
Pound recalled the incident in *The Pisan Cantos* (Canto 80/521). In an April 1936
letter to Eliot, EP criticized the dullness of Bridges' poetry, unsympathetically
referring to him as "Rabbit Britches" (*SL* 280). Yet in a 1962 interview, EP cited
Bridges as one of his important literary predecessors and advisors (the other three
were Hardy, Keats, and Ford). The advice Bridges gave to EP was "a warning
against homophones" ("EP: An Interview," *Paris Review* 28 [1962]: 29).

2 5

---

5 Holland Place Chambers
Kensington. London. W.

Dear A.C.H.

Supposing you to have been the authour of the inquiries re/ the Tagore play, the enclosed series of affirmatives will set your mind at rest.

If you didn't make the original inquiry do send the letter on to Alice Henderson the other art critic.

I suppose Macmillan will forward mss. of play on Monday.

Or go to the *Drama Quarterly* which I never heard of. They ought to know something about the matter.

sorry not to tarry further but am in rush for an appointment.

yours ever

<E. Pound>

<14-3-'14>

---

5 Holland Place Chambers
Kensington, W.

Dear Mr Fox Strangways

The enclosed cable relates to Mr Tagore's "King of the Dark Chamber".

The *Drama Quarterly* wants to print it in their May number. They can pay £15.

I dont know whether you have made any other arrangements, or whether you can make better terms. Not many plays can be used "serially" in magazines. However that's for you to decide. Will you please let me know at your earliest convenience.

yours sincerely

4/3/'14 <Ezra Pound>

<I cant find your address in
Telephone book — nor that of the
India Society. so send this via
Curtis Brown.>

[Enclosure 2:]

From Curtis Brown, International Publishing Bureau, 6, Henrietta Street, Covent Garden, London W.C.

14 March 1914.

Ezra Pound Esq.,
5, Holland Place Chambers,
Kensington, W.

Dear Mr. Ezra Pound,

That letter of yours to Fox-Strangways gets around back to me again, with enclosed letter from Macmillan & Co. I am pointing out to them that the letter should have been addressed to you, and that I am forwarding it to you. There is nothing further I can do in the matter.

Yours very truly,
<Curtis Brown>

CB/RF

enclos.

[Enclosure 3:]

From Macmillan & Co. Ltd., St. Martin's Street, London W.C. (2 Enclos.)

12th March 1914.

Mr. Curtis Brown
 6, Henrietta Street,
  Covent Garden, W.C.

 Dear Sir,
  Your letter of March 5 addressed to Mr. Fox Strangways, with enclosures from Mr. Ezra Pound and a cable on behalf of the American *Drama Quarterly*, was referred to us as we have now taken over the whole management of Mr. Tagore's affairs. After having considered the matter fully we are prepared to accept, on Mr. Tagore's behalf, the payment of £15. for the right to use Mr. Tagore's play "The King of the Dark Chamber" in the May number of the *Drama Quarterly*, of which we understand that only one thousand copies will be printed. We ought to explain, however, that in order that the English copyright may be secured we propose to issue this play separately in this country at a moderate price. We return the enclosures.
  We are,
   Yours faithfully
    <Macmillan & Co Ltd.>

26

\<Apr. 13. '14\>

5 Holland Place Chambers
Kensington. London. W.

Dear A.C.H.

Thanks for your letter. I am, as might be expected, a bit "in the
midst" this week.[1]

Please \<change\> next to last line of BLAST adv.

it should read:

> All subscriptions should be addressed to BLAST
> 4 Percy St. Tottenham Court Road. London. W.C.

Thanks for the advance draft (which aint arrived yet) I'm sorry if I
muddled about the date.

I dont think Sandburg is particularly important but it is the sort of
stuff we ought to print. It is direct from life, tho' he is working on
borrowed \<?\> lines[.] Both he and Frost are however working direct.
Frost is dull and old fashioned and both these qualities obscure his
reality.

Sandburg is obviously modern. That is to say his modernities
are obvious. He and Orrick Johns are the two men so far whom I
should like to see regularly represented. I mean out of H.M.'s lot. I
should like him to get closer, harder, more emotional, and to
develop a personal style.

He is still magnetized by words. Momus is bad.[2]

You understand I am hitting hard, I am being severe because I think he can stand it <???> Most of the other U.S. magazine stuff is just pulp and not worth serious criticism. Sandburg still has his clump phrases. He must break his material smaller before he assembles it.

No, he is not as good as Johns, nor as important as the plodding Frost.

<yours ever,
E.P.>

<13-4-'14> `

<No - Sandburg aint good enough yet. Too loose. Too general. Magazine ideas. Still its the sort of stuff we should print.>

---

1. A week later, on Monday the 20th of April 1914, Pound would marry Dorothy Shakespear.

2. Sandburg's poem "Momus" appeared in *Poetry* III (March 1914): 196-197.

27

<1914>

5 Holland Place Chambers
Kensington. W.

Dear A.C.H.

Thanks for your letter.

I enclose new form of *Egoist* adv.

The May number of *Poetry* is some comfort to a man. I hope we can keep that level.[1]

I am glad Hueffer is in June. I think it a great mistake for H.M. to cut rates on the best stuff she gets. It isn't encouraging, but it may be necessary. I dont know how long his poem really is.[2] Also the cut <in rates> puts me in a very embar[r]assing position, but F.M.H. won't persecute me for the remainder @ 10 dollars per page. And as his "Heaven" will get the guarantors prize I suppose that will salve his possible disappointment.

I thank you very much for bothering about the Noh. I should be very glad to have the American publication arranged for me.

I will send two plays and a prose article mostly Fenollosa's notes, I think, to DRAMA.[3]

~~I wonder, no matter,~~ Hinckley must decide whether he wants to print ALL the Fenollosa notes. DRAMA ought by rights to do it, but, I dont know . . . .

I will talk to Flint and Richard. about translations of plays.

I think I might do the notes on contemporary plays here, probably over a nom de plume. <? will that suit. I don't know whether I wont want [to] sing anyhow.>
But as one won't get free seats on the strength of it I dont know how

far ten dollars per thousand will carry one, if one does "brief notes". However IF the edt will send a printed form for the request of tickets stating WHAT "Drama" is, does, and profits. I dare say it would help some.

I cant exactly recommend Cannel[l], but he is hard up and I'd be glad if Hinckley can give him a chance. His attempts to do Paris notes for the *Egoist* may have taught him something. Je m'en doute.

? How much NOTES does he [Hinckley] want per quarter. I suppose there are five or six decent plays per quarter. Interesting decor etc. would that run to 2500 words. When should the copy be sent. Latest date per number etc.

This IS a dull letter, all details, and it is before 11 a.m.

We, plural, have returned from our honeymoon, none the worse for it.[4] We have not die<d> of boredom or done any of the usual things, no murders or assassinations. I suppose that's something for a start.

D. sends you her best salutations.

I am lecturing on Imagisme at the Ormond Street rooms toward the end of the month. The little Anthology is doing very nicely.[5] Enclosed also receipt for £4. pardon me for bothering to send it via. you. but its one letter less to get off.
I'll send a long rigmarole about book shops and placing *Poetry*, later. I've seen Richard and written to Flint since I began this letter an hour ago, you'll probably hear from them direct or Hinckley will. Thanks for all your bothering.

Yes, Also. Blast adv. is more amusing in the enclosed form. Note change of address to Percy St. s.v.p.

Lawk! I must make an end and get out of this
   yours ever,
      <Ezra Pound>

<When is *Poetry* going to print any more of your verse?>

1. *Poetry* IV (May 1914) contained Fenollosa's "Nishikigi," edited by EP, poems by Bliss Carmen, Skipwith Cannell, and Yeats, plus EP's review of Yeats' *Responsibilities* in which he declared that Yeats was not an imagist; he was "a symbolist, but he has written *des Images* as have many good poets before him" (65).

2. Hueffer's poem "On Heaven," *Poetry* IV (June 1914): 75-94 was one of the longest published in the journal. In the same issue was EP's "Mr. Hueffer and the Prose Tradition in Verse," a review of Hueffer's *Collected Poems* (111-120) with this concluding note: "Mr. Hueffer is not an *imagiste*, but an impressionist" (120). EP also states that "On Heaven" is "the best poem yet written in the 'twentieth century fashion'" (114).

3. ACH apparently offered to help EP in placing his Fenollosa material which EP forwarded to Theodore Hinckley, editor of *Drama* from February 1913 to January 1931. This resulted in "The Classical Stage of Japan: Ernest Fenollosa's Work on the Japanese 'Noh'," *Drama* V (May 1915) 199-247 containing seven Noh dramas plus additional notes. Expanded, it was reprinted as Parts I and II of EP's *'Noh' or Accomplishment* (1916).

4. Pound married Dorothy Shakespear on 20 April 1914. For part of their honeymoon, Pound and Dorothy went to Stone Cottage where the Misses Welfare, who looked after Pound and Yeats during their stay at Stone Cottage in the winter of 1913-1914, cared for them. During their visit, Pound worked on his Noh dramas.

5. Pound was to hold an Imagist Evening at the Rebel Art Centre, founded by Wyndham Lewis, at 38 Great Ormond Street, Queen's Square, London W.C. It did not take place. The "little Anthology" refers to the 63-page *Des Imagistes*, published in April 1914 by The Poetry Bookshop in London. Albert and Charles Boni published the American edition in New York in March.

28

5, Holland Place Chambers, Kensington W.

24-5-'14

Dear A.C.H.

Do keep H.M. up to using my simple & pious verse called "Printemps".[1]

or at least for yr. private delectation have a look at it before she destroys it in a fury of Calvinistic zeal[.]

Does "Drama" want Flint to translate Romains "L'Armée dans le Ville"?

yours
E.P.

[On reverse of sheet:]

I've sent
in 4 new
poems & not
    H.M.
one of them
unserious

■■■■■■

1. "Printemps" is an unpublished poem of an irreligious nature sent by EP to irritate HM who in May 1914 censored a blasphemous line in John Rodker's "London Night." When EP heard of the change, he replied, "keep the Rodker as it is, one can't emasculate everything. I will spit in the eye of Gehoveh in my next lyric if it is necessary to establish free speech, tho I doubt if Jehovah has an eye. . . ." (in Williams 121). On 24 May 1914 EP sent "a few verses of simple piety," assumed to be "Printemps" (Williams 121).

29

EP to ACH   ALS 26 May 1914 I I + I Enclosure. Letter written on cardboard card measuring 8.8 mm x I I.4 mm.

5, Holland Place Chambers, Kensington W.

May 26, 1914

Dear A.C.H.

Here is Flint's letter about French plays. If *Drama* will say what it wants he will go ahead with the translation. I suppose Hinckley had better read through the original & then decide.

I will try to send the Jap stuff in a week or 10 days.

yr ever

E.P.

[Enclosure 1:] ALS I I. F. S. Flint to EP.

17 Canonbury Park North,
Canonbury, N. 25th May 1914.

Dear E.P.,

I have thought over the play question and for the moment suggest the following:

L'Otage   } Paul Claudel
L'Annonce faite à Marie
La Parisienne   or some other play by Henri
                                 Becque
Les Borbeaux
L'Année dans la Ville, Jules Romains

Of these, either *L'Otage* or *L'Annonce faite à Marie* would be most *effective*. Becque's plays less so, perhaps, but an honourable enterprise. Romain's play interesting. *Les Flaireurs*, forerunning Maeterlinck, of which I spoke to you, is only a one-act piece, and might fill a hole later. The other play, *Les Deux Forces*, by Pierre-Jean Jouve is interesting but not sufficiently important to translate. *Théodat*, a short act by Remy de Gourmont might come in later, and perhaps his *Lilith*, much longer, a romantic fantasy of the creation of woman, the first adultery & so on. Among recent work, *L'Inquiète Paternité* by Jean Schlumberger is well spoken of: I have not read it though & this & other stuff can wait until one of the first four at least of the plays suggested on the other side [of the letter] has got across. I am very partial to *l'Otage* myself, though of course *l'Annonce* has the cry.

Yours ever,
F.S. Flint.

3o

Stone Cottage
Coleman's Hatch
Sussex[1]

Dear A.C.H.

If H.M. wont take the slightest effort to learn how stuff is produced, and under what terms it is possible to get decent people to have their stuff printed in Chicago rather than here, I cant help it. There [are] more reasons than "English publication" at the same date, which make it desirable to have things printed in May or June.

Will you have twenty proof copies of Nishikigi sent me at once, I suppose she hasn't printed it in May.[2]

The Hueffer must come in June.[3] I've got here the right to print it BEFORE it's printed in England. i.e. priority of publication. How long does she expect a man of his sort to wait. So far as he is concerned he might as well leave the mss. in a cellar as print it in a paper that wont make the slightest effort to be circulatable on this side of the atlantic.

First she thinks she has ALL the rights on everything printed. Then she wont print at an reasonable date unless the things are appearing here at [the] same date.

Does DRAMA want some japanese plays and some of the Fenollosa stuff about the Noh. The *Quarterly Review* has a big fat prose article and two plays.[4]

I ought to try for some american magazine with a circulation, it would only be fair to Fenollosa but I haven't the energy to fuss with imbeciles . . Will the DRAMA pay decently . . How much could they use. Plays or prose about Jap. stage.

yours sincerely

<E.P.>

<Recd.   <Please detach this receipt
                                & give it to the treasurer.
£15 advance on   s.v.p.>
"Nishikigi"
        with thanks.
            Ezra Pound>

1. Evidence suggests that this letter, sent from Stone Cottage, where Pound spent part of his honeymoon, was written between 26 May 1914 and 12 June 1914.

2. Pound was wrong. Fenollosa's translation of "Nishikigi," edited by Pound, did appear in *Poetry* IV (May 1914): 35-48.

3. Pound refers to F. M. Hueffer's long poem "On Heaven." See Letter 27, note 2.

4. This would appear as "The Classical Drama of Japan [Edited from Ernest Fenollosa's manuscripts by Ezra Pound]," *Quarterly Review* CCI (October 1914): 450-477.

3 1

5 Holland Place Chambers
Kensington, W.

Dear A.C.H.

I am sending herewith Cournos translation of "Sisters" by I.L. Pere[t]z, original in hebrew, the yiddish version was acted in New York by Fernanda Eliscu about four years ago.[1]

Pere[t]z has a great russian reputation. Cournos is badly in need of *immediate* cash, can you do anything with DRAMA.

I sent off two japanese plays direct to said DRAMA some days ago.

This is the first english translation of a play by Pere[t]z, a vol. of his short stories has been done. Pere[t]z himself writes in Russian, Yiddish and Classical hebrew.

yours sincerely
<E Pound>

<12-6-14>

Cournos says I might add that he "needs the money DAMMM soon["].]

---

1. John Cournos (1881-1966), Russian-born poet, novelist, playwright and translator who emigrated to the United States in 1891, lived in London from 1912 to 1930. There he met EP who included one of his poems in *Des Imagistes*. In January 1913 Cournos published a long, laudatory article on EP entitled "Native Poet Stirs London," *Philadelphia Record* (5 January 1913), rpt. *EP/DS* 184-186.

I. L. Peretz (1852-1915), a distinguished Yiddish and Hebrew writer, is considered one of the three great Yiddish authors along with Mendele and Shalom Aleichem. Peretz is celebrated for his poetic dramas, the best known of which is "A Night in the Old Market" (1907), later produced by the Moscow Yiddish Theatre.

32

EP to ACH   TLS 21 December 1914 4 ll + 1 Enclosure.

5, Holland Place Chambers, Kensington, W.

Dear A.C.H.

"Eternally forfeited" NONSENSE. I DISapprove of the War Poem business.[1] I disapprove of poems written to order. Of accepting things done with the tongue in the cheek and refusing serious stuff. Of getting 100 dollars for click clack and taking away Hueffer's just reward AFTER he'd been given half rates.[2] But that's an end of it. I don't demand infallibility of my friends as a sine qua non. And anyhow I dare say you are right from an editorial point of view and that the rotten number was of advantage to the war-chest.

About Hinckley.[3] No. He hasn't written. Of course it would be better if the play and the article went together. But I don't care a hang in what order he prints 'em. He can make it six articles so long as I get paid..... the sooner the better.

There is no official confirmation of a war between me and Les Imagistes. Several of them, I dare say all of 'em by now (except Williams) prefer to select their own anthology instead of having me do it for 'em.[4] Spectamur agendo, let us hope the results justify their anticipations. I have no desire, in fact I flatly refuse to contribute to the se self-logated////anthos said seld self selected boquet. It is a matter in which I think I should be allowed a certain freedom of action. Miss [Lowell] submitted me to a very long harangue upon my initial refusal. I believe several of the contributors to the original book and several of the proposed contributors for the "wider representation" consider that I have insulted them in their tenderest part, i.e. their non-extant critical faculty. Honi soit. I trust that, relieved of my encumbering weight, their charriot will ascend Parnassus at with the greater speed and convenience.

Wilenski's interest in art is, I believe, purely archeological.[5] He

paints society portraits with consumate cynicism. ... entirely apart
from his interest in art ... mostly the quattrocento. I think his article
on German poetry surprisingly good. I thought he was no fool or I
wouldn't have risked asking him, but the result was better than I
expected.

About my "art criticism", I didn't know I had attempted to
make any technical criticism whatever. I like what I conceive to be
"strength" in certain Chinese paintings. I believe the vorticist
painting leads toward a similar strength in occidental work. I believe
very emphatically that Whistler would have been with us, tho' there
is no use arguing such unprovable points. What I insist on IS that
we have a legitimate field of activity. I dont think I've said anything
about technique. Save possibl<y> that Brzeska and Epstein cut stone
and that the result is less like spaghetti <than> the late Rodin and his
weaker immitators.[6]

Here's luck to the possible weekly. I dont think the *New Republic*
will go far. Certainly they won't do anything for the arts.[7]

Thanks for the *Dial* cuttings. I will send 'em a letter if I can get
up the requisite energy.

I have no special connection with the *Egoist*. They send me six
free copies and I occasionally send 'em an article booming something I approve. I can't see that they can improve, and they seem to
me rather a waste of energy under their present composition.
However, there's nothing better at present. I have just done an
article for T.P. and shall go to the *New Age* this afternoon to see if
they've any spare shillings. This does not imply my complete
unanimity with either publication.

About your new weekly. I hereby give you my proxies. If the
crowd want me I will do all I can[.] I will even write for six months
for nothing if that is necessary. I don't in the least think I ought to
write for nothing. I don't think papers with unpaid contributors can
be as efficient, for various reasons, as papers that pay. My living
expenses are so little, and such a d...d bother at that, that <I> think
the <">assisting capitalist<"> ought to look after 'em while I work at
something that matters. But all that's an aside. If its necessary I will
dispense with EEmoluments at least for six months, which will be
time enough to see whether the paper is any good.

I hope Webster <F>ord is in the deal. I am booming him in the
next *Egoist*, in a very poor and hurried article.[8]

I enclose the C.O.A. announcements.[9] Coburn and, I believe, Dolmetsch have each a perspiring apprentice already. The demand for positions *on* the faculty is most brisk.

Guess thats all for the moment.

<yours ever

Ezra Pound>

<2 1-12-14>

▨▨▨▨▨▨▨ [Enclosure 1:]
"PRELIMINARY ANNOUNCEMENT OF THE COLLEGE OF ARTS," 4 pp, listing among its faculty Gaudier-Brzeska (Sculpture), Wyndham Lewis (Painting), Arnold Dolmetsch (Music), Alvin Langdon Coburn (Photography), Edmund Dulac (Illustration), and Ezra Pound (Letters). Communication to be sent, it adds, to "5, Holland Place Chambers."

▨▨▨▨▨▨▨

1. The "War Poem business" refers to the contest initiated by ACH and sponsored by *Poetry* which saw 738 poems submitted and was the feature of the November 1914 issue. Entrants included Wallace Stevens, Carl Sandburg, Maxwell Bodenheim, Amy Lowell, Richard Aldington, and Alice Corbin Henderson. The "click clack" EP refers to alludes to lines from the award-winning poem, "The Metal Checks" by Louise Driscoll. See *Poetry* V (November 1914): [49]-54.

2. EP was irritated at Sandburg's winning the Levinson Prize (limited to an American) of $200 from *Poetry* magazine for "Chicago Poems" in 1913-1914 over Hueffer for "On Heaven" which EP had nominated for the $250 Guarantor's Prize, actually eliminated in 1914. See Williams 123-124.

3. Theodore Hinckley was editor of *Drama* (Chicago) from 1913-1931. EP refers to a series of Noh plays translated by Fenollosa with commentary by Pound which he sent to the journal and published as "The Classical Stage of Japan: Ernest Fenollosa's Work on the Japanese 'Noh' edited by Ezra Pound," *Drama* V (May 1915): 199-247. Expanded and reprinted as Parts I and II in EP's *'Noh' or Accomplishment* (1916).

4. EP refers to Amy Lowell's efforts and her anthologies, *Some Imagist Poets*. In response to her efforts, EP rechristened the movement "Amygism."

5. Reginald H. Wilenski (1887-1975), painter and art historian, later adviser to Faber and Faber. His article on German poetry appeared in two parts in *Poetry*: "Modern German Poetry I," *Poetry* V (January 1915): 178-184; "Modern German Poetry, II," *Poetry* V (February 1915): 234-240. EP suggested Wilenski to John Quinn as a regular contributor on German writing for a new journal he proposed in September 1916 (*EP/JQ* 49).

6. "Vorticism," *Fortnightly Review* XCVI (1 September 1914): [461]-471.

7. *The New Republic* was begun in 1914 by Willard D. Straight with H. Croly as editor. Its announced goal was "to start little insurrections in the realm of their [the readers'] convictions."

8. The pseudonym of Edgar Lee Masters. See EP's "Webster Ford," *The Egoist* II (1 January 1915): 11-12.

9. The Preliminary Announcement of the College of Arts which appeared in *The Egoist* I (2 November 1914): 413-414. EP sent the prospectus to HM on 10 November 1914, adding "I was going to ask ACH to boom it, because I think it can be made a valuable model, or starting point for a much bigger scheme for Chicago" (*SL* 47). For a reprint of the announcement see *SL* 41-43.

33

EP to ACH   TLS ? January 1915 3 ll. Carbon.

Stone Cottage
Colemans Hatch
Sussex

Dear A.C.H.

Have I written to thank you for getting that matter with Hinckley into shape.[1] If not here's thanks.

I am going to bother you with another affair, which however has compensations. . I send herewith Fenollosa's essay on the Chinese Character.[2] read it and you will forgive me. I could have sent it to the *Dial*, but I've forgotten the name of the new asst edtr. and have left his address in London.[3]

I think it might run as three or four articles in the *Dial*. Fenollosa is dead so even the Editor himself cant really object to printing him.

I wonder does H.M. want Yeats<'> new poems He has done several. Two since we came down here, which are quite good.

It is very difficult to know whether I should keep on sending stuff into *Poetry*. Whether H.M. resents my too great persistence.

Letter for Wilenski came this a.m. Have you any idea whether the cheques for Dec. have yet been sent to Rodker and O'Sullivan?[4]

The only good thing I have ever heard of Braithwaite is that for which you reproach him. i.e., <">omitting the Atlantic<"> since Mr. Sidgewick's mama-in-law bought it for him to play with.

I have had another go at Masters in the *New Age* (appearing some time in Feb.), handling him rather more severely than in my first whoop in the *Egoist*. He is better than Lindsay, but he writes too much, no god could turn out a full double column page per week. How old a man is he?[5]

What are you writing on your own?

Luck for 1915, yours ever

<Ezra Pound>

By the way I'm offering "American serial rights" on that Chinese essay. It will be along in a day or so.

<It occurs to me that I might do worse than arrange another anthology on slightly wider lines than "Des Imagistes". Do you, H.M., Masters, want to join in also Bodenheim & Sandburg if either of them have done anything good enough. — and Lindsay if he cares to submit to my editing.[6]

Due acknowle[d]gements, homage or whatever H.M. likes to "Poetry a magazine less known in England than it should be." or whatever she likes.

And are there any suggestions.>

1. See Letter 32, note 3.

2. EP appointed ACH to act as his "agent" in placing this essay in the U.S. *The Dial* was the first choice, although later correspondence indicates many alternatives including *The Seven Arts*, *The Monist*, and *The Yale Review*. Various editorial and postal delays, which frustrated EP, prevented the essay from quick publication; it did not appear until the fall of 1919 when it was printed as "The Chinese Written Character as a Medium for Poetry by Ernest Fenollosa and Ezra Pound" in four installments in the *Little Review* VI, nos. 5, 6, 7, 8 (1919).

3. EP most likely means Lucian Cary (1886-1971) who in May 1914 took over editorial duties at *The Dial*, although he was never listed as Editor. See Letter 35, note 1. The 15 January 1915 issue of *The Dial* contained EP's provocative letter entitled "A Blast from London," arguing for the need among younger poets to believe in literary standards derived from tradition and defending their exile from America because Europe was more accepting of modernity.

4. Reginald H. Wilenski - See Letter 32, note 5.

John Rodker (1894-1955), English writer and publisher whose lengthy poem "London Night" appeared in *Poetry* V (December 1914): 119-124. Rodker later founded the Ovid Press which published *The Fourth Canto* (1919), *Mauberley* (1920), and *A Draft of The Cantos 17-27* (1928). EP included four of Rodker's poems in *Catholic Anthology, 1914-1915*.

Seumas O'Sullivan (1879-1958), pseud. of James Sullivan Starkey, Irish poet and founding editor of the *Dublin Magazine* and later Vice Pres. of the Irish Academy of Letters. Three of his poems appeared in *Poetry* V (December 1914): 107-109 immediately following six poems by D. H. Lawrence.

5. See "Affirmations, VI. Analysis of This Decade," *New Age* XVI (11 February 1915): 409-411; his earlier essay, "Webster Ford," appeared in *Egoist* II (1 January 1915): 11-12.

Vachel Lindsay (1879–1931), American poet from Illinois who contributed to the *Lyric Year* (1912) and *Poetry* (1913) where his poem "General William Boothe Enters Heaven" was runner-up to Yeats' "The Grey Rock" as best poem published in the journal's first year. HM favored Lindsay's work, but EP insisted Yeats receive the prize. Lindsay did win the annual *Poetry* award in 1915 for "The Chinese Nightingale," however, defeating Eliot's "Prufrock" to EP's dismay. Nevertheless, EP told HM that despite "the felicity, the obvious rag-time of the cadence" and similarities to Kipling, Lindsay's poetry was "better than most, than any one else of your lot except Ford and Sandburg who are trying harder" (*SL* 57; cf. *SL* 127). EP parodied Lindsay in a 58-line poem written, he declared, in "4 minutes 31 seconds" in the *LR* (see *EP/LR* 147–148 and *LR* [January 1918]: 54–55).

Edgar Lee Masters was forty-six in 1915.

6. This became the *Catholic Anthology, 1914-1915* (London: Elkin Mathews, 1915). Pound selected and edited the volume which included, in addition to his own work, Yeats, Eliot (five poems, including "Prufrock"), Masters, Harriet Monroe, Bodenheim, Sandburg, Williams, and Alice Corbin Henderson listed as Alice Corbin. Shortly after publication, Francis Meynell and other Catholics protested the title but the book was not suppressed.

34

EP to ACH ALS 21 March 1915 4 ll. The ms. date preceding the body of the letter reads "22 Mar. '15," but the ms. date at the close reads "21-3-15."

5, Holland Place Chambers, Kensington W.

22 Mar '15

Dear A.C.H.

I have spent the day laying out my "*Anthology for 1914-1915*".[1] Mathews will publish it for me = at least we have come to an informal verbal agreement & I think I have rather a stronger table of contents than in my last endeavour. = I have got = the Poetry office. Masters[,] Johns. & Sandburg from the Chicago contingent.

Not Lindsay. I think he gets worse & worse= also I cant find anything of Bodenheims. He is young & can wait.

Of your stuff before me I think yours "An old man appeared out of the dusk" & "what dim arcadian Pastures" are the best for my purpose.[2] I like your "Love me at last" but it is so off the tone of the book that it would seem out of place.

I'd like to see whatever *mss.* you have.

? Do you mind being "Alice Corbin Henderson?" = The rest of the book goes so well in alphabetical order & you fit so much better as "H" than as "C". on the other hand if I can find one or two more of your things that fit in. I should like to use the "What Dim Arcadian Pastures" as the italic head poem for the book. = C'est une image.

Do please "*object*" if you want to, and send in any advice about the book that you like.

I think H.M.'s long "Letter from Pekin" will do her more good here than anything else in "You & I."[3] = I have not yet written her. =

? Does anyone in Chicago want to take sheets or plates for the American edition.? Seymour? McClung?

It will be cheaper to set up the type *he*re. that much is certain.

Also will all American authors please send me.

a̲. List of their published books, publishers. etc.

b̲. formal permission to use their poems. & statement of *what* acknowledgments must be made *to whom*, in the opening note.

I don't want any more lascerated feelings.

yours ever,

Ezra Pound

21-3-15

1. *Catholic Anthology, 1914-1915.* See Letter 33, note 6.

2. Both poems appeared in *The Spinning Woman of the Sky* by ACH, pp. [9], 23.

3. *You and I,* a volume of verse by Harriet Monroe published by Macmillan (New York) in 1914 and reviewed in *Poetry* V (January 1915): 188-191 by Edgar Lee Masters. EP published HM's "A Letter from Peking" in *Catholic Anthology, 1914-1915.* See Letter 48, note 9.

35

EP to ACH   TLS 29 March 1915 1 l.

5, Holland Place Chambers, Kensington W.

<March 29 '15>

Dear A.C.H.

Rest for the iracible is limited to a minimim. Having got my anthology on the way, or out of the way or off my mind, there remain at least two more campaigns for *Poetry* or the *Dial*. A. will either you or Lucian Cary get me a copy of the present law for the tariff on books imported into America.[1] B. a list of the members of the American Academy of Art and Letters, and of the lesser or rather more numerous penumbra of associates of the Institute, or whatever its called.

The first law is iniquitous and forms the excuse for a lot of swindling and a restriction on the circulation of contemporary and even modern books, especially of the non-commercial sort. etc. vide my attack not yet written.

The second affair, is with dead wood, but that rag bag Current Opinion has taken on my letter in the *Dial* and your editorial, etc.[2] And perhaps I can issue some sort [of] challenge that will even move part of that dead skunk the Am. Acad. It ought to be made to get up or get under. Also it should take the part of literature against the old magazines. At present it is only a lot of rusting and idle machinery.

So long as the campaigns are set under way I dont care who does it, but I may as well have an oar in, I can be a shade more insulting than any one else who is likely to take on the job. If *Poetry*, *The Dial* and the *Mirror* can all be started we may be able to get something done.

I shan't vent my indignation here, but will save it for my articles. You might get a copy of the Am. Copyright law also, though I care less about that. Merely I dont want to make misstatements. A la guerre.

<*Poetry* is by now a public institution & there are jobs for it to take on.>

<yours ever

Ezra Pound>

---

1. Lucian Cary (1886-1971), Chicago writer and one-time instructor at Wabash College, Crawfordsville, Indiana. Acting editor of *The Dial* (1913-1914) who praised *Poetry* in the *Little Review* for publishing work "nobody else dared print," "Literary Journalism in Chicago," *Little Review* (June-July, 1915): 2. In the May 1915 issue of *Poetry*, however, he published a letter protesting his alleged connection with *The Dial* from which he had recently resigned (*Poetry* VI [May 1915]: 103-104).

2. EP, "A Blast from London," *The Dial* (Chicago) LVIII (16 January 1915): 277-278; ACH, "Our Contemporaries," *Poetry* V (January 1915): 193-195, an attack on what American magazines believe to be modern poetry.

36

ACH to EP   TS ? May [1915] 2 ll. Beinecke. A postscript dated 12 May [1915] appears in the ms. hand of ACH across the top of page 1 of the typescript.

Pennasanty Wood, Lake Bluff, Illinois

<May 12. I find this wretched note, written a couple of weeks ago, was left out then mailed! — I'm sorry — Please criticise to the limit & send back — >

Dear E.P. — I haven't anything to send you for the anthology but scraps.[1] I've done almost nothing since the magazine started. It's hard to find anything to go with what you've chosen of mine, and what I gather to be the nature of the anthology. I send a few scraps with little confidence of their being worth anything. Sometime I shall take courage and send you more to criticise. The stuff I did at seventeen was more *me* than much I did afterward; alas, that impulse and style do not flourish together! Even now I find very few who care for style irrespective of subject or who love the art beyond anything. The poet cares only for one poet —himself; the public would no doubt be astonished if told that I consider you an exception! Put me in the anthology as Corbin or Henderson, <it doesn't matter. Though I rather like to stick to the first.>

I hope to have something to report on the Chinese. character article before long.[2] It's very fine, but you know the situation over here. I shall do all I can to get it published. Have you arranged for England? The Noh plays are to be in the May *Drama*.[3] The Drama League is rather foolish, but such organizations are necessary.

I've been dreadfully driven all winter — am just beginning to see daylight.

Thanks ever so much for *Cathay*.[4] I read it to W.P.H. the night it came, and we've enjoyed it. I asked H.M. to put an ad for it in this month's *Poetry*. Thank God, I've quit handling the ads. Seymour-

Daughaday are doing it. I'm afraid they'll go down, but I can't help it. . . . .⁵

I wish you'd get Elkin Mathews to send an offer to the Seymour people to take sheets of the Anthology . . . I don't know how such things are arranged. Let me know and I'll do what I can.

Yours, A. C. H.

---

1. Pound included one poem by Alice Corbin [Henderson] in his *Catholic Anthology, 1914-1915*, "One City Only," pp. 20-21.

2. Pound mailed "The Chinese Written Character as a Medium for Poetry" to Henderson in January 1915 for possible publication in the U.S. See Letter 33.

3. "The Classical Stage of Japan: Ernest Fenollosa's Work on the Japanese 'Noh'," edited by Ezra Pound, *Drama* V.18 (May 1915): 199-247, contains seven Noh plays; reprinted in expanded form as Parts I and II of *'Noh' or Accomplishment*.

4. One thousand copies of *Cathay* (London: Elkin Mathews, 1915) were published on 6 April 1915. The copy sent to ACH by Pound, housed at the Harry Ransom Humanities Research Center, contains the following inscription: "A.C.H. / from / E.P. / March 1915."

5. Seymour-Daughaday, incorporated in 1913 as a successor to The Ralph Fletcher Seymour Company, in fact went out of business in 1915, although Ralph Seymour continued as R. F. Seymour Company. Daughaday did not care for EP's work.

37

5, Holland Place Chambers, Kensington W.

<22 May '15>

Dear A.C.H.

There is just the faint nuance of a chance that I may be given a paper (one with which I have never before been connected), a weekly.[1]

If it comes off, what can I count on from Chicago?

I should make the paper, London, Paris, Chicago. Will your crowd there, the crowd that has been wanting THE Chicago weekly join in and back me? How far? and in what ways?

Who are the men who ought to be on it. I take it Lucian Cary, Masters, Sandburg.

What do they expect to be paid?

If I get, say, a trial run of six months, what are they willing to do on the chance that the thing will really succeed and that rates will rise?

Also, damn it, do tell me what ages they have? One must know a man's age more or less if one is to write letters to him.[2]

What number of subscribers can I count on? Mind I shall have the voice of Chicago if I can possibly get it. I shall make a paper where the two sides of the Atlantic can at last really converse.

Do get me an answer as soon as you can. (I know I am always piling things on your back). I think there will be no trouble about the actual publication in America, as the firm who hold the paper has offices both there and here.

Certainly I can get the livest writers here and in Paris, within the limits of what I can pay.

Your crowd apparently is not ready to swing their ideal weekly on their own, but will they fill up and swing a third or fourth of mine until they are ready for their own, just to get their hand in. ???

Can they form any sort of committee or centre.? Of course a weekly devoted to art, prose, politics, wont interfere with "Poetry" once a month. Nor with anything else once a month, for that matter. Neither can a quasi bilingual, bicontinental paper interfere with Reedy's paper (even supposing I were able) or wanted to, which I dont.[3]

Oh well, it's all very sudden. Do let me know who will write and at what rates for a start? And who will subscribe, and if a committee, lady's club, art's club, anything will form and back me?

                              yours ever.
P.SSSSS.   <Ezra Pound>
see next page.

P.S. re/ various matters.
1. The *Drama*, May number hasnt arrived yet. Have they bust? or have they printed me? When will they pay?[4]

2. I sent a very important essay to Cary (from the Fenollosa papers), addressed privately to him at the *Dial* offices. Did he receive it? What has become of it?[5]

    Please ask him to return it, and the other essay on American conditions (my own essay) if he has not used them. I shall want all my cartridges if this deal comes off.

    I am afraid both mss. have been mislaid in his departure from the *Dial*. At least I have had no word from him.

What could you or Sandburg do as a reviewing committee to look at American books and report on same, @ what figure?

    I must get a set of feelers, like the rubricists on the *Mercure*.

hastily
                    <E.P.>
                        <Do let me have
                        something or other
                        in a day or so.>

1. Pound long sought the editorial freedom of his own journal and in the spring of 1915 explored the opportunity of obtaining *The Academy* (1869-1922), a London weekly which Lord Alfred Douglas, implicated in the Oscar Wilde trial, edited between 1907-1910. EP reported his progress and goals for the magazine to John Quinn who encouraged him, but by August 1915 the project had failed. EP then ironically proposed to Quinn the idea of securing the *Saturday Review*, although he preferred to start his own monthly magazine, with the *Mercure de France* his ideal. He also briefly considered Mitchell Kennerley's *The Forum* (*EP/JQ* 31, 35).

2. In 1915 Lucian Cary was 29, Edgar Lee Masters 46, and Carl Sandburg 37.

3. *Reedy's Mirror* (1913-1920), the St. Louis magazine of William Marion Reedy that focused on politics and culture. See Letter 63, note 13.

4. On *Drama* and EP's payment see Letter 39. "The Classical Stage of Japan" by EP appeared in *Drama* V (May 1915): 199-247.

5. "The Chinese Written Character"; for details on its circuitous route to publication, see Letter 33, note 2.

38

EP to ACH   TLS 25 May 1915 2 ll.

5, Holland Place Chambers

<25 May '15>

Dear A.C.H.

No, Most emphatically, NO. "Ford" was NOT in America last winter, but if "Oliver" has robbed a bank, or borrowed money or committed a rape it may be as well to print a definite statement in the notes at the end of *Poetry*, as follows.

"We wish to state, that, contrary to certain rumors, Mr Ford Madox Hueffer, author of "On Heaven", of the articles on "Impressionism" which have appeared in *Poetry*, of "The Fifth Queen Crowned" and many other novels and of "When Blood is their Argument", "The Soul of London", "Ancient Lights" etc. etc. was *not* in America last winter, though a certain Oliver Madox Hueffer was. Mr O.M. Hueffer is likewise an author but the two men are by no means identical."[1]

I dont know what Oliver has been up to, but he is quite capable of taking advantage of the fact that he is occasionally taken for Ford. I believe he had his expenses paid "out" on the condition that he should not return to england but he has not kept to his agreement.

Thanks for the poems. I shall probably use "One city only" in the anthology,[2] it is more of a tone with the rest, though as you say, it isn't quintessentially *you*.

I haven't the energy for a [d]etailed critique at the moment, I am answering your note on Ford not the letter, and as you seem in a hurry to know that Ford was safe in England, I answer at once. Thanks, so much for bothering about the Chinese essay, and for the affair with *Drama*. I await their cheque with "majestic instancy." You will have had a long letter re/a weekly, sent two nights ago. Thanks for the "ad.", I have already thanked H.M., also for the suggestion re/ Mathews and Seymory-Doughady re/the anthology. The enclosed analysis of contemporary American literature may amuse you.[3]

drowsily

<E.P.>

1. Oliver Madox Hueffer (1879-1931) was Ford Madox Hueffer's younger brother; there is no evidence of his visiting America in the winter of 1915, especially since he was a member of the British Army; in 1916 he was seriously wounded.

2. "One City Only" by Alice Corbin [Henderson] appeared on pp. 20-21 of *Catholic Anthology, 1914-1915*. Dorothy Shakespear designed the cover.

3. EP's reference is not clear, although he may have sent a copy of "Affirmations . . . VI. Analysis of This Decade," *New Age* XVI (11 February 1915): 409-411.

39

■■■■■ **EP to ACH**   TLS May/June? 1915 1 l.

5, Holland Place Chambers

Dear A.C.H.

There's the usual hitch and hold up. £500 to "guarantee possible loss." I shouldn't lose it, or at least I should<n't> lose anywhere near all of it. Ma che! The paper is "The Academy", paying for its own printing and having publishing offices potentially both here and in America.

I don't suppose the crowd that wants THE Chicago weekly, has that sum, or would join in. The paper has sixty years tradition and could be published both here and in Chicago, as said above, ... it seems too good a chance to lose.

I haven't absolutely given it up ...... the price of a good automobile would do it.

Please hold that essay on the Chinese character until further notice, if you haven't already rushed to comply with my request to send it back here at once.

yours ever

<Ezra Pound>

<Hang it all. I could swing the thing. if I had six months start.>

4o

5, Holland Place Chambers, Kensington W.

<June 22 '15>
Dear A.C.H.

"Drama" and the cheque have at last arrived as cooling water in a land of great drouth. A nice cheque for 130 dollars. We erect an ivory tablet to your memory and make votive offering to Kuanon for your eternal well being.

The weekly affair is still hung up. I have found 1250 dollars and another indefinite offer which would possibly bring it up to 1500. (2500 was the minimum needed) Yeats, de Gourmont, Hueffer, all keen on it.

However, even if it dont go, the money is, in a way, permanently raised, and sometime we may start something.

What is the Yale Review? They might use that article on the Written Character?[1]

Hinckley asked for suggestions. <I> suggested that two or three Noh plays should adorn each number of Drama, until they run out. They'd make the magazine unique even if it stopped dead in its course.

Also I mentioned some spanish stuff.

Why dont you do a french play yourself? Can I look round for you <& find one or two?> Do let me know if there is anything I can do for you here.

I just this instant note (in the paper that D[orothy] is reading) among the new pensions "Walter de la Mare" £100 per year, which does put an edge on the article that is lying sealed and ready for "Poetry". He has done one rather good little book of verse and some rot. Still it does shame the great western republic. You might tell H.M. in connection with the whoop I refer to. Raby Tagore is knighted as I suppose you know. Some change in the official attitude toward Suspect No.12 Class b.

Note in this that England in the midst of war time can stop to pension De la Mare. Have H.M. put it in a note, or write the note yourself and put it at the end of my article, saying "point is given to E.P.'s article by etc.["]²

New York, or rather new jersey seems to be awakening slowly ????. At any rate they seem to be attempting a vortex and to be bubbling with (beneficent or malificent) enthusiasm. Nascitur ordo etc.³

Thanks again for the bother over Drama.

<yours ever
Ezra Pound>

1. The *Yale Review* (1911–) edited by Wilbur L. Cross, biographer of Fielding, mixed academic/literary articles with general cultural discussions and book reviews. Contributors included William Roscoe Thayer on Dante, Henry Seidel Canby on Yeats, and Gilbert Murray on the tradition of Greek literature. Poems by Madison Cawein, William Rose Benét, and Witter Bynner also appeared.

2. EP, "The Renaissance II ," *Poetry* V (March 1915): 285-287. On the final page EP writes that "above all there must be living conditions for artists"; without support, art will be "individual, separate, and spasmodic; it will not group and become a great period" (287). EP expanded this theme in "The Renaissance III," *Poetry* VI (May 1915): 84-91.

3. "Birth of a new order." The New Jersey reference is to the publication between 1915-1919 of *Others: A Magazine of New Verse*, the successor to *Glebe*, in Grantwood, New Jersey. Founded by the New York poet and editor Alfred Kreymborg (1883-1966) who was assisted by William Carlos Williams and William Saphier, *Others* included verse, criticism, drama, and fiction by H. D., Richard Aldington, Amy Lowell, T. S. Eliot, Djuna Barnes, Marianne Moore, Wallace Stevens, and EP. Its editorial policy encouraged experimental poetry "more imagistic than the imagists" (Hoffman 248a).

4I

EP to ACH   TLS 7 July 1915 2 ll + 3 Enclosures: 3 Noh Plays in TS from the Fenollosa mss.: *Takasago, Genjo, Chorio. Takasago* has remained unpublished and is here printed for the first time as Enclosure I with EP's introduction in which he calls it "the very core of 'Noh'" because of its "flawless structure." For a comment on the play and its importance for Pound see my "Introduction." *Genjo* and *Chorio* appear in revised form in *'Noh' or Accomplishment.* The letter is dated by its postmark.

5, Holland Place Chambers

Dear A.C.H.

If your back is not already broken with my never-ending jobs !!

Anyhow, here are three more Noh plays. I wonder did Hinckley use all the prose I sent him? I can't in the least remember what I sent.

"*Takasago*" is so full of poetry that Harriet might like it, I dont want to hog all the space in the magazine. I dont know whether the new stuff of my own will fill all my ten pages in September, or whatever number it is to go in. If it dont she might take *Takasago*, <or she might prefer *Genjo* which has a little more verse in the translation> or she might print it a few months later, or she may not want it at all. In which case please pass it along to DRAMA, with the rest of this little lot.

I don't suppose Hinckley will ever answer a letter, so you might enquire viva voce whether he can stand any more prose information about Noh.

About the "Written Character", have you tried the YALE RE-VIEW? What is the *Yale Review*, I see that some one has just written "Southey as poet" in it, so I conclude it is antediluvian and that nothing can possibly be too dull.

If they dont want it, please send it back and I will try it on the "Hibbert". if they do want it (for gods sake make sure they pay), if they do want it, please arrange to have a copy made, or proofs sent very early, and I will try for simultaneous publication here.

Am I ever going to be able to do anything for you to make up all this continual bother?

Is Lucian Cary a friend of anybody's, or is he simply an acquaintance? He has not answered my letter, but if he was sacked from the *Dial* I dare say they ate it in the office, out of pure rage.

The weekly is up the stump, at least for the present.

"Others" vol.I. no.1. has arrived.[1] It has *one* virtue namely that nothing in it was intended to please the public. I mean nothing in it was written with a view to its being intelligible "to even the stupidest reader". Two or three of Johns' things are all that seem to have any value, but I think the crowd and its enthusiasm may do some good ???????? At least it is better than the *Poetry Journal* (what a lim[p] rag !!)

Brzeska has been killed, so sculpture will stick where it is for another half century. It does not increase ones love for the Teuton.

<Yours ever

E.P.>

▓▓▓▓▓▓▓▓   [Enclosure 1:]
Takasago by Motokiyo
TS 9 ll. Ms. statement on title page: <Noh plays from the / Fenollosa
mss / edited by / Ezra Pound.> The following 2 pp. TS introduction
precedes the play:

This play "TAKASAGO" might be called the very core of the "Noh". Because of its flawless structure it is called "Shin no issei," the "Most Correct" and other Noh plays are held to vary from it as from a norm. It is a "Shugen" or congratulatory piece and as such it is the hardest sort of Noh play for an occidental to fathom. These "Shugen" (vide "The Drama" for May 1915, p. 208) are used at the beginning and end of the full Noh programme, and this very ending on the opening note is a sort of symbol of perpetuity.

   "TAKASAGO" is not a dogmatic statement, it is, or it "e<x>presses," a *sense* of past time in the present. Or if you are to speak like a Japanese trying to talk English "It is the Pine, it is eternity."

   Umewaka Minoru, or possibly some other of Prof. Fenollosa's friends, in trying to explain it has used these words, which I take verbatim from the note book: "The old man and woman say: we are symbol. In heart of young men is many dusts, old men must help allay them. When one does not sweep his dirt heaps away, he will be buried in the dust".

<If> ~~The first half [of] the play, in this translation is stiff and prosaic but it does get the reader primed, as it were, intellectually prepared to~~ *feel* ~~the last half~~, <The play> is nearly intranslatable and is fairly incomprehensible until you get the clue, first to the "sense of past time in the present", second, to the symbolism of Takasago (the past age) and Sumiyoshi (the present).

When I say it is perfect in construction I do not refer to anything like occidental "dramatic construction". <In> Takasago the various parts of a Noh play: the speech telling the names, the speech saying: we have arrived, the *issei*, or hero's voice raised for the first time "very powerful, just as if it could pierce", the *sashi koye* or "flow-along tune" and the various other divisions of Noh, are by authorities held to be each in its proper position.

The Cast

The Waki, the wandering priest, Tomonari
The Shite, an Old man
The Tsure, an old woman
Chorus.

TAKASAGO.
BY
MOTOKIYO.

PRIEST.

I am Tomonari, priest of <the> shinto temple at Aso, in the province of Hijo in Kinshu. I have never seen the capital before and I am now coming thither. I shall visit Takasago by the way.

I have sailed over the calm spring sea, and Takasago, which I thought to be very distant in the clouds, is before me.

OLD MAN and TSURE TOGETHER.

The spring winds blow over the pine trees of Takasago. And it is twilight now. The bell of Onoye rings.

TSURE. <(Old Woman)>

The waves are hidden in mist.

TOGETHER.

The sound alone says 'tis full tide.

OLD MAN.

Whom shall I make my friend? Even the pine does not know me. The past days are like snows gathered and gathering, and I am like an old stork left on the bare nest at dawn. Even in the cold evenings of spring I have heard only the wind of the pine trees. My heart is my only friend.

(They sing together)

O, we will ask the pine trees for tidings of the world. We will sweep dust under their shade and stand in the fallen pine-needles here, together, in Takasago.

The pine tree of Onoye is older, the waves of age are upon us, and we have lived through and lived through, piling the fallen needles beneath the boughs of this pine, how long shall we last out? How long? As long as the life of this pine here?

PRIEST.

I was waiting in the village and I saw this old man and old woman. I have something to ask the old man.

OLD MAN.

He means me. What's the matter?

PRIEST.

Which tree is the great tree of Takasago?[2]

OLD MAN.

This tree under which we are sweeping.

PRIEST.

Well why do they call it "Ai-oi?" Why do they call all the pines in Takasago and in Suminoye "Ai-oi?" the two places are very far distant, and the word means "growing together."

OLD MAN.

Yes, I know anyone can read in the preface of Kokin that "It seems the pine trees of Takasago and Suminoye grow together" but I am a man of Sumiyoshi, of Tau No Kumi, so you had better ask the old woman, she's of this place.

PRIEST.

What, I see the old pair here together and yet he says they live apart, he says he is of Sumiyoshi!

TSURE.

That's a stupid thing you are saying. Though the mountain and river lie between us we are near in the ways of love.

OLD MAN.

Think a little[.]

TOGETHER.

The pine trees of Takasago and Suminoye have no breathing life and they call them "growing together". Yet we who are from Sumi[y]oshi have long life in these pine trees.

PRIEST.

Yes, but what is the story that you are half telling?

OLD MAN.

As men have said in the old times, "It's a sign of the happier reign."

TSURE.

Takasago means the old age of the emperor Manyoshu.

OLD MAN.

Sumiyoshi means our own time of Engi.

TSURE.

The pine-needles are like inexhaustible words.

OLD MAN.

Their glory is the same through all seasons.

TOGETHER.

They are symbols to honour the reign.

PRIEST.

My doubt goes like a spring day's cloud at hearing your story.

OLD MAN.

The light is smooth on the water.

PRIEST.

It is surely smooth on the western sea there, out towards Suminoye.

OLD MAN.

And here in Takasago.

PRIEST.

The colour of the pine-trees grows deeper.

OLD MAN.

The spring sky _ _ _ _

PRIEST.

_ _ _ being calm . . .

CHORUS.

The waves of the whole sea are quiet,
The whole country well governed
The wind does not even rustle through the branches,
It is surely a happy reign.

As happy as are pines growing together
Indeed it is an age that we can look up to
And that we can not show forth in words,
A kindly deed of the gods.

PRIEST.

Tell me the full tale, if it please you.
The full story of Takasago.

CHORUS.

Though grass and trees have no mind
They have their time of blossoming and of bearing their fruit, they have the virtue of bright spring and their blossoms come out first on the southern branches.

OLD MAN.

And the look of this pine is eternal.

Its needles and cones have one season.

<They are all out on the one bough Together.>

CHORUS.

And so for all the four seasons

The green of a thousand years is deep against the snow, they say the pine is in blossom but once in a thousand years.

OLD MAN.

It was that I was wanting,

It was that I would learn from the pine-trees.

CHORUS.

The gems of dew on the pine boughs

Burnish my heart.

OLD MAN.

O All-who-have-life

CHORUS.

Come near to the Shikishima.

Come near to the island of verses

Like a light skiff on the wave,

Chaio, the bard, said in the days of Ichijo:

The voices of all things,

The voices of every living heart

Will come to the isle of verses,

The voices of all things that have heart.

There will be the grass and the trees and the sand and the soil together and the winds and the sounds of water, they have all of them heart for verses. And the forest waving with spring wind from the Eastward, the crickets and small things of autumn that whirr in the northern dew, these are all the form of our verses, and the pine-tree is over them all. It is the dress of the eighteen princes, the green of a thousand autumns lasting forever. The <emperor> Shiko decreed that it was noble, all countries acknowledged its rite.

OLD MAN.

A bell sounds over Takasago, the bell of Onoye.

CHORUS.

At dawn frost comes on the branches
The leaves retain their one green,
And every morning and evening
We sweep the shed flakes
We clear this space beneath boughs.

There is no end to the falling. Yet now they have ceased to scatter, the colour grows deeper and deeper, as a sign of the lasting reign. The pine-tree is known for its glory. The pine is the giver of joy, how splendid are all the pine-trees growing together.

[Enclosure 2:]
Genjo by Kongo. TS I I II. The translation appeared in *'Noh' or Accomplishment, A Study of the Classical Stage of Japan* by Ernest Fenollosa and Ezra Pound (London: Macmillan, 1916 [1917]), pp. 229-241. The title page of the TS in the letter to ACH reads:

Genjo

The second part of this play shows clearly the descent of Noh from the God-dance.

Cast.
An old man (1st Shite)
An old woman (1st Tsure)
Fujiwara no Moronaga
Waki, an attendant of Moronaga,
2nd Shite, The Emperor Murakami
Riujin, the Dragon God.

"Genjo"

by

Kongo

The scene is in Settsu.
<*note*. The *biwa* is the large chinese & indian lute.>

<Noh plays from the Fenollosa mss
    edited by Ezra Pound>

[10 pp. TS of Genjo follow.]

[Enclosure 3:]
Chorio by Nobumitsu. TS 7 ll. The title page in MS reads <Chorio / by
/ Nobumitsu / Noh plays from the / Fenollosa mss. / edited by Ezra
Pound>. The translation appears in 'Noh' or Accomplishment, pp. 223-
228.
        The following paragraph introduces the play:

This play show<s> the Noh in very simple form. It is nothing
more than a little story narrated and there would hardly be any
excuse for its being presented as a play were it not for the magnificent chance of dancing in the final scene where Chorio fights with
dragon.

1. See Letter 40, note 3.
2. Here EP inserts a single footnote numbered "1": <"Takasago" = "the
past">.

42

EP to ACH   ALS 9 August 1915 6 ll. This letter contains EP's first reference to *The Cantos*.

5, Holland Place Chambers.

<August 9th - [15]>

Dear A.C.H.

Sorry you are worn out, however, be of good cheer, London begins to move again, faintly. Life is not wholly extinct.

It can not be too clearly understood that I have no longer ANY connection with the *Egoist*. I have not had any for nearly a year. I forget when I departed, but there has been no communication (save re/ some details of Joyce's affairs) since about Xmas.[1]

I am very much displeased with Richard, more displeased with Flint, and within the last week I have found it necessary to eliminate Cournos <also> from my list of acquaintance (re/ Brzeska's death, not on a point of style or literary activity)

There has been not[h]ing but fuss since I first ventured to become more interested in Brzeska and Lewis than in certain jeune poetes. Of course R.'s marriage increased the difficulty of criticising either his work or H.D.'s to any advantage.[2] Latterly he seems to me to be falling into his constitutional dangers of words and sentimentalism. The alliance with Storer is an alliance with the mushiest head in London.[3]

At any rate I wash my hands of the lot of 'em. The whole affair is perhaps my punishment for interfering between budding artists and their public, at any rate it is over.

The second BLAST has almost made itself into an institution and I think the third number can be almost wholly serious with only a dash of satire here and there, only it wont feed us yet a while.[4]

Hueffer has got a commission, and in the regular army at that, which is very sporting of him considering how much over age he is.

Bodenheim shows up very well in his letters, and he has sent two good poems. I can very well imagine that any very young poet in America may be a bit bear-headed, and as Sandburg and Masters are so much older and as they are neither of them precisely flawless I dont wonder that there is some friction. He (Bodenheim) seems to swear by H.M., and as nearly everyone else <(us included)> does not but swear *at* her, that may be perhaps counted unto him for a righteousness. His appreciation of Bill Williams poetry, also, interests me.

From the present state of the papers I think the day may soon come when we may overhear in the corner "pub", two voices at the bar, sic:

"Ai, Joe, Wot about this 'ere vers leeber?"
second:

"Well naow yeh see, it's like this ....etc."
costumes from Ally Sloper.[5]

As to actual writing, I think nothing new is done here. The war, and war verse takes all their energy. Rodker has done four things quite unlike his dot and dash stuff, and I shall include them in the anthology.[6] For the rest I think english verse is temporarily dead, deader than mutton. And *Poetry* can use all its space on the home product with a perfectly clear conscience.

Amy's talent seems to be chiefly forensic? I think my anthology will start for the printers some time in Sept. (If H.M. hasn't yet sent me a copy of W.B.Y.'s "Bald Heads" poem, will you please send it, as I am using it in the anth. and want it to be here in time, and W.B.Y. is in Ireland and I dont want either to disturb him about it, or to have to redecipher it from his script. If it has appeared in the Aug. *Poetry*, dont bother, of course.[)][7]

Returning to your questions. Aldington's <I don't know that I exactly regret having put him in charge of the *Egoist*.[8] I couldn't have taken it myself at the time and they do do a few notes on current French stuff. ma che!> *prospective* ability? . He seems to me stuck, dead stuck. But then, as I intimated above, we are not on terms, and I may be too pessimistic. Considering that all his ideas, save a feeble hellenism, are either Hueffers or mine, his constant jibes at Ford in the *Egoist* are unpardonable, or perhaps they are pardonable, God forgive us our sins (writing by gas light at 10/30 a.m. in August.)

Drama has saved my life, paid the rent, etc.[9] <T>he gods will reward you. Thanks for sending on the other mss.

I started to do an article of Lope de Vega, for Hinckley, but found it easier to write nice things about the Spanish stage than to believe them when written.

I am working on a long poem which will resemble the Divina Commedia in length but in no other manner. It is a huge, I was going to say, gamble, but shan't, it will prevent my making any money for the next forty years, perhaps.[10]

There are of cour[s]e *no* significant phases of drama. If I dont sell Joyce's play to the Oliver Morosco (or -cow) Co. I will have it sent on to you for the theatre you mention.[11]

About the imagistette controversy. I hav<e> as a matter of fact sent a letter or article to the *New Republic*, mostly recommending 'em to read the first Imagiste statement in "Poetry" of the century before last.

For the rest, Lewis and Joyce are the two men of genius, Rodker has a small vein, but his own. Eliot has a quaint mind full of intelligence. And that is about the circle of my interests. Lewis now and again gets a good bit of work out of one of his followers.

Has a copy of the second *Blast* been sent to Chicago, if not I will send it. W.L.'s notes on the new schools of art are interesting.

It is curious that we should be drifting into a serious review when we set out for larks and explosions. And the pitiful wail of the press "How are we to know that Mr. Lewis *never* jokes?" is so very pathetic.

Did I ever send over a *Fortnightly Review* containing an article on Vorticism?[12] The present attacks have taken the form of defining "vorticism" to suit the attackers' taste and then saying that Brzeska, or I Am, are, was, *not* vorticists. etc. ad infinitum

Re/ the weekly, it has been sold to the imitators of Oscar, so that's an end of it for the present.[13] I am glad, however to have gathered some information from you, Reedy, etc. It will come in useful sometime. <at present I want to work on my chryselephantine pome.>[14] Hueffer's going off to fight, would have crippled me very much if I had succeeded in getting started.

However, everything, save finance, seems to be livening up a little, which is a comfort.

It is undoubtedly time you had another vacation on this side of the salt.

I have sat here at this machine for an hour and a half, some of it spent in silent and stupid meditation. and I seem to have written you an almost endless letter, about nothing in particular. However, it may as well be sent off. <L>et us hope it contains some aroma of the capital.

yours ever

<Ezra Pound>

I think i must have answered all your questions, most of them twice. vale et me ama.

<no I haven't. — the $2500 was to have been *risked* not spent. I think that would apply in any new effort. *Blast* now pays for itself. though there is still a debt on the 1st number (which was so huge. & so much remade & corrected and altered after it had been set up).

Mathews has written to Seymour re/ anthology.>[15]

1. In the winter of 1913-1914, EP had a falling out with *The Egoist* over his role as literary editor (see *SL* 27, 29, 31; also Letter 32 this collection). In 1915 he published only two articles in the journal (January and October), but resumed his association in March 1916. The reference to Joyce relates to the serial publication of *A Portrait of the Artist as a Young Man* which ran in *The Egoist* from January to September 1915.

2. With EP present, Richard Aldington married H. D. at the Kensington Registry on 18 October 1913. The Kensington Registry Office was also the site for the marriages of Frieda and D. H. Lawrence, Katherine Mansfield and John Middleton Murray, and Nora and James Joyce.

3. Edward Storer (1882-1923?), English poet and classicist who attempted imagist verse in 1908 but soon turned to publishing verbose translations of Sappho in the *Poets' Translation Series* and reprints from *The Egoist* of less familiar Greek and Latin poetry and prose. Other contributors were Aldington, H. D., and F. S. Flint. A notice on the series appears in *Poetry* VII (November 1915): 99-101, while T. S. Eliot's review of the series, praising H. D.'s translation of Euripides, is in *Poetry* IX (November 1916): 101-104.

4. *BLAST* 2, edited by Wyndham Lewis, appeared in July 1915 containing two poems by Eliot, eight by EP, and a comment by Wyndham Lewis describing EP as the "demon pantechnicon driver, busy with removal of old world into new

quarters" (82). Gaudier-Brzeska, Ford Madox Hueffer, J. Dismorr, and H. Sanders also contributed.

5. Ally Sloper was a fictitious late Victorian comic dandy originating in a popular weekly illustrated periodical published by the Dalziel Brothers from May 1884 to April 1923 entitled *Ally Sloper's Half Holiday*.

6. Four poems by John Rodker appeared in *Catholic Anthology, 1914-1915*: "Twilight I," "Twilight II," "The Lunatic," and "Fear." The last two were poetic experiments in prose.

7. The opening poem of *Catholic Anthology, 1914-1915* was Yeats' "The Scholars" which begins with the line "Bald heads forgetful of their sins"; also published in *Poetry* VII (February 1916): 226.

8. When he reduced his activities at *The Egoist* in the winter of 1914, EP recommended that Aldington continue as Assistant Editor with increased responsibilities in carrying out the daily tasks in running the magazine at the same time he suggested to Amy Lowell that she take over as editor (*SL* 31-32).

9. EP received payment for his lengthy contribution "The Classical Stage of Japan," *Drama* V (May 1915): 199-247.

10. EP's first mention to ACH of *The Cantos*. In February 1917 he would send her the so-called "Ur-Cantos" which she, in turn, would forward with an enthusiastic letter to Harriet Monroe in Chicago. See Letters 61, 62, 63.

11. From Zurich Joyce mailed *Exiles* in sections to his agent J. B. Pinker in London in July 1915; by October EP had read it and sent an article celebrating the work to *Drama* ("Mr. James Joyce and the Modern Stage," *Drama* VI [February 1916]: 122-32). Believing he might be able to get the play staged, EP refers to the theatrical impresario Oliver Morosco (1876-1945), a one-time acrobat and successful West Coast theatrical producer who with the Schuberts would open the Morosco Theatre in New York in 1917.

12. "Vorticism," *Fortnightly Review* XCVI (NS) (1 September 1914): [461]-471.

13. EP refers to his interest in purchasing *The Academy* (1869-1922), edited from 1907-1910 by Lord Alfred Douglas, implicated in the Oscar Wilde libel case of 1895; hence, the reference to "the imitators of Oscar." See *EP/JQ* 31 and Letter 36, note 1.

14. EP favored this adjective for *The Cantos*, especially in its early stages, using it again in a 21 September 1915 letter to Milton Bronner (see Stock 184).

15. EP was investigating the possibility of having Ralph Seymour in Chicago publish an American edition of *Catholic Anthology, 1914-1915*. However, no American edition was ever printed of the work.

43

5, Holland Place Chambers

Dear A.C.H.

Your "One City Only" looks very well in print. I hope your copies of the anthology will be ready to send next week.[1]

The *Yale Review* wrote to me in August, in reply to a note of mine. They said they hadn't rec'd the Fenollosa mss. on "The Written Character". I suppose they must have it by now, but I have heard nothing more from them.

I am really writing this letter on account of the Preface to Lionel Johnson's poems. Mathews paid me for the preface and it appears in the English edtn. of the book. Macmillan in New York, I suppose thinking to annoy or injure me in revenge for my having pointed out to them that they were and are liars, have asked to have the preface omitted from the copies sent to them.

It is a very trifling affair, but it is typical and I think it may be as well<,> in *Poetry*'s review of the book<,> to include some such phrase as

"Poems of Lionel Johnson". Elkin Mathews, London. This edtn. contains a - - - - - preface by E.P., the price is the same and those desiring to have preface as well as the poems should be careful to order the English edtn."[2]

I send simply the preface as I suppose a copy of the *Poems* will be sent to "Poetry" from N.Y.

The matter is very small but it is characteristic of the Macmillan firm and the "elder generation" of swine in general. They have illustrated themselves. It does not hit me in man's tenderest spot, as I have been, as I said, paid a lump for the job. *ma che* ....

I wonder, do they think this sort of thing can keep a man permanently down ??

I see that Werner Laurie is publishing "Spoon River" here. That was another star play of the Macmillans, the english end of the concern. They got over the S.R. and then sent all the copies back to the U.S.A., however a few people had seen it first, so the[ir] obstru[c]tion wasn't much use.

The book on Brzeska is on the way. At least I hope my part of it is finished.[3] The anthology is presumably having its covers put on.

Is H.M. ever going to have room for anything more. ??

I am sending Hinckley some notes on events, so I wont run over 'em in this letter.
Lewis has done a korking novel.[4] Joyce's book not yet published.[5] Eliot has a job and I am afraid it uses up too much of his time.[6] "London" will have to be run by the japs, the americans and the aged for the next ten months.
    De Gourmont's death needless and a great dampener to one's spirits. I shall try to get Tailhade to "replace him" on the magazine (the mythical magazine, that never comes to a head.) but of course nobody can replace him in any sense that matters.[7]

Itow's dancing is a great success, [but] between him and the Brzeska's estate matters I have been rushed to death. However .... I hope to make my last trip to the French embassy in 85 minutes.[8]

Anna Wickham says she is going to send in some verse, but since I have seen her book I am less interested, it is very very uneven.[9]

Rodker has a trace of something. The others seem stuck dead. Eliot alone seems likely to matter. Yeats has finished his mad play. I wonder what will happen with it.[10]

<yours ever
E Pound>

1. Alice Corbin [Henderson], "One City Only," *Catholic Anthology, 1914-1915* (London: Elkin Mathews, 1915): 20-21. For a review of the anthology see Max Michelson, "The Independents," *Poetry* VIII (May 1916): 94-96.

2. Published in October 1915, the *Poetical Works of Lionel Johnson* (London: Elkin Mathews, 1915) contained a fourteen page "Preface" dated 1914 by EP; the U.S. edition printed by Macmillan in December 1915 dropped the material. Later impressions of 1917 and 1926 published in London and New York also excluded the "Preface."

An unsigned review of both the London and New York editions entitled "A Poet of the Nineties" appeared in *Poetry* VII (March 1916): 313-317.

3. *Gaudier-Brzeska: A Memoir* was published on 14 April 1916 by John Lane, The Bodley Head. It included published writings of Gaudier-Brzeska, a selection of his letters, and 38 illustrations of his sculpture and drawings plus text by EP.

4. Wyndham Lewis' first novel *Tarr* was serialized in abridged form in nineteen parts in *The Egoist* from April 1916 to November 1917. In December 1915 Lewis told EP sections of the novel would be forthcoming and asked him to read it in "an incredulous and argumentative voice" (*EP/WL* 17). Harriet Shaw Weaver did not like the novel but supported its publication (see *EP/WL* 21, 22).

Tarr, an autobiographical novel drawing on Lewis' 1907/08 period in Paris, contrasts the bohemian life of the artists Frederick Tarr, an Englishman, and Otto Kreisler, a German. The philosophical Tarr, who believes that "an artist requires more energy than civilization provides" and that "everyone who does not fight openly and bear his share of the common burden of ignominy in life is a sneak," is in conflict with the psychological Kreisler, driven by sex, money, and the artlessness of existence: "life did not each day deposit an untidiness that could be whisked off by a Gillette blade, as Nature did its stubble" (*Tarr*, ed. Paul O'Keeffe [Santa Rosa, CA: Black Sparrow Press, 1990], 360, 33, 77-78). Kreisler, whose father has not only cut him off financially but stolen his fiancée, has devastating emotional problems; Tarr, by contrast, approaches life intellectually, seeking to liberate the artist from human weaknesses. In the *Little Review* (IV [March 1918]: 35), EP celebrated *Tarr* as "the most vigorous and volcanic English novel of our time" (*LE* 424).

5. Joyce's *A Portrait of the Artist as a Young Man* would not exist in book form until 29 December 1916 when B. W. Huebsch published it in New York. Its serial publication in *The Egoist* began in January and ran to September 1915.

6. Married in June 1915, T. S. Eliot needed work and became a schoolmaster in September 1915 at High Wycombe Grammar School. He also started to publish book reviews in the *International Journal of Ethics* and the *New Statesman*, thanks to Bertrand Russell.

7. Remy de Gourmont, French novelist, critic, poet and, along with Alfred Vallette, founder of the *Mercure de France* in 1889, much admired by EP, died in Paris on 17 September 1915. See EP's appreciation in *Poetry* VII (January 1916): 197-202.

Laurent Tailhade (1854-1919), French poet and man of letters cited by EP in his "Approach to Paris," *New Age* 13 (2 October 1913): 662-664. Pound met him in Paris in 1913 and published the poem "Our Respectful Homages to M. Laurent Tailhade" in *BLAST* 2 (July 1915): 21.

8. Michio Itow (1893-1961), Japanese artist who in late October 1915 performed five "dance poems" translated by EP. See *Pound/Joyce: The Letters of Ezra Pound to James Joyce* 58; EP, "Sword-Dance and Spear-Dance: Texts of the Poems used with Michio Itow's Dances," *Future* 1 (December 1916): 54. Itow danced while the poems were read aloud (Longenbach 202; *Pound/Joyce* 58).

Itow rented EP's old apartment at 10 Church Walk after John Cournos. EP recalled Itow and his unusual speech in the *Pisan Cantos* (77/483). For EP's early praise of him see *SL* 63; for additional details on Itow see EP, "Remy de Gourmont," *Fortnightly Review* XCVIII (N.S.) (1 December 1915): [1159]-1166 and Longenbach 198-202.

9. Anna Wickham (1884-1947), English poet who lived in Australia from ages 6 to 21 and then went to study at the Paris Opera. She married an English astronomer and published work described by Louis Untermeyer as intense, crude, and ironic; her poetry, however, was little known and not widely read. See her *Songs of John Oland* (1918).

10. Most likely *The Player Queen* which Yeats returned to in 1914 and then revised again during September 1915 when he was at Coole Park. He probably reported his reworking of the text to EP in London which he then read to EP when he returned to London in December 1915. Yeats would continue to revise it, however, until 1919 (Longenbach 298).

Yeats began *At the Hawk's Well*, the better-known text which was directly influenced by EP's Noh translations, at Stone Cottage around 4 February 1916. By the 16th of February plans for a performance in the first week of April were outlined with EP to prompt the production, Dulac to design the masks and costumes, Itow to dance the Hawk, Henry Ainley to play the Young Man, and Alan Wade to act the Old Man.

44

EP to ACH   TLS 24 January 1916 2 ll. Postmark: "London S.W. / 2.15 PM / 24 JAN 16."

> Stone Cottage
> Colemans Hatch
> Sussex

Dear A.C.H.

I like your "one city," very much, as you know. I think the Sarasate poem also comes off. And the little Yeatses are pas mal in their way.[1] At any rate you do not butcher the language. Can you not, as you are on the spot[,] prevent other murders. I fulminate to H.M. ... I dont know whether she pays any attention to my letters ..... ma che ..... You are at least in Chicago and can see proofs etc.....

Is there no way to prevent

"A crimson flame *my heart above*"[2]

He "stood the door behind", says the senile poet.

BAHHHHHHaaa.   What did he stand it behind?

This sort of p<y>ing the order shows nothing but sheer impotence. It is not used in a whirl of emotion too violent to show itself in orderly speech. It is just bad.

Kreymborg and his gang are going to pace-make for the last yell. I suppose the double-Chestnuts are going to make some sort of a stand <against> the Kreymborg crowd and I hope and suppose that the[ir] slogan will be "good english" and "form".

Poetry has a tremendous advantage by reason of its endowment, but but that lead wont hold us up forever, and the office will have to look sharp if we are to stay certain of the summit.

Incidentally "A.L." should have signed in full (page 207)[;] the suspicious might think that the author of the work reviewed and the reviewer were one and the same person.[3] I did not notice it, but it was brought to my attention and criticized.

I wish Rodker wouldn't write about things being "friable", all these damn cockneys will do th[a]t sort of thing, emphasis on a word with no lineage, a word that might just as well be 20 other words. When one drags in an outre word it must so certainly be the mot juste.

I have damed most of the other writers to H.M. direct. If she keeps up the whooping enthusiasm of the concern you (in your spare moments) must look after the style, for H.M. probably dislikes style [as] something un-National and therefore pernicious.

ebbene

<Yours

E.P.>

---

1. *Poetry* VII (January 1916) opened with six poems by Alice Corbin. The first was "One City Only" on pages 163-164, which also appeared in EP's *Catholic Anthology, 1914-15*. For his enthusiastic response to the poem see *SL* 67.

Pablo Sarasate (1844-1908), Spanish violinist and composer. Saint-Saëns and Dvořák dedicated works to him; Whistler titled his 1884 portrait of him "Arrangement in Black: Pablo de Sarasate." Alice Corbin [Henderson] refers to Sarasate in her poem "Music," *Poetry* VII (January 1916): 165-166. EP would cite the Whistler painting of Sarasate in Canto 80/517 and the difficulty of the Bavarian painter George S. Sauter in understanding the work until "one day after Whistler's death / I think it was Ysaÿe [Belgian violinist] was with him / who saw the Whistler / for the first time and burst out: / What a fiddle!" (517).

The "little Yeatses" likely refers to "Color Note" and "Song," *Poetry* VII: 168.

2. Pound misquotes a line from "Footnotes," by Muna Lee in *Poetry* VII (January 1916): 176. The line correctly reads "A crimson scar my heart above."

3. A. L., "Miss Lowell on French Poets," *Poetry* VII (January 1916): 202-207. A. L. is not Amy Lowell but Agnes Lee (Mrs. Otto Freer) of Chicago, author of *The Sharing* and other books of poetry, as well as a frequent contributor to *Poetry*.

45

EP to ACH   TLS [? February 1916] 1 1 + 2 Enclosures: ms. letter from Elkin Mathews dated 21 February 1916; pamphlet on *Gaudier-Brzeska*.

Stone Cottage
address. 5. Holland Place Chambers
Kensington. London. W.

Dear A.C.H.

Here is Elkin's submissive reply. I sent on your note as it stood.

I suppose you. H.M., Quinn and everybody else will some time send me a set of long letters all about everything.

To return to an ancient affair, wherewith you must be bored to death. The *Yale Rev.* which is probably devoted to the dead. wrote to me that they hadn't rec'd Fenollosa's "Chinese Written Character".[1] I suppose they've ate it and hid it. Any way, if you haven't placed it, please dont bother any more, and please return it as the *Quarterly* has at last forgave me for being concerned with BLAST and there may be some chance of my placing it with them.

I have just written to Sandburg. Perh<ap>s you will see the letter, you might remind him to show it to you, as it contains part of what I had on my chest this a.m. and I cant rewrite all of it.

<yours
E.P.>

[Enclosure 1:] ALS 1 1 from Elkin Mathews, Publisher Cork Street. London, W. Printed at the top reads "Telegrams: Verbaliser, London".

Feby 21st 1916

Dear Ezra Pound

I promptly attended to Mrs. Henderson's and your suggestions — to wit:

a review copy of the "C.A." [*Catholic Anthology*] has been sent to the
Boston Transcript 36 copies-----------have---------------- on Sale to
Poetry
    543 Cass Street, Chicago
a review copy of L.J. [*Lionel Johnson*] with Preface to Mrs.
Henderson
    c/o Curtis & Davison
a review copy of the latter also with Preface was sent to Milton
Bronner

    I return herewith Desmond MacCarthy's letter — thanks for
sight of it.
Yours sincerely
Elkin Mathews

[Enclosure 2:] Four-page pamphlet on *Gaudier-Brzeska, A Memoir* by
Ezra Pound published at 12s 6d containing a reproduction of the
title page including a photograph of Gaudier-Brzeska's bust of EP.
One page of text describing the book and EP's "intimate" association with the sculptor; a specimen illustration showing Gaudier-
Brzeska standing next to one of his pieces; an order form for the
book to be sent to "John Lane, The Bodley Head, Vigo Street, W."

1. See Letter 33, note 2.

46

EP to ACH TLS 18 March 1916 1 l. Addressed to "Mrs. W.P. Henderson, 10 E. Ohio St., Chicago, USA" crossed out and corrected to "Sun Mount, Santa Fe, New Mex." This is EP's first letter sent to ACH after she moved to Santa Fe in 1916 because of her tuberculosis.

5, Holland Place Chambers

< 18 March 1916>

Dear A.C.H.

You really oughtn't to have been caught with Masefield's molasses. He *is* a weak backed mackerel. I hope you wont mind my onslaught (sent to H.M.), but *really* !!!!!!!![1]

The other "really," is why does H.M. only allow me my softest notes?

The other point is, can you send me back my Johnson preface, there is some talk of my having *at last* a book of my prose blasts done.[2] I suppose it will come to nothing, but still, if it isn't too beastly a bore, could you return it. I find I haven't another copy, and may want to use it.

Really that note on Eliot *ought* to get in. Why all you people are so gentle and careful when dealing with imbeciles I do not know, one might think the death of a fool was a national calamity.

<yours ever
E.P.>

1. EP refers to ACH's "Mr. Masefield's Lecture," *Poetry* VII (March 1916): 301-303, a report of Masefield's talk at the Chicago Woman's Club on the phases of English poetry, emphasizing the poet/audience relationship. EP opposed this stress on the audience shaping a poet and objected to the Whitman quote reprinted on the backcovers of *Poetry*: "To have great poets / there must be great audiences too."

For a critique of Masefield see EP, "This Constant Preaching to the Mob," *Poetry* VIII (June 1916): 144-145. EP's original criticism of Whitman's statement and the question of audience appeared in his essay "The Audience," *Poetry* V (October 1914): 29-30.

2. Johnson: see Letter 43, note 2. For information on EP's collection of essays, see Letter 47, note 5.

47

EP to ACH   TLS 3 May 1916 4 ll + 1 Enclosure.

5, Holland Place Chambers

Dear A.C.H.

D A M N. Aunt 'Arriet has just written me that you are
tucked away in a sanitarium (writing illegible so this has to go via
Chicago.). If you were only Sara Teasdale or any other one of the
9000 illustrious American imbeciles you would have the constitution
of a dray horse.[1] America is a very bad place.

'Arriet says I am to write to you, from the smoking ashes of
europe, words of cheer. The words of cheer are various, Lewis has
got into the artillery so there is less chance of his being shot than if
he were in something else. (But then you may not like Lewis ...).
Shall I send you my "Gaudier-Brzeska" book?[2] I've hidden one copy
against emergency. It may only annoy you, you and your family
being addicted to a different sort of modern art. ????

The Japanese book, you have seen most of it, I think, and
Yeats' preface isn't set up yet.[3] Still I'll send you the proofs if you
want 'em. Do you see the beastly *Egoist* where you are, or is the
exchange copy kept in Chi.?
Lewis novel began last month.[4] I'll send you the thing as it comes, or
anything else you can think of, that might amuse you.
Arriet says my new poem isn't nice, and that Masefield is a dear
good man full of the Xtian virtues.
America is an awful country.
I believe Marshall in N.Y. is to publish a large prose work of mine,
on "This Generation". Most of it has gone and the rest is about to
depart.[5] I hope it will do some good. The last American I saw said
"nothing will do the damn place any good, save carnage *so* great that
they wont be able to sentimentalize over it." .

The *Times* is two columns respectful over the Gaudier.[6]
The *Quarterly* has forgave me. My news seems to cling to one spot.

New poems went to Mathews on Monday and he hopes
they'll be printed by September.[7] He phoned for the printer and for
the reserve of paper at once. (Actions showing to what an extent the
war is regenerating this island.)

Marshall may also do Joyce's novel in America, and I hope
a book by Eliot.

Yeats' noh play went better than could have been expected.
Have done three very brief "plays" myself. Also edited papa Yeats'
letters to his distinguished son.[8] They are very entertaining and
ought also to "do some good". I'll send on the *Egoist* anyhow, in case
you don't get it in Cal. I don't know how my Fontenelle reads.[9] It
seems short, choppy in print, but reads out fairly nicely I think.
Would god, that America could be put through a course of Voltaire
and the 18th century frenchmen.
My news is very restricted, everybody else is off to the wars.

The drunken lady in the rooms under Yeats<'> set the place on
fire and has been kicked out, so he has taken on the floor, painted
the stairs sky blue, ordered a large board table like mine, and
Woburn Blds. is shaken to its foundation.

DuLac is the only real comfort left in this capital. Meeting
between him and Lewis (on leave for a few days) very thundery.
Dulac better at all things than painting. His masks for the play [*At
the Hawk's Well*], and the costumes very interesting. There are also a
few amusing japs left out of the trenches. A few good poems
gathered in from Iris Barry, the last entertainment.[10]
I enclose proofs <(have to go separate)> of a couple of pencil designs
poor Gaudier had done in the margin of his copy of "Ripostes". One
a first idea for the bust, the other a tail piece to "Acr Carr". The
paper is much too white but I can't help it.
I wonder what else there is that would amuse anyone.
Vorticist show has been shipped to New York.[11]
Irish ruction will give that country another set of anecdotes to keep
it going another hundred years.[12]
I cant send "thee violets" from this distance, do use the enclosed for
chocolates or flowers or whatever the sanitary experts allow [you] to
have for your health.[13]

And above all do get well and come to Europe. even in the midst of Armageddon it is probably better for sensitive temperament than our broad patriarchial desert.

<you seem to have started off Miss Buss on a violent press campaign.[14] She just sends me a half pages on Gaudier.

etc.   I have done nothing but letters letters letters all day and am at about the end. besides I must put on my feet & go forth to the estimable Belotti.[15]>

<yours ever

E Pound>

<3/5/'16>

▬▬▬▬▬ [Enclosure 1:]
   A check from Ezra Pound to "Alice Corbin Henderson" for $10.00 dated May 3, 1916 to be drawn on the Jenkintown, Pa. Trust Company, Jenkintown, Pennsylvania. The carefully written signature reads "Ezra Pound."

▬▬▬▬▬

1. Sara Teasdale (1884-1933), popular American lyric poet who wrote wistful verse of sparing imagery and who won the Pulitzer Prize in 1917 for *Love Songs*.

2. *Gaudier-Brzeska*, published 14 April 1916. For details see Letter 43, note 3.

3. *Certain Noble Plays of Japan, From the Manuscripts of Ernest Fenollosa*, Chosen and Finished by Ezra Pound, With an Introduction by William Butler Yeats (Churchtown, Dundrum: Cuala Press, 1916). In his eight-part introduction dated April 1916, Yeats evaluates the impact of Noh theatre on his own work, declaring that "with the help of Japanese plays 'translated by Ernest Fenollosa and finished by Ezra Pound,' I have invented a form of drama, distinguished, indirect, and symbolic . . . an aristocratic form." Yeats furthermore celebrates the power of the mask and the discipline and nobility of the actors. He also notes that the Noh fascination with dance is "not in the human form but in the rhythm to which it moves, [while] the triumph of [the] art is to express the rhythm in its intensity." "We only believe," Yeats later writes, "in those thoughts which have been conceived not in the brain but in the whole body." Comments on the art of Dulac, the dance of Itow, and Yeats' own production of *At the Hawk's Well* run throughout the essay. Yeats, "Certain Noble Plays of Japan," *Essays and Introductions* (London: Macmillan, 1961), 221, 231, 235.

4. The first installment of Lewis' *Tarr* appeared in *The Egoist* III (1 April 1916): 54-63.

5. "This Generation" (1915-1917) was originally a collection of EP's prose pieces from ca. 1910-1915 titled "The Half Decade." By March 1916 terms were drawn up with a new publisher, John Marshall of New York, who had once worked for the bookseller Laurence Gomme (owner of the shop EP made his

"headquarters" during his 1910-1911 visit), was a partner in The Little Bookshop Around the Corner, and who had briefly financed Kreymborg's magazine *Others*. EP sent the manuscript to Marshall in early May. However, Quinn, in New York, discovered that Marshall was not financially sound and attempts by Quinn to see Marshall on EP's behalf failed. From Alfred Kreymborg, Quinn learned that Marshall had taken off for Canada with the manuscript and his ill young bride. A portion of the typescript, however, has survived and is in the Pound archive at the Beinecke. Also see *EP/JQ* 83.

6. "The New Sculpture," *Times Literary Supplement* No. 745 (27 April 1916): 199. Although the review begins with "this book like the sculpture in it, will irritate many; and we could write a column and more about the provocations of Mr. Pound" (199a), it is generally favorable.

7. *Lustra* was issued by Mathews in September 1916.

8. *At the Hawk's Well* premiered 2 April 1916 in the drawing room of Lady Cunard. For a comment on the work by ACH, see "The Hawk's Well," *Poetry* X (June 1917): 163-165. Michio Itow danced the role of the hawk. His photograph appears accompanying the large mask created for the play by Edmund Dulac in an article entitled "Are you in the No?" *Vogue* 48 (1 July 1916): 69. The androgynous-looking Itow is described as "the young Japanese dancer who has this season created a furor in London" playing "the subtle role of the mysterious bird, half hawk, half beautiful woman, that guards the Well of the Water of Immortality" (ibid.).

One of the "three very brief plays" EP refers to was *The Consolations of Matrimony* which was to be presented with Yeats' work but was cut because of little time to prepare for the evening (Longenbach 209-12). That work, along with *The Protagonist*, De Musset's *A Supper at the House of Mademoiselle Rachel*, and *Tristan*, appear in *Plays Modelled on the Noh*, ed. Donald C. Gallup (Toledo: Friends of the University of Toledo Libraries, 1987).

Passages from the Letters of John Butler Yeats, selected by Ezra Pound (Churchtown, Dundrum: Cuala Press, 1917). EP reviewed his own text in *Poetry* XI (January 1918): 223-225.

9. The first of EP's "Dialogues of Fontenelle, Translated by Ezra Pound," appeared in *The Egoist* III (1 May 1916): 67-68.

10. Iris Barry (1895-1969), a young English poet from Birmingham. EP had seen her poetry in Harold Monro's *Poetry and Drama* and wrote to her attempting to solicit some work for *Poetry*. Her prompt answer led to an important and instructive correspondence by EP on the art of poetry (*SL* 76 ff) followed by a move by Barry (at EP's suggestion) to London where she eventually became involved in film, establishing the London Film Society in 1925. Barry became a film critic for the *Spectator* and, later, librarian and then film curator of the Museum of Modern Art in New York.

11. The Vorticist exhibition shipped to John Quinn during the war was a costly and time-consuming undertaking; it included work by Wyndham Lewis, Edward Wadsworth, Frederick Etchells, William Roberts, Abel Sanders, and Henri Gaudier-Brzeska (see *EP/JQ* 58-60, 69-70). The long-delayed show

opened in New York City's Penguin Club on 10 January 1917 and ran for three weeks.

12. EP refers to the Easter Rebellion of 1916 which actually began on Easter Monday, 24 April 1916. Overtaking a city virtually deserted because of a bank holiday, the Citizens' Army and Irish Volunteers took control of Dublin for six days with Patrick Pearse as President of the Irish Republic at Headquarters set up in the General Post Office. The seven signatories of the Proclamation declaring an independent country included three poets, two teachers, one musician, and one self-educated workman. Nearly 1500 volunteers took part in the Rebellion against 16,000 British troops stationed in Ireland—although that number rose to 50,000 within a week. By the afternoon of 29 April 1916, the rebels surrendered, leaving 450 from both sides dead. On the day EP wrote this letter to ACH, 3 May 1916, the British executed by firing squad the former President, Pearse, the poet Thomas MacDonagh, and the Fenian Tom Clarke at Kilmainham prison.

At first condemned by the majority of the Irish, the Rebellion quickly achieved monumental importance because of the martyrdom of its leaders. "Right down to the heart of Irish nationality it cut," declared the playwright Lennox Robinson (in G. Costigan, *A History of Modern Ireland* [NY: Pegasus, 1969], 333).

13. EP enclosed a check for $10.00 to Alice Corbin Henderson dated 3 May 1916 to be drawn on the Jenkintown Trust Co., Jenkintown, Pennsylvania.

14. Kate Buss (1884- ?) American author, playwright, and journalist whose work appeared in the *New Republic*, *Vanity Fair*, and *Poetry*. A friend of Amy Lowell, Buss also corresponded with EP and praised *Lustra* in the *Boston Evening Standard* (6 December 1916; rpt. in *EP: The Critical Heritage* 24-25; see also *SL* 71, 101, 174, 186). EP later asked her to distribute in America the "Bel Esprit" circular printed by Rodker and designed to generate support for Eliot. See *SL* 174-175 and Letter 71, note 6.

15. EP's favorite London restaurant located at 12 Old Compton Street, "the cheapest clean restaurant with a real cook" he told Iris Barry when outlining how she should survive in the city (*SL* 97). In the late summer and early fall of 1915, EP and Violet Hunt held weekly dinner parties at Bellotti's whose owner is mentioned in Canto 80/515 as reading from the pedestal of the statue of Shakespeare in Leicester Square, London, a quotation from *Twelfth Night*. EP also celebrates him for bringing in "about 2 ounces of saffron / for a risotto during that first so enormous war" (ibid.).

48

5, Holland Place Chambers, Kensington W.

<May 5, 1916>

Dear A.C. .

Your's to hand. I sent a note to you yesterday on receipt of Harriet's statement that you were ill.

Of course the plain damn unvarnished fact is that Harriet is a fool. A noble, sincere, long strugglin impeccable fool. That is infinitely better than being Amy-just-selling-the-goods, but it is damd inconvenient, AND we are all, (I in particular) in a position where it is impossible, base, treacherous to admit that Harriet is a fool. The better the stuff I send in, by me or by anybody else, the more God damn worry, fuss, bother to get it printed.

I ought to have had strength of mind enough to erase America from my consciousness when I last sailed from New York, or before then.[1]

As for Amy, damn Amy. I was a fool to let in that one poem. Did you see the yankee salesman in Potash and Pearlmutter?[2] Amy without the disarming pathos. Still even Amy will pass <pass away, pass into Henry Van Dykeness>.[3] The New York crowd is *on*. I didn't do it, little Bill just naturally arrived and various others arrived with or about. Bill calls it "that tub of guts". Amy will pass. Amy *is* rather annoying.

I believe Marshall in N.Y. is publishing a book of mine on "This Generation". A dignified work, mentioning only things worthy of mention.[4]

Get well, dont worry about Amy. ref/ Abe Lincoln on gullability.[5] And, dear heart, Amy did come to me with references from

<C>hicago <It was H.M.>. You said, I think, "300 pounds and a
charmer". Her dinners were excellent, She has charm. She is a
delightful acquaintance, or would be if one were a civil engineer.
Poor Amy, poor Amy. It is all very distressing, and my Arm Chair
has never been the same since she sat in it, or rather bounced with
glee over some witticism. No upholsterer can do anything with it,
the springs still do *such* funny things.[6]

And "Remy", yes I would write beautiful essays if you found me
twelve Remys a year, to <be> praise <in> the <essays>.[7] But most
things are not even worth cursing. AND Harriet is *so* humane. Last
night I had almost strength of mind enough to say "I'll resign. I'am
not angry, I just recognize the utter hopelessness of ever teaching
you anything ma chere H.M. It is very inconvenient, I need the
money, but still I will pull out, It is damd cheek for you to think
anyone with the design of being a classic author is going to suit your
Dorcas society."

Dora [Marsden] on the *Egoist* is another trial. She don't interfere but
she is ignorant and eaten up with conceit and there is her four pages
of slosh on the forehead of every number. <But she hasn't H's mania
for genteelness. & she believes in individual differences.> H.M. *still*
yearns for a parish gazette. Despite all we've both done for her
education, elle est inattaquable (spelling<?>).
        BURN THIS DOCUMENT
She has done a noble work, but she is a fool, with NO sense about
poetry, , no that is too strong, she has more sense than any other
American editor, save Kreymborg (who has no sense whatever, but
excellent intentions).[8] He will do in N.Y. with no capital all that she
has done in CHI with it, and he could have all her strong cards if he
could pay. voila.

Your prose is the only prose save mine that is worth a damn in the
paper. I'm landed with her damn stuff in my anthology (not that it
matters, ma che, one *has* got artistic beliefs.[9] <O>f course one *couldnt*
leave her out after all she has done, but damn it all it aint art.

Amy knows more. That is <the> damn trouble. America is so bloody
bone ignorant tha[t] anyone with time and money enough to learn

anything can take in the whole show. Fletcher has got some sort of sincerity, damn fool, ma che .... <excitable - no controll.>

This is not kick. It is simply recognition that nothing can come in America. The best will continue to come over here. Masters seems to be going to <p>ieces. Climate again, no reason to finish anything, all whoop.
The new stuff is mostly bad copies. <Even> Masters is simply a grab at a method, new subject matter, and a good man doing it. But still <it is> application, its not the germinal thing.
                                   Keep this letter in <New Mexico>. Think of your own work. Nothing else matters, we have been mad with crusading. Nothing matters save the occasional good poem. Nothing else lasts out ten years. The bad stuff will go. Our own follies will be forgotten. We can live 'em down with a few decent poems.

There is 4000 dollars waiting for my magazine, they want $10,000. And now that Remy is dead, and Ford gone to the wars, I don't want the damn magazine. I <want> a quiet life and a pension. Cheaper for all concerned.

You'll probably get this letter before the one I mailed yesterday, as that had to go via Chicago, *your* address is legible. Though not all of your letter.

My "Lustra" is in the press. Saw the sample page this a.m.[10]

The war is remaking the country, took the poems to Mathews on Monday. He telephoned at once for paper. Then telephoned to the printer. Still I dare say it will take 'em till Sept. to print it.

Did I put in a list of my works, yesterday.
                 Gaudier-Brzeska, out
                 Certain Noble Plays of Japan, in the press,
                     waiting for Yeats to finish introduction.
                 Lustra, in the press (all the new poems, with "Cathay")
                 This Generation, prose "kulturband," on everything:
                 poetry in Paris, here and in the U.S. during the last
                 eight years. I believe this is to be brought out at once

in N.Y. via Kreymborg and his friends.

Letters of old Yeats to W.B. (edited by E.P.) rather amusing.

Three playlets, ten minutes long, in type-script.

<I suppose I must next do a "Lewis" as a
             companion book to the Brzeska.>

Harriet would have been so happy with Masefield. Masefield would have been happier with Harriet. I enclose a tintype, there'll be a prettier one in the book (Lustra).

D. is raging *for me* to *come forth* to supper.

O<h> about Yeats and the anth. I don't know what can be done. We've <just> had our months <together> in the country, and I am so tired of a lot of dead ideas.[11] There is no breech but I can't, oh well maybe I can, but still, damn personal favours in a matter of art. Can't the thing be an american anthology? None of these people want to go into it. I don't know. - - - - All this personal element is so rum. It needs all my diplomacy to get stuff for the magazine. None of 'em really like being printed in Chicago. I've used my personal credit so often.

OF COURSE the editors ought to be in <the> magazine every month. And I in my pride and vanity think I ought to have ten pages of verse every six months. O superbia<!>
O stiff necked pride of E.P. <!!>
There never was but one intelligent editor, that is Vallette of the *Mercure de France*, who never appears in the magazine, save once in five years to make an announcement about the printing or something of that sort. <(Perhaps it is *sa femme* Rachilde who prevents it. — why believe in a miracle!)>

I always feel that H.M. would be happier if she hadn't me on her back like a parasitic old man of the sea, talking about international standards.

Dear girl, forget it all, none of it matters. Don<'>t write to the magazine, dont write to Chicago. Write to me. I don<'>t know who<m> you've got in Paris to write to. Anyhow write to this side.

Write to me all that you feel like and I'll answer all that I can. Also write a few good poems.

Lewis says "they call me aggressive, *Blast* aggressive etc.["] Damn it all <when> I sit in my room making a drawing I am ten times more <aggressive than ten> dozen *BLASTS* and all the press put together.

Thanks for bothering about the Chinese essay. The L.J. don't in the least matter. I can easily rip out the leaves from a bound copy.[12] I wonder which DeGourmont you mean<?> The "Fortnightly" or the "Poetry" Remy<?>[13]

As to Harriet. I have always tried to suggest that you should write more of the magazine, without definitely saying "See here 'Arriet, you are an ignorant if strong minded female, you can<'>t expect to be saved, and the only person in Chi. who knows black from dove grey is your assistant." <I did recommend "One City Only." I'll always reship your stuff if you send it to Poetry *via me*. You needn't phrase it that way. — you can send it to me for "criticism" or whatever you choose to call it. & tell me what you want to go in.>

Notre honette directrice is much too strong minded to stand criticism of her own stuff. I think there was nearly a ruction over my choosing <for the Cat. Anth.> the only thing out of her book that could possibly have got by *anything*. She don<'>t really much want to learn. Her conscience tells her she ought to want to, but *la volonta* is at strife.

Now about her anthology, I have heard nothing in particular.[14] I supposed it was her attempt to prove that I shouldn't have tried a Cat. Anth. and that the breezy western manner was more suited to the readers of *Reedy's Mirror*. It was a special and unique act of grace that W.B.Y. should have come into the Cat. Anth. rather against his feeling, but out of willingness to stand by me. I have never consented to appear in any American or any English anthology, for that matter. Couch wrote to me and I refused the poems he asked for and then he simply took some others.[15] I can't see why W.B.Y. can possibly want to appear in company with a lot of people selected by H.M. I can't see what argument I am to use on him. He loathes all sorts of pursuasion and is pretty well proof against it.

Harriet has a fine upright character and one can trust her to do the best that she knows, which lifts her infinitely above Boston politics, but which do not help in the "art woild" much beyond that. if you were doing the book, or even if I had been told six months ago that you were using some restraint over H. in doing it, I might have been able to do something.

<">The wisest of men abandon the <world>, the next wisest abandon their own count[r]y, and the third wisest abandon the dominion of catch-words" says Confucius.[16]
I dare say "Imagism" is a catch word, and that Koung the master had mixed with a new school of poets in his young youth. We are not all born with the serpent[']s wisdom. Amy was very disarming. Perhaps she would have returned to America a paroxyste, if she hadn't returned with the Imagist ark of the covenant, varnished and empty.[17] I doubt if the lack of that particular label would have kept her in absolute silence. *chi lo sa*? I had one brilliant inspiration. I was about to declare the imagist movement *over*, when the first anthology came out. Like a damn fool I didn't.

Oh well, you've got some leisure, stop reading modern verse. any of it. Stick to the classics, at least till you come out of Sun Mount.
thats enough for this evening.
<yours ever
Ezra>

1. EP sailed to England from New York on 22 February 1911 on the *Mauretania*.

2. EP published Amy Lowell's "In a Garden," in *Des Imagistes* (New York: Boni, 1914), 38.

"Potash and Pearlmutter" refers to the anthology *Representative American Poetry*, ed. William S. Braithwaite and Henry Thomas Schnittkind (Boston: R. G. Badger, 1916).

3. Henry Van Dyke (1852-1933), American poet, essayist, and short-story writer, was a minister who published sentimental verse and later became Professor of English at Princeton. In 1910 he published *The Spirit of America* and in 1912 became President of the National Institute of Arts and Letters. From 1913 to 1916 he was American Ambassador to the Netherlands and Luxembourg. *The Blue Flower* (1902), a translation of a work by Novalis, is his best-known

book. Pound satirized him in "L'Homme Moyen Sensuel" (*P* 256-263); see *EP/JQ* 63.

4. See Letter 47, note 5.

5. In a speech at Clinton, Illinois, on 8 September 1858, Lincoln said "you can fool all of the people some of the time and some of the people all of the time, but you can't fool all of the people all of the time."

6. EP may be recalling an incident when Amy Lowell visited his rooms in the summer of 1914 following her 17 July 1914 dinner, a belated celebration of *Des Imagistes* at which she was ridiculed by EP who dragged in a bathtub and announced that the *Imagistes* were being superseded by the *Nagistes* (swimmers). EP is here still smarting from Lowell's attempt to usurp imagism as her term and establish her own anthology, *Some Imagist Poets*, although he had already turned to Vorticism.

7. Remy de Gourmont. EP expressed his appreciation of him following his death in September 1915 in two essays: "Remy de Gourmont [Part I]," *Fortnightly Review* XCVIII (N.S.) (1 December 1915): [1159]-1166 and "Remy de Gourmont [Part II]," *Poetry* VII (January 1916): 197-202. In 1922 EP would translate Gourmont's *The Natural Philosophy of Love* (New York: Boni and Liveright, 1922), adding a thirteen-page "Translator's Postscript."

8. Alfred Kreymborg, editor of *Others*. See Letter 40, note 3. EP included two of Kreymborg's poems in *Catholic Anthology, 1914-1915*. EP met Kreymborg for the first time in Paris in 1921, the same year Kreymborg and Harold Loeb founded the little magazine *Broom* in Rome. In 1927, with Paul Rosenfeld, Lewis Mumford, and Van Wyck Brooks, Kreymborg founded the successful *American Caravan* series.

9. EP included HM's "A Letter from Peking" in his *Catholic Anthology, 1914-1915* (London: Elkin Mathews, 1915) on pp. 46-53, the longest poem in the collection. See his comment on the poem in Letter 34, this edition.

10. Two hundred copies of a privately printed edition of *Lustra*, containing a frontispiece photograph of EP by Alvin Langdon Coburn, would be published in September 1916 by Elkin Mathews, printing having been delayed because of concern over the indecorum of certain poems. Three poems were withheld when the volume finally appeared, and nine additional poems were suppressed when the second impression, a trade edition, was offered by Mathews in October 1916.

11. Pound refers to Stone Cottage and the winter 1915-1916 period. EP arrived in late December 1915; they did not return to London until March 1916. More importantly, through ACH, HM wanted EP to ask Yeats for a contribution to *The New Poetry* anthology to be published by Macmillan (New York) in February 1917. Reluctantly, EP asked Yeats who agreed to send ten poems, including "The Wild Swans at Coole."

12. EP may be referring to his "literary journal," his designation for "Status Rerum - The Second," *Poetry* VIII (April 1916): 38-43, a detailed summary of "the state of affairs in contemporary poetry" (38). He most likely asked for unbound sheets but tells ACH that he will remove the pages from a bound copy

of *Poetry*. This would be in preparation for sending off copy to John Marshall in New York for the proposed collection of his essays "This Generation," which in fact was mailed in May 1916.

13. See note 7 above.

14. *The New Poetry*, organized in 1916 and published by Macmillan (New York) in February 1917. EP had twenty poems in the collection.

15. Sir Arthur Quiller-Couch, "Q" (1863-1944). In October 1912 Quiller-Couch asked EP if he could include two of his poems in the *Oxford Book of Victorian Verse* (Oxford: Oxford University Press, 1912). EP objected to the two selected, "Ballad for Gloom" from *A Lume Spento* (1908), reprinted in *Personae* (1909), and "Portrait" from *Exultations* (1909), both of which he was planning to omit from his next edition of the revised *Personae* published with *Exultations* in 1913. Nevertheless, Quiller-Couch printed them in his anthology. See EP to HM, 22 October 1912, *SL* 12 and F.G. Atkinson, "Ezra Pound's Reply to an 'Old-World' Letter," *American Literature* XLVI (November 1974): [357]-359.

16. EP's version of a passage from the *Analects of Confucius*, Book XIV, Ch. XXXIX, a work he would translate and publish in 1951 as *Confucian Analects* (New York: Square $ Series, 1951). In the James Legge translation, the passage reads

> XXXIX. 1. The Master said, '*Some* men of worth retire from the world.
>
> 2. 'Some retire from *particular* countries.
>
> 3. 'Some retire because of *disrespectful* looks.
>
> 4. 'Some retire because of *contradictory* language.'

James Legge, *The Life and Teachings of Confucius* 7th ed. (London: Kegan Paul French Truber & Co., 1895), 218.

17. *Paroxyste* was a term for violent, explosive lyricism associated with the Symbolists, especially the Belgian poet Émile Verhaeren (1855-1916).

49

EP to ACH   TLS 18 May 1916 2 ll. Dated by postmark and ms insertion. This letter contains Pound's request for ACH to prepare a selection of his work and includes two poems by EP, one unpublished.

5, Holland Place Chambers, Kensington W.

<May 18 *1916*>
Dear A.C.H.

The I-am-its lightens one corner of "May" number.[1] Cannell has a song, I dont know where he got it, it may be widely dispersed.

   I'm de guy wot made all the commotion,
   I'm de guy wot put the salt in the ocean,
      I'm de guy.

etc. through forty verses.

   Are *any of these* new people *any* use ??? I wonder how ill you are, and how much you are to do and not to do, and what is diversion and what is dam'd boredom.

   For the 950 th. time I am trying to decide how much of my first three or four books ought to be scrapped before another edition. I cant tell whether one should throw out 3/5ths, or only throw out the worst. And even then it is so beastly hard for me to tell what IS the worst (with a few exceptions). I have never been content with the Small Maynard selection (*Provença*), the sap seems to have gone.

   I wonder if you have the books with you, by any chance, or if H. would send you the *Poetry* copies, or if it would bore you to extinction, or divert you, to make out a list of what ought to go into a new edition, and what ought certainly to be left out, and what you have doubts of.

   If the thought tires you beyond measure, dont for gods sake think of it again. If on the contrary it is just enough mental activity to keep you <from> bored idleness ....

   It seems nearly impossible to get an opinion. People are so bloody polite at the wrong moment. My most trouble is with

Personae, Exultations and *Canzoni.* "Ripostes" hasn't <I think> much waste matter in it, I dont feel that it matters much whether I cut it or not, but the other books are only good enough to be taken one at a time. Bound into one they are too dull for bearing.

I have had a good deal of fun with "This Generation". It has at last got posted.[2] Lewis' novel "Tarr" is here in mss. and very good. I am going out to hunt for a cast for my "Noh" play, occidental not japanese noh.

The "Mercure" is too dull to [be] borne, these days. I have vague hopes of getting the first fat vol. of Fenollosa off my chest or at least out of the flat, *sometime.*

I have sent some stuff by Iris Barry, to H.M., it has been the one new contribution, new find, or whatever one is to call it.[3] I cant see that the new vols. of jeunes printed here have much in them, not the last crop.

I have written two brief verses. We give them with a wan smile. Impermanent petals.

IN LONDON
On hearing that the daughter
       had just written a novel;
And that the mother wrote essays
       and that the friend of the family was a reviewer;
And that the son worked in a publishing house,
       the young American traveller
Said:
    This is a darn'd clever bunch.

The DOUBLE PENTAGON,
THE THRICE UNAPPROACHABLE SPLENDOUR
At a feast of honour to Masefield
The following people sat for their photograph:
Mr Lawrence Houseman,
Mr Witter Bynner,
Mr Cale Young Rice,

Mr Edwin Markham,
Mr Louis Untermeyer,
Miss Amy Lowell,
Mrs Josephine D.D. Something-or-other,
                Mr Masefield
                Mr Noyes.[4]

The last has at least the virtue of simplicity. Monro is preserving the reproduction.
        <Vale et me ama>

                        <yours
                        E.P.>

----

1. ACH's "A New School of Poetry," *Poetry* VIII (May 1916): 103-105, a satiric description of the new "I-am-it school of poetry . . . not to be confused with *Les I'm-a-gists*, who are already out-classed and *démodé*" (103). The satire created a strong protest from the *Others* group led by Kreymborg and Bodenheim, with William Carlos Williams acting as mediator. Henderson, however, didn't wince. (Williams 192-4).

In the same number Max Michelson reviewed EP's *Catholic Anthology, 1914-1915* under the title of "The Independents," *Poetry* VIII (May 1916): 94-96.

2. See Letter 47, note 5.

3. See Letter 47, note 10.

4. Contrary to the wishes of EP, this satire was published with one change (l. 9) in the *Little Review* IV (January 1918): 56 and retitled "The Quintuple Effulgence or the Unapproachable Splendour." See *EP/LR* 148 and *G* C318b. The appearance of the poem in this letter confirms EP as the author.

5o

ACH to EP   TS [30 May 1916] 2 ll. Beinecke. The envelope, stamped "opened by censor," is addressed to "Ezra Pound, Esq. / 5 Holland Park Chambers / Kensington W. / London, England." On verso of envelope EP has sketched several Chinese ideograms.

Sun Mount
Santa Fe, New Mexico

Dear E.P.

It was lovely of you to think of sending me "violets," but really, I "want but little here below." Everything I want is on the other side! I am going to keep the check as a decoration and remembrance, but please cancel it in your book and send me instead your Breszka, which I shall be delighted to have. ("Family" ditto.)[1]

And please *do* send me the *Fenollosa Jap* book and the *Yeats letters* and your *Lustra* as soon as they come out. You can order them sent to me by Curtis and Davison where I have an account, and if it's not too far out of your way, please inscribe them.[2]

I shall be interested to see the Yeats letters.[3] When we were in N.Y. we went with the Colums to have dinner with Mr. Yeats Sr. The day before at John Quinn's, who was showing us, including Mr. Y., some of his latest modern art, Lady Gregory took me aside and explained apologetically that Mr. Yeats belonged to the Watts period, but did very well for that! And that night Mr. Yeats pointed out an old gentleman in a black skull cap at the other end of the table, of the Civil war period, who painted pictures of cattle in streams and still had a good enough market to keep him contented. "Nothing on earth," said Mr. Yeats, "would convince him that Monet and Whistler etc. were not monstrosities!" So runs the world away.

You mention Yeats' noh drama, mention it only, but that's all I've heard of it. Hope it was good. I'd like immensely to see your brief plays. Do send them if you have extra copies.

I was delighted to get your letters — both of them. I think *we* can be frank with one another without being disloyal! Please *don't resign* . . . . . . I am not supposed to use the type-writer at all, so I can only do a little at a time, but I'll write to you right away --- tomorrow if I can and tell you *everthing I know of the situation*. I am getting along so well that I don't want to take any chances. I am still in bed most of the time. I was given a little Corona typewriter before I left — just like a war correspondent — but I should have been given a dictaphone!

I'm awfully glad to have that little picture of you. It looks just like you to me![4]

Please don't bother about the Yeats and the anthology. I'll tell you about it next time.

. . . . You say to write a few good poems — ah, yes, *if I can*! I don't really know what I want to write or how I want to write. I know that the good poem is partly an accident, though the foundation isn't. What classics shall I read? I can't read Greek or Latin. What translations? . . . . Mañana I will write the rest . . . .

Many thanks again and best greetings!

Yours, A.C.H.

<May 30 1916.
No, I don't see the *Egoist* — and I'd like
to. If its a bore to send it, ask Curtis &
Davison to enter a 6 mons. sub.>

1. See Letter 47, dated 3 May 1916.

2. At the Harry Ransom Humanities Research Center there is an inscribed copy of *Lustra* (London: Mathews, 1916), no. 46 of 200 privately printed copies with an inscription by EP which reads "Alice Corbin Henderson, Santa Fe Sept. 23, 1916."

3. *Passages from the Letters of John Butler Yeats*, selected by Ezra Pound (Churchtown, Dundrum: The Cuala Press, 1917).

4. This is probably the photograph by Coburn used as the frontispiece for *Lustra* (1916).

5 1

EP to ACH   TLS [15 June 1916] 3 ll + 1 Enclosure. Dated by postmark.

5, Holland Place Chambers, Kensington W.

Dear A.C.H.

You are to get well, and not talk of "other sides" save in reference to "*this*" side of the Lantic Ocean.

The "Brzeska" has been posted you this. a.m. *Egoists* containing "Tarr" will follow in a few hours. The novel will have to be very much abbreviated to get it into the paper. I am not protesting, as I only got it into the *Egoist* for the sake of getting Lewis the £50 AT ONCE.[1] The sooner they get through with it the sooner we can get it out in book form.

Heaven knows when I shall get copies of the Noh Book. The proofs are all rushing about trying to find a publisher for the big edition of the Fenollosa papers. And the Yeats' senior hasn't started to be set up.

"Lustra" has got as far as the enclosed. I may have a spare set of proofs in a week or so. and will send them along.

I have not resigned. H.M. seems in a calmer state of mind and rather more cordial.

Great God, what classics are you to read, without greek or latin? I read greek like a hen, but it is just possible to get good latin translations from the greek. I have always intended really to go into the matter of english translations from both latin and greek and see if there were ANY fit to read. I dare say you have read as much french as I have. Villon, Gautier, Corbiere, Charles d'Orleans. I dont know that there's much new to be said. Anglo-saxon is harder than greek or latin. and then there is hardly more than the Seafarer and a few lines in Wanderer. There remains always "Cathay" a small leaflet of translations from the chinese, but that you by now have exhausted.

In English<,> Rochester and Dorset and possibly some of the other more scurrilous restoration poets might entertain you. They are little read. Rochester has not left a great deal but some of it is as good as Heine.

Drummond of Hawthorneden is fine in spots and so also is William Dunbar.

I still think Byron amusing, but Browning and Fitzgerald are about the only later english poets that one can keep on reading. Do however read Landor<'>s Imaginary Conversations in bulk if you haven't done so already. There are vast dull tracts but there are also priceless dialogues. The chinese one<s>, and the Petrarch-Boccacio-Chaucer, and the Aspasia, and some of the earlier one<s>, also the <N>apoleonic period, and scraps elsewhere. Dents' edition is not over expensive I believe.

In German there is only Heine, and some of the very early Minnesingers, Von der Vogelweide etc.

Spanish next to nothing since the Poema del Cid. except stray ballads.
Italian; Dante, Guido, Leopardi.

I am temporarily off mediaevalism. I dont know that it will do anyone the slightest good to read Chaucer and the very early english poets. I mean for practical practicing contemporary writers to do so.

Butler's "The Way of all Flesh" will amuse you if haven't yet read it. ages ago.

I think, about classics: I will send in as my next swot in *Poetry* some fragments from my l o n g poem. I dont know. I dont know whether it would do me any good to print scraps until it is finished. There is one gob of classic in it that you might like.[2]

I dont know, If you dont read latin I should think the next best thing was Flaubert's "Trois Contes". One might have a lot worse "poetic" training than that of committing all three to memory, or rather the first and third. St Julien gets a little distressing.
I suppose they contain all that anybody knows about writing.

------- INTERRUPTIONS ------------- *3 hrs. later.*
MacDonagh has done you a fine compliment in quoting you at
length in the introd. to his "Literature in Ireland" (I have just sent in
a review of it to H.M.). It is your remarks on patriotism in the
poetry of a subject country <that he quotes>.[3]

I have met W.H. Davies, and like him.[4] H.M. has rubbed him the
wrong way. I doubt if I can get any of his stuff for the magazine.
Interruptions have put me off the main line of this note and now I
must array myself and depart.

You musn't write long letters if it tires you

<yours

E.P.>

<I will try to write you a decent letter - not a mere list of names &
dates like this one — in the course of the next few days.>

▬▬▬▬▬ [Enclosure 1]:
Revised proof copy (1 leaf) of the advertising circular for *Lustra*
published by Elkin Mathews headed "LUSTRA of Ezra Pound with
Coburn Photogravure." The volume contains "all the Poems in his
newest manner, together with the 'translations' from the famous
Fenollosa Chinese MSS., the collection known as 'Cathay.'" The
leaflet reproduces Ford Madox Hueffer's review of *Cathay* from *The
Outlook* (19 June 1915). The circular adds that "the volume is, for
Mr. Pound, a very thick volume, containing many Poems on modern
and several on Provençal subjects." The circular also lists the
"POEMS OF EZRA POUND": Vol. I. "PERSONAE" and "EXULTA-
TIONS" ; Vol. II. "CANZONI" and "RIPOSTES." Under "First
Editions" it lists *PERSONAE, EXULTATIONS, CANZONI, RIPOSTES.*

▬▬▬▬▬

1. This explains the considerable difference between the serial and book
form of the novel as published in New York by Knopf in 1918. For a comparison
of the two versions and a bibliographic comment see Bradford Morrow and
Bernard Lafourcade, *A Bibliography of the Writings of Wyndham Lewis* (Santa
Barbara: Black Sparrow Press, 1978), 29-31.

2. The first three, or so-called "Ur-Cantos," would be sent to ACH in early
February 1917.

3. Thomas MacDonagh, *Literature in Ireland: Studies Irish and Anglo-Irish*
(Dublin: Talbot Press, 1916). EP's review, "Thomas MacDonagh as Critic,"
appeared in *Poetry* VIII (September 1916): 309-312. In the review EP refers to
ACH as "probably the best critic now writing in America" (309). MacDonagh
was executed for his role in the 1916 Easter Uprising. See Letter 63, especially
note 14.

On pp. 14-15 of his "Introduction," MacDonagh quotes from a passage dealing with patriotism and poetry in ACH's "Too Far From Paris," *Poetry* IV (April 1914): 105-106. MacDonagh comments that "this writer has stated almost sufficiently for me the case of Irish patriotism as an inspiration" (15).

4. William Henry Davies (1871-1940), Welsh poet and novelist who until the age of thirty chose the life of a peddler and then a vagabond in America resulting in his popular *Autobiography of a Super-Tramp* (1907). He settled in London and soon became part of a literary circle including Conrad, Gosse, and Pound; he eventually moved to the country, however.

EP reviewed his *Collected Poems* in *Poetry* XI (November 1917): 99-102.

52

■■■■■■ **EP to ACH**   TLS 22 June 1916 1 1 + 1 Enclosure.

5, Holland Place Chambers, Kensington W.

Dear A.C.H.

    I sent off the *Egoists* last week. There is a new postal regulation coming on and I dont know that I shall be allowed to send out printed matter after July 1.

    I have just done a note on DeBosschère for *Poetry* and will send it with one of his poems as soon as he sends me a typed copy.[1] I shall also send two longer poems of his to the *Little Review*.

    I have writ to Hinckley to get copies of 2 jap plays "Chorio" and "Genjo". I suppose he has 'em. Macmillan have ordered a big Noh book and I am in the throes.[2] I seem to have sent my only copies of those two plays to the U.S.A., that is to you (??? I think) for Hinck.

    Also that wretched Chinese Character essay has *not* arrived.

    Alas that we who are strong should wail to you the afflicted. !!!!!!!

    DuLac has done a magnificent caricature of E.P. MOST noble.

    I am presiding at some bloody dinner or other and must wash and get out of this.

    You should have rec'd the "Gaudier" by now. Wadsworth goes off to the Eastern Mediterranean tomorrow.[3] Naval job. That about cleans out the gang.

        <Yours

         E.P.>

            <22-6-'16>

[Enclosure I:]

Four-page Cuala Press notice of *Certain Noble Plays of Japan* "from the translations by Ernest Fenollosa and finished by Ezra Pound, with an introduction by W.B. Yeats" plus Cuala Press notice of *Letters from John Butler Yeats: Selected by Ezra Pound.* The editor is identified as "a young man who is a leader of one of the more violently modern schools in literature. . . ." A general notice on the Cuala Press, founded in 1902, outlines its aims and printing standards, and forms the last two pages of the circular which has as its cover the Cuala Press colophon.

1. This apparently did not occur, although in September 1916 EP published *12 Occupations by Jean de Bosschère* (London: Elkin Mathews, 1916). EP provided the English prose translations, although anonymously. The pamphlet is a selection from de Bosschère's *Les métiers divins* (1913).

2. *'Noh' or Accomplishment* (London: Macmillan, 1916), actually published 12 January 1917. "Chorio" by Nobumitsu and "Genjo" by Kongo both appear in the volume.

3. Edward Wadsworth (1889-1949), artist and friend of Wyndham Lewis, who contributed to *BLAST*, and was to be a part of EP's proposed College of Arts. His work was included in the Vorticist show sent to Quinn in New York which opened on 10 January 1917. In 1914 EP published "Edward Wadsworth, Vorticist. An authorised appreciation," *The Egoist* I (15 August 1914): 306-307.

53

5, Holland Place Chambers, Kensington W.

Dear A.C.H.

The "Chinese Writ. Char." has arrived. Thanks very much. I have sent H.M. some more poems, including a Voltaire series which, at least for the moment, pleases me. As she refuses to use the Cabaret, I hope she will be able to get these in and bring my Sept. batch up to fighting or *eating* strength.[1] I hope to be able to send your "Lustra" in a week or so.

The infant lispings in July are in spots interesting. The McKaye is however as dam'd with rhyme as its elders.[2] Heredity in guinea-pigs, I presume.

Dulac has done a noble and ferocious caricature of me sighting a bore. The vorticist show has arrived in New York. Marshall having ordered various books by Joyce, me, and others has subsided in domestic tragedy, but I dare say literature will recover.[3] The *Quarterly Review* has forgiven me for cooperating in BLAST.

I have done a distortion of one of LaForgue's "Moralities" for Dulac to illustrate. By the way, I think we should take a course in LaForgue, those of us who have not done so, BUT ONLY the very elect. I do not think we should mention him to anyone but ourselves. Publicity is too dam'd democratic.

DuLac on the more serious side has been about looking at Minoan sculpture. We may do a book on it if we can find anyone to pay for the reproductions.

I wonder what other news there is. I have done a little booklet of DeBosschère into English, and Mathews is bringing it out.[4]

Apropos of your note in July number. IS there any reason why we
should print verse by people who wont subscribe to the magazine.[5] It
might be a very salutary thing to refuse to read poems by anyone
who is not a subscriber OR who is not recommended by THREE
subscribers. (or an editor or foreign correspondent.). There are few
people who cant afford 1.50, and if they are too poor the chance is
very much against their poetry being any good IF they cant find
three people to pull wires.[6]

The recommendation by the "editor or correspondent"
should be kept secret.

And damn it all if the ASSpirant isn't sufficiently interested
[in] the art, the art as a whole, the art of others people besides his
stuffy self, to take in the magazine which has etc. etc. etc., then let
him go hang.

I think this is the answer. The impecunious could try a six
months subscription if they happen to belong to the tribe of Judah.
<This plan is a lot more humane than it sounds. =
"Owing to the tremendous influx of mss. the editors must refuse to
consider mss. save by subscribers etc.["] = The alternate plan of
stupid lazy readers. being rejected>
<Yours
E.P.>

<hr>

1. Appearing in "Poems Old and New," *Poetry* VIII (September 1916): 275-
282 is "Impressions of François-Marie Arouet (de Voltaire)." The poem was
reprinted in *To-Day* (London) I (July 1917): 185-186 and in the first and second
impressions of the American edition of *Lustra* (New York: Knopf, 1917).

"Cabaret" refers to EP's version of Rimbaud's "Au cabaret-vert" translated
by EP as "Cabaret Vert." The French text is in EP's "A Study of French Poets,"
Little Review IV (February 1918): 3-61. His translation was published with the
French version in his *Rimbaud* (Milan: All'Insegna del Pesce d'Oro, 1957).

2. A portion of *Poetry* VIII (July 1916) was devoted to "Poems by Children"
(191-194). Arvia MacKaye's "The Purple Gray" (191) is the object of EP's
remarks.

3. On the Vorticist show see Letter 47, note 11; on Marshall see Letter 47,
note 5.

4. See Letter 52, note 1.

5. In "The Rejection Slip," her editorial comment for July 1916 in *Poetry*
VIII: 197-199, ACH begins with a comic suggestion that if the subscription list of

Poetry equalled the receipt of manuscripts, the journal's circulation would flourish—hence, EP's remark that a subscription should be a prerequisite for publication. In her essay ACH then defends the formality of *Poetry*'s rejection slips, explaining that despite the tone of the letters, all manuscripts receive serious reading by the editors. She goes on to criticize the idiosyncracies of individual submissions and their form, while noting the dangers in relaxing one's standards. Nevertheless, with each morning's mail "hope renews itself that genius may be discovered beneath the flap of each envelope" (199). Editors, she adds, experience more disappointment when having to reject contributions than do poets.

   6. The one-year subscription rate for *Poetry* was $1.50.

54

ACH to EP   ALS [10 August 1916] 5 ll. Beinecke. (This letter answers EP's of 22 July 1916.)

Sun Mount
Santa Fe, New Mexico

Dear E.P. —

Your letter mailed July 22nd — came two days ago — I am always so glad to hear —

I was so *stupid* about the *Chinese* article: — but I want to make some suggestions.[1] You spoke of getting it published in the *Quarterly* or *Fortnightly* — when you have arranged this, try for American publication, simultaneously. I would try Ellery Sedgwick, the *Atlantic Monthly* — unless you have too much against it. Fenollosa did a lot for Boston — and they ought to take it on that ground if for nothing else: — and then, there is the *Open Court* magazine — Chicago — about which I forgot entirely — the great irony being that the magazine is better known elsewhere than in Chicago. Dr. Paul Carus — *The Open Court* — 378 Wabash Ave. Chicago. London agents are Kegan, Paul, Trench, Trübner Co. — Dr. Paul Carus has translated Lao-Tze's *Tao-teh-king* — and ought to be interested.[2]

I've enjoyed Brzeska very much indeed —[3]

I have scraps of a longer letter to you lying around — I'll gather them up and send them soon — a sort of Status Rerum — as I see it. Also I have gone over your poems again and again.

Thanks for reminding me of Laforgue — the biggest bookstore in Chicago confirmed a complete ignorance of Rochester. I don't know him, although I know the others.

Would it be worth while sending you one or two letters from this country for the *Egoist*? I have a notion that it might cure me. I've absorbed quite a bit — although I spend most of my time in bed. "The Rejection Slip" which served, you might say, as my rejection slip — I wrote before I left Chicago.[4] Never mind, I don't think anybody else will wear him or herself out looking for the poetic seed. There isn't anyone to publish, I think, who does not subscribe.

"August" is pretty sad, I think — I told H.M. so — of course Sturge Moore should have had first place[5] — although I don't see why one should want to re write the Bible. Amy is tiring — but at least one has to admit that she is better than the rest of the padding.

What did you think of Wallace Stevens' play?[6] — it reminds me of a Nō in a way, but without enough Nō *communication* I should say to act.

By the way — I can send you some good silhouettes of Masters, and Sandburg that would reproduce well in a zinc plate — if you want them for the *Egoist* — i.e. if you have connections with that paper now? —

How can anyone be as mindless as Aldington was in his poem about Brzeska?[7] ------ ----------------- ---------- and incidentally — is Louis Wilkinson's name worth trying? Would it arouse me even mildly?[8] ---

I wish I could see the Dulac caricature.[9] I think you said the Coburn portrait would be in *Lustra*.[10] I'll be delighted to have the book. — Have review copies sent to Frances Hackett, *The New Republic*; and Kate Buss, *The Transcript* — (she'll be out here after Aug. 23rd.[)] — it can be sent in my care. It might not be a bad idea to have a copy sent to *James Huneker* — care [of] Scribners is the only address I know. I think by the way that he has an article on LaForgue in "Ivory, Apes and Peacocks."—[11]

Was it Jas. Frederick Gregg who wrote the article on the Nō in *Vogue*?[12] *Vogue* and *Vanity Fair* are far more exclusive than any of the literary magazines! Isn't it funny? If it was Gregg — he's quite a wonderful publicity man! see that a copy of *Lustra* is sent to him.

What about Holt?[13] Should I see what I can do about having them handle American editions of your poems?

Enough of these mundane matters!

Yours —

A.C.H.

Aug. 10, 1916 —

1. "On the Chinese Written Character" sent to Alice Corbin Henderson in January 1915 (Letter 33); Pound's letter of 22 July 1916 acknowledges its return. See also Letter 39 (22 June 1915) and Letter 45 (? February 1916).

2. Paul Carus (1852-1919), German-American philosopher who settled in Chicago in the mid-1880s after losing his post in Dresden for his liberal political views, edited both the *Open Court* and the *Monist*. Carus translated Kant and in 1907 published *Chinese Thought*, in 1914 *Nietzsche and Other Exponents of Individualism*, and in 1916 *The Venus of Milo*.

3. Ezra Pound, *Gaudier-Brzeska, A Memoir* (London: John Lane, 1916). Official publication day was 14 April 1916.

4. Alice Corbin Henderson's "The Rejection Slip" is a two-and-a-half page essay on the difficulties of editors, like herself, in writing rejection letters; see *Poetry* VIII (1916): 197-199. See Letter 53, note 5.

5. The August 1916 issue of *Poetry* (VIII) featured T. Sturge Moore's long poem "Isaac and Rebekah" as the last item in the poetry section, 239-250. Other contributions included the opening poem, "1777" by Amy Lowell, "At Thirty He Sings of A Day in Spring" by Clinton Joseph Masseck, and "Branded" by Amy Sebree-Smith which begins with this couplet: "The spell of the desert is on me — it's got me fast and sure, / And I must leave the easy trail to follow the desert's lure" (232).

6. "Three Travellers Watch A Sunrise," *Poetry* VIII (1916): 163-179, winner of *Poetry*'s one-act play in verse contest. Announcement of the $100 award occurred in *Poetry* VIII (1916): 159-162.

7. Aldington's poem about Gaudier-Brzeska's death, "A Life," appeared in *The Egoist* 3 (May 1916): 69; rpt. in Norman T. Gates, *The Poetry of Richard Aldington* (University Park: Pennsylvania State University Press, 1974): 257-258. For Pound's response to the work, see the following letter.

8. Louis Wilkinson (1881-1966), a minor writer who after being sent down from Cambridge became a staff lecturer at Oxford, Cambridge, and London universities; co-founder of the University Lecturers Association in New York. Published two novels: *The Buffoon* (1916) and *A Chaste Man* (1917), and contributed to *The New Age* and the *Forum*. Married to Frances Gregg. See Letter 15, note 4.

9. See Letters 52 (22 June 1916) and 53 (22 July 1916) to ACH.

10. *Lustra*, published by Elkin Mathews in September 1916, also had a circular stamp by Edmund Dulac.

11. Kate Buss' positive review of *Lustra* appeared in the *Boston Evening Transcript* (6 December 1916): sec. 3:5.

James Huneker (1860-1921), "The Buffoon of the New Eternities: Jules La Forgue," *Ivory, Apes and Peacocks* (New York: Scribner's, 1915), 32-51. The dedicatee of the book is John Quinn. There are also essays on Schoenberg, Wedekind, Cezanne, and Italian Futurists. EP published "Irony, LaForgue and Some Satire" in *Poetry* II (November 1917): 93-98.

12. "Are You in the No?," *Vogue* 48 (July 1916): 69. Contains a photograph by Alvin Langdon Coburn of Michio Itow performing in Yeats' *At the Hawk's Well* holding a mask designed by Edmund Dulac. Itow played the mysterious bird, half hawk, half woman. See Letter 43, note 8 and Letter 47, note 8.

13. Henry Holt & Co. In 1914 ACH brought the manuscript of Sandburg's *Chicago Poems* to Alfred Harcourt at Holt who published it. Pound, however, never chose to place work with the firm, choosing, instead, E. P. Dutton, Small, Maynard & Co., John Lane (New York), Albert and Charles Boni, and Knopf as his American publishers between 1910 (*The Spirit of Romance*) and 1918 (*Pavannes and Divisions*).

55

5, Holland Place Chambers, Kensington W.

Dear A.C.H.

No. I've no connection with the *Egoist*.

Miss Weaver is ALL RIGHT. And their spotting up for Joyce and Lewis is most commendable. Its her spotting up, though she would probably deny it, and prefers to consider herself a committee, still I have a fair notion who pays.

Richard's verse on Gaudier is best left to natural oblivion. I can not hold myself personally responsible for his actions. Sending a letter to me would be a fairly sure way of NOT getting it printed in the *Egoist*. I have no monthly or weekly "organ" at present. I dont know that it much matters. The vorticist work is selling better than I could have hoped.[1] Joyce has got a grant from the government.[2] Lewis' affairs are almost presentable. I have no particular need of a magazine. Am very busy with books. Macmillan here have begun printing the big Jap play book.[3] The other stuff will get through being printed sometime, possibly.

I am now on the Chinese vol. of the Fenollosa material.

No, not the *Atlantic*, Sedgwick would see himself crucified before a line by me should appear in his parish gazette.

The "Seven Arts" writes in a friendly manner. Do you know anything of the editor "James Oppenheim"?[4] I dont imagine they are much OF my party, or very strongly pro-me, but they have apparently no strong determination against.

Spent yesterday doing a story with a nice thick nauseous indian atmosphere. I dare say no one will print it. Mostly cribbed from the Kamasutra. It may be litteratoor. Am uncertain.

I believe DuLac is going to cut loose from his illustration

contracts and burst out into something really his own, and that he will provide a few surprises.

I have not read the Stevens play.[5] Is it any good?

I am very busy with Wang Wei at the moment, should I divert my attention to Stevens?[6]

Oh yes re/ Wilkinson. The novel is trashy with clever spots.[7] Wilkinson never saw any vorticists, Lewis, Brzeska, or any of them. He has the Aldington family, and I think a man named Squire who writes on the *New Statesman*, si<gn>ing himself Solomon Eagle. I dont know who else save a sort of gilded and tinseled me. I think it is Richard[']s duty to punch his head. At least he would have challenge[d] him in any civilized country, ma che ...

The novel is mostly devoted to <J>ohn Cooper Powys. I'd send you a photogravure separate but one is not allowed to ship photos. so you'll have to wait for the book. Thanks for review. copy suggestions.

Surely the *New Republic* is no good. At least I certainly have no fr<ie>nds in that gallery.

I think the "vanity fair" or *Vogue* or wherever it was mush about Itow was done here by an amiable trashy idiot called Willard.[8]

Holt is no use.[9] Even the most patiently long suffering over- hyper-bloody-christian May Sinclair says Holt is dishonest. Besides I've met his daughter, THE most tumid excrescence that america has exported ... not excepting even Kate Douglas Wigwaum.

Quinn is trying to place my stuff in N.Y. Just at present Kreymborg's friend Marshall <has> engulphed himself in domestic tragedy (or else done a bunk) and no one seems able to find the mss. (unique mss.) of "This Generation." which Marshall promised to publish.[10]

Columbus was eminently misguided.

Petrie has just brought out a book on Egyptian sculpture, haven't read text, but choice of illustrations is amazingly fine. He must KNOW.[11]

If you find a publisher who wants a book on greek sculpture before it went to pot, or a "Wyndham Lewis" to match the Brzeska, speak up. I have a fine lot of photos for the pre-periclean book. Greece produced at least one sculpture but being on the verge of their cataclysm into democracy they took pains to forget even his name. The illustrations to the Petrie book are stupendous.

There is also a german book, badly selected but containing some fine heads of the time of Amen Hotep IV. presumably the first intelligent man. King Wan coming a century or so later on the other side of the globe.

<Yours ever

E. P.>

<26-8-'16>

1. *Gaudier-Brzeska* (London: John Lane, Bodley Head, 1916). The focus of Chapter XI is "Vorticism." The English edition of 450 copies appeared on 14 April 1916. See *G* A10 for publishing details.

2. In August 1916 Prime Minister Asquith granted Joyce a Civil List pension of £100. Those writing for him included Yeats, George Moore, and Pound. See *Letters of James Joyce* II, ed. Richard Ellmann (New York: Viking, 1966), 380-382.

3. *'Noh' or Accomplishment;* the 267-page volume was published on 12 January 1917.

4. *The Seven Arts* was a monthly devoted to new American talent published in New York from November 1916 to October 1917. James Oppenheim was editor and his two associate editors were Waldo Frank and Van Wyck Brooks. The advisory board included Louis Untermeyer and Robert Frost. The magazine was founded by the novelist and critic Floyd Dell who praised EP's *Provença* in the *Chicago Evening Post* and celebrated the controversial "Contemporania" poems EP published in *Poetry* II (April 1913): 1-12. The journal sought to promote art in America and its open letter to artists in its first issue (November 1916) is an important manifesto of art as an expression of national life. The pacificism of the magazine, however, caused it to lose its subsidy and it soon folded, having published only from November 1916 to October 1917. ACH wrote a welcoming commentary on the journal in *Poetry* IX (1917): 214-217. Also see EP to ACH, Letter 56 (30 August 1916) and Letter 63, note 8.

5. Wallace Stevens, "Three Travellers Watch a Sunrise," *Poetry* VIII (1916): 163-179. See Letter 54, note 6.

6. Pound refers to the Chinese poet, "an eighth century Jules Laforgue Chinois," he explained to Iris Barry (*SL* 93), he found in the Fenollosa notebooks which he was studying at this time, their having been transferred to him by Fenollosa's widow in late 1913. "Light rain is on the light dust" by Wang Wei, translated by Pound from notes by Fenollosa, forms the epigram to "Four Poems of Departure" in *Cathay* (London: Mathews, 1915), 28.

7. Louis Wilkinson, *The Buffoon* (1916).

8. Pound answers ACH's question in Letter 54 concerning the authorship of the *Vogue* article on Noh.

9. Henry Holt, American publisher. See Letter 54, note 13.

10. In a 19 August 1916 letter to Quinn, EP explains that he told Kreymborg "to go steal the mss. before the owners of Marshall's premises seize the whole stock and security for the rent" but that "This Generation" was "written on order and designed for a new revolutionary house like Marshall, and I think it will raise the hair on the aged heads of any older firm" (*EP/JQ* 83). Quinn soon discovered that Marshall had decamped for Canada with what was thought to be the only copy of the ms. See *G* E6b and my forthcoming edition of the unpublished prose of EP. Also see Letter 47, note 5.

11. Sir William Matthew Flinders Petrie (1853-1942), Egyptologist who provided the first accurate measurements of the Egyptian pyramids in 1883 and discovered the royal tombs at Abydos. His philosophy of excavation paralleled Agassiz's approach to biology cited by Pound in *ABC of Reading*. Petrie believed that "the true line lies as much in the careful noting and comparison of small details as in more wholesale and off-handed clearances."

Petrie published no general study of Egyptian sculpture in 1916, but EP may be referring to his visitors' guide, *Handbook of Egyptian Antiques, Collected by Flinders Petrie*, exhibited at University College, Gower Street (London, 1915), reprinted in 1916. EP celebrates the untitled work again in a 31 August 1916 letter to John Quinn (*EP/JQ* 84).

56

5, Holland Place Chambers, Kensington, W.

<Aug *30*>

Dear A.C.H.

Various letters to hand. clippings etc. I dont know anything about the "Seven Arts'" plans.[1] I dont imagine they are very fervid. Probably want to be safe, and noncommittal and "open-minded" in a limited sense. There is room for their sort of endeavour. They may exist for a while and perhaps send one a few cheques. That is about all I hope for.

It is a comfort to know that that old braying idiot Brown[e] and all his tribe are ousted from the *Dial*.[2] I have sent 'em a line to say so.

Thanks for the Gaudier reviews. Kilmer *is* a soft-pated wobblewotch.[3] I think England has done rather better.[4] Lewis' Paintings are selling well in N.Y. so the book has not been in vain.[5] At the present moment I feel that I have no one to look after but myself. Which is odd after four years of propaganda.

I don't think there is any news since my last. I mentioned the Flinders Petrie book on Egyptian Sculpture, I think.[6]

My next job is "Chinese Poetry" by E. Fenollosa and E. Pound ready in 1918 unless hindered by circumstance. I suppose it wont be ready in 1918.[7]

<Yours
E.P.>

1. On *The Seven Arts* see Letter 55, note 4.

2. Francis F. Browne, founding editor of *The Dial* from 1880 until 1916 when the Chicago-based magazine was purchased by Martyn Johnson. Under

Browne, *The Dial* had a midwestern but academic emphasis stressing political and social, not literary, subjects. In 1918 it moved to New York with Conrad Aiken, Randolph Bourne, and Van Wyck Brooks among its contributing editors.

In the twenties *The Dial* became the principal American outlet for Pound's *Cantos* with the appearance of Cantos IV, V, VI, VII, VIII, and XXII, plus part of XXVII. In addition, "Mauberley" appeared in the September 1920 issue and from September 1921 to February 1923 it contained his "Paris Letters" series. Pound's translation of Cavalcanti's "Donna mi prega" appeared in the July 1928 issue. Between 1925 and 1929 Marianne Moore co-edited the journal with Scofield Thayer.

3. Joyce Kilmer (1886-1918), the American poet best-remembered for his popular poem "Trees" which appeared in *Poetry* II (August 1913): 160, reviewed *Gaudier-Brzeska* in *The New York Times Magazine* of 25 June 1916 (section V: 13-14). Kilmer refers to Pound as a "fellow insurgent" of Brzeska's in an essay that is critical of Vorticism whose doctrine is called "mystifying and boyishly erudite." Nevertheless, Kilmer admires the altered aesthetic of Gaudier-Brzeska, the result of his war experiences which were charged with blood and smoke, not "Soho restaurants and Bayswater studios." Kilmer copiously quotes from letters Pound includes, while a picture of the Hieratic Head of Pound accompanies the article. Pound's complaint about Kilmer derives from the latter's misunderstanding of Vorticism and the value of *BLAST* as stated in Kilmer's *New York Times* article entitled "How the War Changed a Vorticist Sculptor."

4. *Gaudier-Brzeska* was reviewed in the *Times Literary Supplement* No. 745 (27 April 1916): 199, where reaction to the book and Vorticism was more sympathetic, although still critical, than in America.

5. The January 1917 exhibit of the work of Wyndham Lewis and other Vorticists was underwritten by John Quinn. A passage in *Gaudier-Brzeska* celebrates the art of Lewis with Pound claiming that Lewis' abstractions and their composition are "so successful that *I feel right in seeing them the start of a new evolution in painting*" (32). Lewis is cited throughout *Gaudier-Brzeska*.

6. See Letter 55, note 11.

7. Pound did not publish Fenollosa's essay, which he edited and to which he added notes, until September 1919 when the first of four parts appeared in the *Little Review* VI (September 1919): 62-64. The final installment appeared in the December 1919 issue of the periodical (VI: 68-72). *Instigations* (New York: Boni and Liveright, 1920) is the first appearance of the essay in book form. In *ABC of Reading*, Pound declared that "the first definite assertion of the applicability of scientific method to literary criticism is found in Ernest Fenollosa's *Essay on the Chinese Written Character*" (*ABC* 18). See also Letter 33, note 2.

57

EP to ACH   TLS 14 October 1916 2 ll. Dated by postmark.

5, Holland Place Chambers, Kensington W.

Dear A.C.H.

We are still indulging in Armageddon. That consummate cad and liar W. Wilson is "uncertain" what the conflict is about, but even without his archangelical sanctimonious permission the war continues.[1] AND such delicacies as fine-woven or whatever it is paper for sketches etc., artists materials generally, which come mostly from france etc. etc. holland etc. are not easy to find.

Try Japan. Everybody who might know about such matters is in the army, at least about everyone I know is. At any rate I'm afraid I cant help you.

Ah well, let us turn to pleasanter matters. By the time this reaches you America will have confirmed her shame and reelected Woodie Wilsie, and all questions of national existence will be at an end.

I'm sorry I can be of no use about the paper, Let us return to your earlier letter.

You are quite right in saying that W.B.Y. in his *Wind Among the Reeds*, gets a sort of unity which my books have never had.[2]

He also produces the effect of having only one note or one key or one colour.

I know that I loose [*sic*] a certain amount, but then ....

Then there's so much unacknowledged cribbing. And a personal cult is usually rot. Look at the Tagore muck. And if what rotten personality I've got cant stand the strain of admitting that Q. Septimius translated some greek epigrams four centuries ago, the said personality had better "git out or git under."

If I am merely a collection of antiquities there is no use in pretending the contrary. Nihil humanum nisi nom meum gets more and more difficult as time goes on, or perhaps it doesn't. .

There is undoubtedly a present loss. A fake would get more immediate notariety, but I cant see that its worth it.
I have again spoken to Mathews about sending books to K. Buss.

It bores me. America has disappeared. What does it matter whether one's books are sent there, or read there or reviewed there. <It is Braithwaites country not mine. Why shouldn't he have it. if it likes him.>

Get well and come back here when the war is over.

I'll write to the Cuala people, to have them send you J.B.Y's letters.

<Yours ever
E Pound>

---

1. Woodrow Wilson (1856-1924), 28th President of the U.S. (1913-1921), would be re-elected in November 1916 by a narrow margin on an isolationist or neutral platform. The deteriorating situation in Europe, however, forced him to enter the war on 17 April 1917.

2. W. B. Yeats, *The Wind among the Reeds* (London: Elkin Mathews, 1899). For EP's early praise of this book and its importance to him, see EP to his father quoted in Longenbach 13; for Yeats' difficulties with the publication and design (especially the cover) of the book, see Nelson 75-86.

58

EP to ACH   ALS 20 December 1916 2 ll. On envelope in ACH's hand: "Ans. Jan 16 '17."

5, Holland Place Chambers, Kensington W.

Dear A.C.H.

Thanks for the clipping & your defense in the *Transcript*. I am glad to see you so full of fight & hope it presages a full return of health.[1]

re/ dear Amy. it would be more correct to say that E.P. declined to continue the association. however these are matters of no importance whatever & suavity is perhaps better,
Mr. P. having invented the terms imagiste & imagisme, to define a particular thing, & having nothing in common with Mr. [D. H.] Lawrence, & next to nothing if not nothing itself in common with Mr. [John Gould] Fletcher. & having no sympathy with the aims of Miss Lowell, graciously declined to continue in the august association which extended the terms "imagist" & "imagism" to the works of D.H.L., J.G.F. & to endless immitations of Paul Fort. — or perhaps that is unjust & too vigorous.

Let us say E.P. declined to sell out without receiving definite compensation.[2]

However this is of no importance.

I wonder will I get up steam enough *to* write to the *Transcript*.

One might note that Eliot is the only advance since the first imagist stuff.

It is assenine to call Sandburg a failure at this stage of the game simply because a lot of his work is rough.

However, as I have said before "A coon! a *Boston* coon" what *can* one expect.

There is very little to write. Best luck for your Xmas. *Poetry* has just sent me $3.75.

get well & come over

Yours

Ezra Pound

20/12/'16

1. W. S. Braithwaite attacked EP and *Poetry* in "Another Year of Our Poetry — Promising a New Emerson-Longfellow Group," *Boston Evening Transcript* Pt. III (28 October 1916): 4. Braithwaite labeled *Poetry* "the instrument of Ezra Pound's radicalism" and called EP "the idol and master" of "the social-revolutionists, the Imagists, and the Radicals of the 'Others, a Magazine of the New Verse' group" (4). Favoring Kreymborg, Lowell, Masters, Frost, and Oppenheim, Braithwaite denigrated Sandburg and, of course, EP whose "collected poems" have "so little interested the American public that they find it difficult to discover an American publisher, and the magazine 'Others' largely supported by his disciples, has ceased publication" (4).

ACH presumably responded to Braithwaite's exaggerations in the *Transcript*, although research has not identified her contribution. Harriet Monroe, however, provided a strong attack on Braithwaite's views in "Sir Oracle," *Poetry* IX (January 1917): 211-214, pointing out in a final paragraph that despite his criticism of *Poetry*, Braithwaite was proceeding to reprint eight poems copyrighted by *Poetry* in his forthcoming anthology without even securing the permission of its editor.

2. EP is summarizing his break with Amy Lowell over her anthology, *Some Imagist Poets (with a Preface on Imagism)*, published in 1915 and followed by Volume II and III in 1916 and 1917. Pound neatly surveys his view of their disagreement in this letter. For another account, see Jean Gould, *Amy Lowell, The World of Amy Lowell and the Imagist Movement* (New York: Dodd Mead & Co., 1975).

D. H. Lawrence and John Gould Fletcher both appeared in Lowell's anthology (Fletcher had been left out of EP's *Des Imagistes* volume).

Paul Fort (1872-1960), French experimental poet who favored printing his work as prose to emphasize its rhythm, cadence, and assonance.

59

ACH to EP   ALS [4 January 1917] 3 ll. Beinecke. This letter appears to be written in answer to EP's 20 December 1916 letter to ACH.

Sun Mount
Santa Fe, New Mexico

Dear E.P. —

Not another day in this year shall go by without my writing to you. The trouble is that my writing is so bad that I hate to impose it on you — And I didn't think I had even thanked you for *Lustra*. I wasn't able to write, when it came — Of course I've so enjoyed it — I didn't know whether I wrote you of liking your *Cabaret* — when it came in to *Poetry*?[1]

Everything seems so far away now — and out here I am in reality much further away from *America* than you are — of course I see the papers & magazines. But I don't read the papers — can't stand'em: and very little of the magazines! My own fear is that I shall get "soft" — and that, after your word of praise, would never do! Send me a strenuous word from the depth of China —

I can still react, however — to some extent: — against the weakness of the last no. of *Poetry*. It is pathetic. H. M. can't help it. She does the best she can. She needs to have her hands held up. like Joshua — Eunice Tietjens is a loving creature — raptures & impulses and no discretion.[2] Since I came out here I've realized how you must have felt, many a time, in London. That is, realized it more keenly — of course I realized it before —But I wonder if it matters? — After all the crusading, the poetic renaissance seems to be degenerating into "mush" — more on account of the open-mouthed critics I should say, than on account of the poets, although they forget "the fascination of voices difficult."

Kate Buss has sent me her review of *Lustra*.[3] Says she has reviewed the *Noh* Plays, & *The Transcript* has asked to have it made longer! —

I'm sending you some more [poems]. Please be merciless. Some of it may amuse you — which verses, if any, in *The Spinning Woman*, would you reprint in a new book? — a very slim one. Do you still want my choice of poems in your early books?[4] If so, I'll send it. That is, if I didn't send it. I don't remember —

I am *much* interested in the Indian dances — have seen two. Not at all what one might expect — The Eagle dance as fine as Pavlova[5] — Their sense of costume — works, etc. in manner of these pueblo Indians were as even Paris, as they are Chicago or New York — They would not lack interpretation. A *theatric* interpretation, I mean. There has never been a shred of it that I can find! — I hope to see the *Buffalo Dance* on the 23rd. — (My remissions are rare, however.) When you get through with China, come out here and do the Indian. Not the "big injun" of commerce but the ones that *you* would find. W.P. H. is making some fine things of the dances. Do write now and then. We all send our best wishes to you & Mrs. Pound for a *fine* New Year —

Yours —

A.C.H.

Jan. 4, 1917.

---

1. See Letter 53, note 1.

2. *Poetry* IX (January 1917) contained a series of unsuccessful poems by relatively minor figures: Wilfrid Wilson Gibson, Clement Wood, Travis Hoke, Gordon Bottomley, Anna Wickham, Anna Spencer Twitchell, and Ridgely Torrence. Eunice Tietjens contributed a self-congratulatory and self-serving essay entitled "Appreciation" (198-199). ACH, however, had a useful critique of *The Seven Arts* (214-217).

3. See Letter 47, note 14.

4. See Letter 49.

5. EP cited "gilded Pavlova" in stanza two of "The Garret," in his controversial "Contemporania" series, *Poetry* II (April 1913): 1-12, rpt. in *Catholic Anthology*, 86.

60

EP to ACH   ALS 23 January 1917 11 + Enclosures. The first of two letters by EP written on this date. Enclosed are eleven unpublished satiric poems completed in April 1916 by ACH and praised by EP.

5, Holland Place Chambers, Kensington W.

Dear A.C.H.
    Yours just rec'd.
This lot must go into "Poetry" *at once*.[1]
        Will send comment on *others* soon.
      =
Note two pencil scribbles on text of these.
           yours
           Ezra Pound
      23-1-17

[Enclosures:]

a. I.

This is the most popular poetess in the United States,
And in every one of her four hundred and fifty lyrics
She is either dead or dying,
Or wailing about love.
Some people call her Sappho,
But Sappho, as I remember it,
Took the Leucadian leap once and for all.
~~She didn't waste words about dying~~
~~And leaving her lovers,~~
~~Her poems were about life,~~   [EP cancelled these lines.]
....
~~And even on the night when~~

~~her lover failed her,~~
~~She made a garland of it.~~
Her poems were of
Weddings and festivals.

II.

This, ladies and gentlemen, is a debonair poet,
But his gaiety covers sorrow.
He has a fictitious lady-love,
Who is no longer living,
Like Dante's Beatrice,
(He calls her by the name of
Ben Jonson's mistress),
(She is very much less in the way
Than if she were a real mistress),
And to her he indites pleasing sentiments
That may be read between the tango and the tea,
— He dances divinely,
And all the young girls whisper about him,
And say, 'Poor dear!'
But the matrons give him no time
To flirt with the rose-buds.

III.

You have a certain respect for good honest wh ---
Which you cannot extend to one
Carrying corruption into the bosom of the family
Like Alfred Noyes . . .
I did not start out to talk of him,
But of Ella Wheeler Wilcox,
And yet I do not mean
That the name above is for her;
She is rather a lowly but faithful concubine of Apollo,
As was Hagar to Abraham -----
I will not carry this farther,
For I see that I have said
All I intended.

IV.

This lady is a poetic Tammany,
She is the boss, the delegates, and the whole works,
And when she is not too busy
Writing advertisements
And campaign documents
And publicity dodgers,
She writes something
That looks like poetry,
But tastes — different.

V.

Here you will find a man
Afraid to talk too much,
And so he says a great many words
That give you a hunch
That there is something behind them,
And if you never find out what it is
You are comforted nevertheless
By the thought
That perhaps he knows!

VI.

She has no fear of the sanctuaries
Of our Lord Apollo.
She does not linger in the portal.
If the god's eyes are closed,
She will prop them open with sticks
And dance before him.
And he is so much astounded
That he forgets to wither her
As he did poor Marsyas,
Or lay rods across her back . . . .
Besides, she is a woman
And commands the society columns
Where the Amateur is a Genius.
- - - -After she had left off dancing
Before the shrine,

I purified the place,
And when I had taken the sticks
Out of the god's eyes
He winked at me!
And I lay down at his feet
And laughed!

VII.

This boy with pale blue eyes
Wears a pale blue tie
When he goes to read his poems
On the Lake Shore Drive.
I envy him, because he is not yet blasé.
With a thin, slim smile
Strained through a sieve
He will try to convince you
That his present intense enjoyment
Is the depth of boredom.

VIII.

This nice young girl
From a little town in Indiana
Is an anarchist —
A believer in free love
(Her adventures are spiritual),
A rebel against family
And authority.
She has entered the lists
Of vers libre
Because she finds in it an outlet
For <her> emotional sentimentality.

IX.

It is very like Boston
To accept as poetic arbiter
In the cradle of liberty,
And <here> in a country where all men
Are created *free and equal*,
One so obviously handicapped
By nature.

But tell me this, O ye guardians
Of the stern moral fibre,
Have the arts no rights?

[marginal comment by EP for last line reads "cadence not quite right"]

X.

You know if you brush against a tiger lily,
Some of the pollen may come off on your clothes.
Just so all these countless little ones
Have caught the flair of the "new movement,"
And have deserted hexameters, triolets, rondeaux, sonnets
Long before they had learned to crawl in them.
Of what use is a rebel
Who has nothing to rebel against?

XI.

This poor gentleman has been sadly abused:
At some time or other
He lost his gentle mistress,
His sweet ladye,
And while his wits were wandering
Somebody substituted a lean witch
Called Civic Drama.
It is truly distressing
To see the poor creature
Lavishing caresses
Upon a broomstick!

N.B. It is impossible
[To] induce eugenic matrimony
Between art and the people.   <April 1916>

---

1. Eleven short satires on typical American poets by ACH favored by EP; on 21 August 1917 EP queried Harriet Monroe: "Are you printing Alice's poems on American poets? They are the only entertaining native products I have seen for some time" (*SL* 116). However, they did not appear in *Poetry* and are printed here for the first time from the typescript accompanying Letter 60. See Letter 63, note 2, where ACH in her 16 April 1917 letter to HM mentions her "Wax Works."

61

EP to ACH   TLS 23 January 1917 4 ll + 21 Enclosures: Poems by Alice Corbin Henderson edited by Pound. This section documents EP's critical sense and aesthetic goals of clarity and precision. His comments are direct, from "use 'em in the book" to "not up to the rest" and "too long, too many prose phrases." Cadence and sound are also important principles for him. Following a list of the 21 poems, three are reprinted.

5 Holland Place Chambers

Dear Alice

I sent you the poems on Amurkhn Potes AT ONCE, you'll probably get both this and them by the same mail.[1] I had only two minute suggestions about that lot. Harriet must insert em at once.

I should put em in by themselves, not add any extraneous poems to them.

When does the book come out?

I have chalked up this lot considerable, and perhaps too hastily. Perhaps "Song" and the one to Pluto are the best. The houses ["Old Houses"] has good matter and I like some of the Indian things. The Inscriptions entertain me. I should advise you to have the miraculous restraint of keeping them for the actual book.

Do you know whether Harriet is still grumped with me, or if there is any use [in] my trying sweet reasonableness at long range.

Of course I dont know Eunice [Tietjens], but the type you describe is FAMILIAR (OH HELL YES) to me.

Of course I cant write to her. H.M. would never stand two sets of subterranean subpontine influence from me to Chicago.

Besides I suspect I have long left Eunice cold.

Still if you can direct me HOW to stir warm and affectionate pulses in the Eunician boozum, IN SUCH A MANNER as to support Harriet's Joshuan (? wasn't it Mosesian?) arms, during this contest !!!! I e'en would attempt it.

What is there to say? I sent you the three cantos only a week or ten days ago.[2] They are my virtuous deeds. I am paying the rent with the translation of a libretto.[3] Strange are the uses.

Eliot has chucked schoolteaching and steps forth with only his writing to protect him. (result: lumbago or something of that sort.)

Padre José (whom I mention in the preface to *The Spirit of Romance*[)], has turned up here in London. The last man I ever expected to see out of Spain. I am very glad to see him again. A meeting by sheerest accident.[4]

Lewis under pressure has finished or cleaned up another fine lot of drawings. [They] Are left here, and an intelligent man has bought twenty which will go to the nation if Lewis is used up in the war.[5]

I have had no word about the exhibit in New York save the notice in *Vogue*, and that merely said the show was about to open.[6]

The sheets of Joyce's novel have arrived here, and I believe it is out in New York.[7]

I paid my debts at the beginning of the year and since finishing my three cantos, I have done nothing but sit about feeling that it is time to do something.

Did Braithwaite mean to imply that "Poetry's" influence had waned in proportion as my influence in "Poetry" has waned? Oh awful dilemma for the black man of Beacon St. !!!!!

Does Harriet want me to write a vindication of *Poetry*? (on these lines) Or am I to be cast adrift in compliance with popular clamour?[8]

Rodker has done a few more entertaining poems. Rather to my surprise. I wonder if he will beat Aldington after all. Is it better to be silly than stupid? Upon which temperament does Apollo smile with more vigour.

Make them get you Jules LaForgue's poems. I believe they are out of print for the present, but there may be a stray copy of them in America. I cant get them here.

More anon.

Yes, of course I still want your selection from my early books, if it isn't too much trouble to you. You haven't sent it.

　　　　　　　yours ever

　　　　　　　　　　<Ezra>

　　　<23-1-17.
　　　Ezra Pound>

▓▓▓▓▓▓▓▓   [Enclosures:] 21 Poems by ACH. [Asterisks denote poems which were included in ACH's *Red Earth: Poems of New Mexico* (Chicago: Ralph Fletcher Seymour, 1920).]

Indian Songs
　　　*Listening
　　　*Buffalo Dance
　　　*Where the Fight Was
　　　*The Wind
　　　*Courtship
　　　*Fear
　　　*Parting
Wax-Works from a Dime-Museum
Inscriptions for a Forth-coming Volume of Poetry
　　　To My Publisher
　　　To My Reviewer
　　　To My Salesman on the Road
　　　To My Bookseller
　　　To My Reader
Why Be A Poet?
Old Houses
Song
*[Pluto]
*Here in the desert
*Four O'Clock
*Once every twenty four hours
*The hill cedars

　　　　All ms. insertions in the following three poems by ACH are in EP's hand.

Song

I know you beautiful and fair   <keep this
Beyond delight,   good
I know our bodies bare   despite
In love unite,   _in_versions>
Yet weep for passion's flight.

I weep because the rose
Must fade away,
I weep because of words
That lead astray,
I weep that passion never tells
What it longs to say.

Though your breast lies on my breast,
Still in vain the lover's quest;
Like the dryads in the woods
Powerless to tell their moods —
In a world of forest spells
Never half the lover tells.

[Pluto]

I have seen you, O king of the dead,
More beautiful than sunlight.

Your kiss is like quicksilver;   <OK
But I turned my face aside   good.>
Lest you should touch my lips.

In the field with the flowers
You stood darkly.

My knees trembled, and I knew
That no other joy would be like this.

But the warm field, and the sunlight,
And the few years of my girlhood
Came before me, and I cried
Not yet!
Not yet, O dark lover!

You were patient.
— I know you will come again.

I have seen you, O king of the dead,
More beautiful than sunlight.

Four O'Clock

Four o'clock in the afternoon.
A stream of money is flowing down Fifth Avenue.

They speak of the fascination of New York
Climbing aboard motor-busses to look down on
             the endless play
From the Bay to the Bronx.
But it is forever the same <& lifeless>

Watching a cloud *on* the desert,   <? over>
Endlessly watching small insects crawling in and out
             of the shadow of a cactus,[9]
A herd-boy on the horizon driving goats,
Uninterrupted sky and blown sand,

[EP drew a   Space — volume — silence —
box around   Nothing but life on the desert,   <not quite
these 3 lines.] Intense life.   right yet>
                                                              <?>

Once every twenty-four hours
Earth has a moment of indecision:
Shall I go on?
Shall I keep turning?
Is it worth while?
Everything holds its breath.
The trees huddle anxiously
On the edge of the arroya,   <something
And then with a tremenduous heave,   in
Earth shoves the hours on towards dawn.   it>

<can you make it more compact =
I think Eliot in *Blast* did almost the same thing as part of this with
more grip & tenseness>[10]

1. See Letter 60.

2. The so-called "Ur-Cantos." See Letter 63.

3. EP translated the libretto of Massenet's *Cendrillon* for Sir Thomas Beecham's Opera Company. This brought him stalls for the Aldwych opera season but, despite being paid nearly 40 guineas for the work, the opera was not performed (Carpenter 308; *SL* 104).

4. Padre José is Padre José Maria de Elizondo who aided EP in obtaining a photostat of the Cavalcanti manuscript in the Escorial, Madrid. See "Praefatio," *SR* 7; *Guide to Kulchur* 158; Canto 77/480.

5. Captain Guy Baker (1874?-1918), a wealthy professional soldier and friend of Wyndham Lewis who left Lewis' drawings to the Victoria and Albert when he died in the influenza epidemic of 1918. Guy Butcher in *Tarr* is modeled on Guy Baker.

6. The long-delayed Vorticist show opened in New York in January 1917 (Reid 292-293).

7. *A Portrait of the Artist as a Young Man* was published by B. W. Huebsch in New York on 29 December 1916.

8. See Letter 58 and note 1.

9. Compare with lines from Canto 80/527, "if calm be after tempest / that the ants seem to wobble / as the morning sun catches their shadows," and Canto 81/535, "The ant's a centaur in his dragon world." ACH curiously anticipates EP's absorption with the minutiae of nature in *The Pisan Cantos*.

10. EP is most likely recalling Eliot's "Preludes I-IV" and "Rhapsody of a Windy Night," *BLAST* 2 (July 1915): 48-51.

62

EP to ACH   TLS 9 February 1917 4 ll.

5, Holland Place Chambers, Kensington W.

Dear Alice

You will by now have the long poem, for *nutriment*.[1]

Nothing will replace "Poetry's" fat subsidy. H.M. must have credit for that always and anyhow. If *Poetry* peters out it will deplete one's income. BOMBBBBB.[2]

I have however fair hope of getting a start for prose. A regular stand where I, Joyce, Eliot, and Lewis if he comes back, can appear regularly and without delay, and be paid a workable rate. I hope you will join in if it comes off. The subsidy would be for the four males named above, but there may be a little over, and I should hope to be able to send you a spare guinea now and again. I've done a fair number of "1000" [words] at no better rate.

Poor Fletcher has married a loidy wit gold teeth, so I hear. He has something to him, but he writes too bloody much.[3] However he would gladly be crucified and dear Amy would NOT, no, not under any circumstances.

As to the Dudley family, I saw a mulatto-like female with a hippo-potamus jaw at the Aldington's years ago, I dont know which one she was. I was given to understand that she regarded my work as a mistake, and that she did not wish my acquaintance. Also she flocked with the Meynells. I think her name was Helen, like bride of Menelaus, but perhaps it was not, perhaps it was that of the Saints of Siena and Byzantium. Still I *think* it was Helen.[4]

I am glad Tagore hasn't gone to pot personally. His work has and Yeats says he will no longer stand criticism, and that he has

taken to composing in English, which will destroy all the advantage
he had in using familiar idiom, and also led him to express only
thought that will fit into such English as he knows. The descent
from Yeats to Evelyn Underhill, was *facilis* like the more famous
descensus.[5] Poor Rabby!

I dont know that much is going on. Lewis has finished about sixty
more drawings, and been posted to a battery, twenty have been
bought to go to the nation if the owner is (also a soldier) is killed.
The vortograph show opened this week, jaw by Coburn, me , G.B.S.
(in the order named) last evening, audience mostly photographers,
about a third of them ready to "admit" abstract art. Fletcher's friend
Arbuthnot, made a few intelligent remarks also.[6]

Joyce's novel is actually a bound fact. America stung by the negroid
lash of Mr. Braithwaite seems about to rise and publish my works,
and also to make a bid for her national honour.[7]

Among second rate novels, Dorothy Richardson has done one called
"Backwater", Violet Hunt "Their Lives", and Mrs Turner (Borden's
condensed milk, I think) signing herself "Brigit Maclagen", has done
"The Romantic Woman" and got back *some* on Chicago.[8] All these
are worth reading for entertainment. Nothing much to do with
literature, but better than the average.
     De Bosschère has got a job, Heineman paying him well for a
series of drawings, Lane had also taken a few and paid damn badly.[9]

The big Fenollosa "Noh" book is out. The *Times* has given it two
columns.[10] It will appear in N.Y., try and get a free review copy.

Cannell wrote from N.Y. long ago re/ Fletcher "I think he is tiring
of the Flesh-Pot". That gang in N.Y. dont seem to have liked her. I
do, of course, and wouldn't have lost her for worlds were it not for
my interest in poetry, and in a more or less responsible position.
Were I [a] painter I would cling to her, fold my wings close and sing
to her, her and her dinners.[11]

     Yea even had she no dinners to offer for she is, as you said in
your first letter about her, a charmer, and she has an excellent heart

when her passhuns do not obscure things, and her *gran disio dell'*
excellenza or *dell' rumore* does not lead her to folly.

Be sure you print the series about Amurkn potes.[12]

　　　　yours ever
　　　　　　　　<Ezra Pound>
　　<9-2-'17>

1. "Three Cantos," mailed to ACH in early February 1917.

2. EP's relationship with *Poetry* began to falter in the fall of 1916 when,
without permission or consultation, HM suppressed a word from EP's
"Phyllidula and the Spoils of Gouvernet" and a line from TSE's "Mr. Apollinax."
The resulting quarrel between EP and HM over her authority and ability to
manage the magazine confirmed a long-standing disagreement, marked by her
earlier rejection of EP's "To a Friend Writing on Cabaret Dancers" in December
1915. ACH encouraged HM to believe that EP's disaffection was temporary
(Williams 197). However, EP had no direct contact with the Chicago office
between January and April 1917. "Three Cantos" were mailed to ACH in Santa
Fe, and were then forwarded by ACH to HM at *Poetry*. See Letter 63, note 2.

At the end of 1916 HM also altered the editorial emphasis of the journal
stressing young and unknown writers rather than established and recognized
poets. Hence, the relative absence of Yeats from the journal, combined with
TSE's refusal to publish in it because of HM's editorial censorship, and EP's
reluctance to participate (despite the appearance of "Three Cantos"—although
without the support or enthusiasm of HM), signalled an important turn away
from recognized voices. "And don't my services as foreign correspondent rate
something higher than $7.68?" EP asked in a letter to HM of 18 April 1917
(Williams 204). However, his opening statement in the *Little Review* for May
1917 reiterates his continued association as "Foreign Correspondent" for *Poetry*,
perhaps in part a positive reaction to the news that his "Three Cantos" would
appear over the summer of 1917 in the magazine (Williams 205-206; cf. *SL* 110,
a conciliatory letter of sorts to HM).

3. On 5 July 1916 John Gould Fletcher married Florence Emily (Daisy)
Arbuthnot, with whom he had been having an affair since the fall of 1913. A
conventional middle-class woman whose hobby was raising canaries (she kept
some fifty in a basement), she quickly found Fletcher unsuitable; they eventually
divorced in 1936.

4. Possibly Helen Dudley (1858-1932), American settlement worker and
pacifist, who attended MIT and then Bryn Mawr and eventually took over
Denison House in Boston. She participated in the trade union movement,
becoming one of the founders of the National Women's Trade Union League in
1903, and later joined the Women's International League for Peace and

Freedom. She made various trips to Europe and likely visited H. D., an acquaintance from Bryn Mawr, where EP met her.

5. Evelyn Underhill (1875-1941), English poet, novelist, and mystic whose *Mysticism* (1911) and collection of poems *Immanence* (1911) were popular successes. Among her recreations, according to *Twentieth Century Authors*, were "gardening, walking, and talking to cats" (1431).

6. The Vortograph show of 13 paintings and 18 Vortographs by Alvin Langdon Coburn opened at the Camera Club, London, on 8 February 1917. EP wrote an anonymous preface to the catalogue, reprinted in a modified form as "Vortographs," *Pavannes and Divisions* (New York: Knopf, 1918), 251-255. George Bernard Shaw made the opening remarks, while Malcolm Arbuthnot (1874-1967), another photographer and signatory of the Vorticist Manifesto, also spoke (see *EP/JQ* 119).

7. *A Portrait of the Artist as a Young Man*, printed by Harriet Shaw Weaver's Egoist Press, appeared officially on 12 February 1917.

Quinn had made arrangements with Knopf to publish EP's work following the collapse of Marshall. *Lustra* appeared in October 1917; *'Noh' or Accomplishment* in June 1917; *Pavannes and Divisions* in June 1918, all published in New York.

8. Dorothy Richardson (1872-1957), *Backwater, A Sequel to Pointed Roofs* (1916; New York: Knopf, 1917).

Violet Hunt (1866-1942), *Their Lives* (1916), with a second printing that year and a third in 1917.

Brigit Maclagen, pseud. of Mary Borden (1886-1968), who later married Sir Edward Spears who brought Charles de Gaulle out of France in 1940. She organized and directed field hospitals for the French in WWI and WWII. *The Romantic Woman* was published by Constable in 1916.

9. Jean de Bosschère (1878-1953), Belgian painter, illustrator, poet, and novelist who frequently visited and published in Paris. In 1915 he fled Belgium for London where he remained for several years. In 1916 EP translated a collection of de Bosschère's poems entitled *12 Occupations* (London: Mathews, 1916). Two of de Bosschère's poems in *The Closed Door* (London: John Lane, 1917) were translations by EP who in a 30 June 1916 letter to Margaret Anderson referred to de Bosschère as "undoubtedly about the most 'modern' writer Paris can boast, not excluding Apollonaire" (*EP/LR* 1).

10. "Japanese Mysteries," *TLS* (25 January 1917): 41a-b.

11. John Gould Fletcher returned to New York in late 1915 and became entangled with Amy Lowell, the "she" referred to here and following, and her efforts to promote Imagism. Sarcastic EP expresses his continued displeasure with Lowell and her actions. The New York gang included Skipwith Cannell, William Carlos Williams, Marianne Moore, Maxwell Bodenheim (who migrated there from Chicago in 1916) and Alfred Kreymborg (who was to move to Chicago in 1917). EP alludes to the sumptuous dinners Amy Lowell provided in 1913 and 1914.

12. See Letter 60.

63

ACH to EP TLS 17 February 1917 3 ll + ALS 3 ll. Beinecke. ACH's response to reading "Three Cantos," possibly the earliest direct criticism of the poem.

Santa Fe, New Mexico. Feb. 17. 1917.

Dear Ezra:

Romana's twisted columns, and that hunting scene
Set in a bare chamber, and the maps
Laid out in colour with more charm
Than many a modern painting: summer morning,
Wind rippling water in the land half-marsh ...
Sunlight, stark emptiness, and cold bare walls,
Gonzaga's barren splendour,
Shown to the idle tourist for two bits a head —
And underneath it all that touch of spring,
That hint of youth and summer . . . . .
"Drear waste, great halls" -----[1]

Your cantos are very beautiful and I long for more to come. I've sent the mss. on to Harriet though I hated to give it up. I hope she will put them in April.[2] I really like them tremenduously. You've explored worlds beyond worlds, and it's a pleasure to follow you. *Bueno, Bueno!*

No, I wouldn't bother at all about the Black Man of Beacon Street.[3] Enough has been said and too much. What he needs is *action*. I don't know whether you had grounds for a suit for libel, but it seemed to me that Sandburg had, and I would have dearly loved to see a man like John Quinn take it up. I think the POETRY magazine had grounds for damage, and I urged it, but I guess Mr. Hamill didn't want to do anything.[4] Of course it would have done no good to bring suit against Braithwaite, but against *The Transcript*. However, that's past, and I think B. has done *himself* more harm than us <as indicated by clippings which speak of his *"venom."*>. He would never dared have said what he did about you or Sandburg about anyone with as much money as Amy! He's not black — he's *yellow*. I've joined The Author's League for the express purpose of collecting from him for using one of my poems without permission. I'll report on my progress. In the meantime let him *drop*.

But your influence with POETRY hasn't *waned*, you know, except as *you* have been willing to let it wane! I didn't know Harriet was grumped with you? What have you been doing or saying that she should be? I'm sure she's not really. She was much concerned awhile back lest you should get a false interpretation of some sort of a split between herself and Bodenheim. (Bodenheim is really very much of what you call over there "a bounder.") I mean that she cares very much what you think. I don't think there's the least use or necessity of your addressing E[unice].T[ietjens]. Carl [Sandburg] is better than anyone in Chicago, and then there's Masters. And there's still ME. But Harriet herself is a good deal of a brick, all things considered. I don't know anyone else of her generation who would prove so elastic — unless it might be Hen. Fuller, who has always been a joy to me personally. Do you know his "Chevalier of the Pensiere Vani"? Huneker calls it a neglected American masterpiece.[5] You'd enjoy it if you haven't read it. I wish you would. Oh, and please do me another favor. For de Lawd's sake, read that play "Grotesques" in *Poetry* and tell me what you think of it. I can't find it anything but tawdry, sentimental, slush and drivel: yet H.M. and a chorus of other Chicago "lights" proclaim it a masterpiece.[6]

But as I was saying, you have a perfectly good stand-in with Harriet direct. I'm sure of it. The magazine *needs* you. The review section has been very sad lately. And if you want cash, I'd suggest that you fall to and bolster it up. I wish you'd write a review of Doughty. It's new material, utterly, for America. I liked *The Clouds*. Places in it delighted me. *The Titans* I have here, but have not got through. And then there's Cranmer Byng's *Feast of Lanterns*.[7] What of it? Is there *any* poetry at all coming out of France? Is Vildrac still living?

And after all what is there but POETRY to tie to? The 7 Arts more like a "college magazine" than anything else![8]

Harriet writes that about sixty percent of the guarantors have renewed their pledges so far. That looks good.

How about you and Masters? Have you seen *The Great Valley*? I am strong for Masters — not because he is even, or a perfect stylist by any means: but because he has *bulk* — is strong on the "humanities" — (what makes the humanities; of course I am not so banal as to mean humanity.) because he has some background and depth and width. Take "The Steam-Shovel Cut" which Harriet was afraid <or didn't like enough> to print. Isn't it as good as Hardy's "Sunday Morning Tragedy" in a way?[9] <of course its not all good *art*, perhaps — but its modern — *crude, western*. It may be slightly melodramatic — but I like it! — also others in the G[reat] V[alley] —> The G.V. is getting the usual sort of condemnatory criticism from *The Dial* etc. and the "*little radicals*" if you know what I mean. (*Spoon River* is *now* a good book!) No *clarity* of criticism whatever. Harriet's talk of "the tale of the tribe" apropos of Frost and Masters of course wasn't *criticism* at all.[10] Nor do I think his psychology shallow. His Lincoln poems, to my mind, suggest a new vision of the man. ------- Well, what do you think?

Thanks awfully for your criticisms. <They are *most* helpful —>[11] Some I accept at once, and I'll ponder the others. I'm not *sure* but you chop your cadence off too short at times ??? for the full value of a mood and sound too ???? By now you've seen the aboriginal number, ye gods![12] I had no idea that my things were to be so determined! I'll work on the things before they go into a book. I haven't made arrangements yet for a book, my strain is rather small, but still it might be amusing? Is there anything in the *Spinning Woman* that you would include? <Please let me *know soon*.> I sent the Inscriptions to Reedy, but he returned them! — so I won't find it hard to save them for the book! The Wax-works, which is what I called the Potes, Harriet would never publish, I fear![13] However, I'll give her a chanc't. They're pretty obvious!

Got to stop now, will write soon again.

<yours.

A.C.H.>

<P.S.>
<Why don't you cover the new English books of poetry in a group review? They always come out in England first — and you ought to do it as *foreign correspondent* — (If H.M. doesn't pay you enough, tell

her so.) — There's Hewlitt's, *Song of the Plow* (is it any good?) & *Gai Saber*

What about Fletcher's Poems?

Davies' Selected Collected Poems?

Lawrence's *"Amores"* —

MacDonagh's Poems — ?

Padraic Pearse

    etc., etc., etc.[14]

Also, *as a piece of news* you might say just what Eng. poets are now in service or at the front — Masefield, I hear, is in France? Hueffer? — Manning, Aldington, etc. — Dunsany, the Irish poet — what *side is Joseph* Campbell on? (over).[15]

I would have made these suggestions — editorially speaking — long ago, but I thought perhaps you were too deep in China to care about coming out of it — But when the "wolves eat the mind & the lute is under the & ..." — eh what?[16]

    I'm enclosing a check for $2.00 for which please buy & inscribe and send me the Macmillan "Noh"[17] — I gather that you have an American account — or don't bother to get an order — HM's hoping no substitute gets the book! —

    Do you see anything of Fletcher, or are you permanently estranged? I think he's quite the best of the New Adventurists. I get tired of H.D.'s one pessimistic note. Too much *pointillism*.

    P.P.S.

How about a new American *one-Volume* selection of your Poems? ------why not do this? ----

    Has Irwin done anything? — What American publishers have been tackled, if any? ----[18]

    You'd probably *hate* my selection, but I'll bet if you'd let me make it, it would go — with a one-page incisive forward by

                        A.C.H.

----

1. ACH's metrical response to EP's *Cantos* alludes to the opening lines of Canto II of "Three Cantos" received by her in early February 1917. "Three Cantos," *P* 234-235.

2. In a letter of 6 February 1917, ACH told HM that "E.P. has sent me a long poem for POETRY. He sent it so I could read it and then send it to you. Of course it will be caviar to the general, no doubt, but I like it. I am mailing it,

registered, tomorrow" (HM Poetry Collection, Chicago).

The 7? February 1917 note accompanying "Three Cantos," located in the HM Poetry Collection, Chicago, reads:

> Dear H.M. Here are Ezra's Cantos. I really hate to let them go. I really like them tremendously. Another hard answer that could be made to idiots like Braithwaite. Of course they are erudite —but there is life — and a poet's life — in it & through it all— considerable vision and depth — and beauty of style. You need to read it several times — at least I did — to get the full value. In fact, it can be read *indefinitely* — & give up new meanings — which is a *good* deal to say — I am sending the mss. to your house, so you can read it away from "official" distractions. Let me know what you think about it. It was nice of E.P. to send it through me so I could read it & I am sorry I kept it longer than I meant! -
> Yours. A.C.H.

On 19 March 1917, HM replied to ACH in Santa Fe, New Mexico, from 64 E. Elm Street, Chicago (HRHRC):

> I read two or three pages of Ezra's Cantos and then took sick — no doubt that was the cause. Since then I haven't had brains enough to tackle it, and the other day I let Robert Frost take it east with him. But lord! — think of his expecting us to print 24 pages of that sort of thing in one number. I don't know what to do about it.

Nearly a month later, HM completed her reading of the *Cantos*, writing to ACH on 9 April 1917 from Tryon, N.C. (HRHRC):

> Well, I have read Ezra's poem at last. Of course it has his quality — though more diluted than usual, but I can't pretend to be much pleased at the course his verse is taking. A hint from Browning at his most recondite, and erudition in seventeen languages. Of course it would be suicidal to [do] the three cantos — or even two — in one number; I shall make it a serial in three numbers, if he consents, beginning probably with June. Is he petering out, that he must meander so among dead and foreign poets? has he nothing more of his own to say?
>
> I tremble frequently to think how Ezra must condole with you over the way *Poetry* has slumped since you left it. Is his language very strong?

On 16 April 1917, ACH replied to HM, repeating her admiration for "Three Cantos" (HM Poetry Collection, Chicago):

> I liked Ezra's poem —in spite of it being a tuning up of fiddles, it seemed to have some body of its own[.] Of course if nothing crystalized further on, I can't see that it would be sufficient excuse for itself, except in method and quality. It is a preparation, and a linking up of times and classics, etc. prepara-

tory, let us hope, to an individual vision. Of course as far as popularity is concerned, that's different. I don't think that's your prime concern after all — it never has been, and that's why *Poetry* has been worth something. But I think your suggestion of printing one canto a number ought to do.

Don't worry about Ezra's condoling with me over *Poetry* — he hasn't done it, and I have imagined that his thunders must have gone direct to you. I think he must have adopted a 'middle-aged' calm. He seemed to have felt premonitions of it in his book on Brezska! Apropros of your wondering about this, I had just read it when I saw Benet's cartoons in the April *Bookman*. They are quite amusing.

. . . . Apropos of Ezra again, some time ago I sent him a series of Wax Works, being portraits of contemporary poets. He was urgent that they be printed in POETRY. Of course I knew that you'll do no such thing, but I'll forward them for your amusement. I wrote them shortly after I came out last year.

"Three Cantos I" appeared in *Poetry* X (June 1917): 113-121; "Three Cantos II," *Poetry* X (July 1917): 180-188; "Three Cantos III," *Poetry* X (August 1917): 248-254. In a 24 May 1917 letter to Margaret Anderson, however, EP confidentially tells her that

> I revised and condensed my long poem, i.e. the first three cantos of it, between Saturday 11.15 p.m. and Sunday 8 a.m. It goes at the end of the volume Knopf is bringing out [*Lustra*] and also runs as a serial in *Poetry* June, July, Aug. (At least that's what they wrote me they were doing with it.) Dont say I have revised it. I want them <i.e. "Poetry"> to go on with the text they've got. (*EP/LR* 54)

3. Braithwaite. See Letter 58, note 1.

4. Charles H. Hamill was a distinguished Chicago lawyer and a member, with William T. Abbott, of *Poetry*'s Administrative Committee. His name appears on the masthead of the journal.

5. Henry B. Fuller (1857-1929), Chicago novelist and admirer of Harriet Monroe who became a member of the advisory board of *Poetry*. *The Chevalier of Pensieri-Vani* by Stanton Page [pseud. of Fuller] appeared in 1890 published in Boston by J. G. Cupples. Fuller's review of *'Noh' or Accomplishment* appeared in *The Dial* 63 (1917): 209.

James Gibbons Huneker, music critic, novelist, essayist, associate editor of *M'lle New York* and contributor to the *Smart Set* known for his satire of American institutions; author of *Egoists: A Book of Superman* (1909) and *Painted Veils* (1919).

6. "Grotesques: A Decoration in Black and White" was a verse tragedy written by Cloyd Head appearing in *Poetry* IX (October 1916): 1-30. Four photographs of the Chicago Little Theatre production of the play accompanied the text. The author described the play as episodes "conceived as a pantomime,

the words being often a rhythm superimposed upon that pantomime" (*Poetry* IX [1916]: 32). The play won the $200 Levinson prize for the best poem by an American in *Poetry* for 1916-1917.

7. Charles Montagu Doughty (1843-1926) published *The Clouds* (London: Duckworth) in 1912 and *The Titans* (London: Duckworth) in 1916. He is best known as the author of *Travels in Arabia Deserta* (1888) and perhaps for his 6-volume epic, *The Dawn in Britain* (1906). EP read portions of both works to Yeats at Stone Cottage. See Letter 64.

Launcelot Alfred Cranmer-Byng (1872-1945), *A Feast of Lanterns* (London: J. Murray, 1916). Two years later he published *A Feast of Jade: Selections from the Classical Poets of China* (London: J. Murray, 1918).

8. Among contributors to *The Seven Arts* were Sherwood Anderson, John Dos Passos, Dreiser, Frost, and Lowell. See Letter 55, note 4.

9. Edgar Lee Masters, *The Great Valley* (New York: Macmillan, 1916). HM reviewed the book with hesitant praise in *Poetry* IX (January 1917): 202-207, along with Frost's *Mountain Interval*. Thomas Hardy, "A Sunday Morning Tragedy," *Time's Laughing Stocks* (London: Macmillan, 1909).

10. HM began the second paragraph of her review "Frost and Masters," *Poetry* IX (January 1917): 202, with this sentence: "These two poets, Frost and Masters, are telling the tale of the tribe, the varying tales of their separate tribes." In the opening paragraph, Monroe referred to Kipling's story of primitive men where the bard becomes a prophet because he can "'tell the tale of the tribe'" (202). The Kipling source is apparently his 1906 address to the Royal Academy Dinner entitled "Literature" in which he narrates the story of a speaker who told "the tale of the tribe." See Kipling, "Literature," *A Book of Words*, Vol. XXXII, *The Writings in Prose and Verse* (New York, 1928), 6. Pound in *Guide to Kulchur* cites Kipling as the source of the phrase (194). However, Pound may have first come across it in HM's 1917 review.

11. See Letter 61, 23 January 1917.

12. ACH refers to *Poetry* IX (February 1917) which contains a series of poems on aboriginal people including her series "In the Desert I-V," and "Indian Songs," 232-238. HM's editorial on the Indian number appears on 251-254. ACH includes a paragraph explaining her "Indian Songs" on 256.

The same volume contains reviews of D. H. Lawrence's *Amores* (1916) by Eunice Tietjens and H. D.'s *Sea-gardens* (1916) by John Gould Fletcher. An editorial note on the volume reads "all but one of the poets represented in this number live, or have lived, in the wilder West of the United States or British Columbia" (274).

13. See Letter 60 dated 23 January 1917, the first of two written on that date, and note 1.

W. M. Reedy edited *Reedy's Mirror* (St. Louis, Mo.), a weekly book review, from 1913-1920. Among its contributors were Sara Teasdale, Fannie Hurst, Orrick Johns, Vachel Lindsay, Babette Deutsch, Carl Sandburg, Edna St. Vincent Millay, Maxwell Bodenheim, and Edgar Lee Masters, whose *Spoon River Anthology* appeared from 29 May 1914 until 15 January 1915.

14. Maurice Hewlett, *Song of the Plow* (London: Heineman, 1916) and *Gai Saber* (London: Elkin Mathews, 1916); John Gould Fletcher, *Goblins and Pagodas* (Boston: Houghton Mifflin, 1916); W. H. Davies, *Collected Poems of W. H. Davies* with portrait by William Rothenstein (New York: Knopf, 1916); D. H. Lawrence, *Amores* (London: Duckworth, 1916); Thomas MacDonagh, *Poetical Works of Thomas MacDonagh* (New York: Frederick Stokes Co., 1916). Involved with the Abbey Theatre and the independence movement, MacDonagh, like Padraic Pearse, was executed following the Easter Rebellion of 1916. See Letter 51, note 3.

15. Edward John Dunsany, an Irish Baron, published *Fifty One Tales* (London: Elkin Mathews, 1915; 2nd ed. 1916). Yeats wrote the introduction to *Selections from the Writings of Lord Dunsany* (Churchtown, Dundrum: Cuala Press, 1912); Joseph Campbell, an Irish playwright and nationalist, translated the Gaelic works of Padraic Pearse and edited his *Collected Works* in 1917.

16. ACH may be recalling here two lines from EP's early "Villonaud for This Yule": ". . . when the grey wolves everychone / Drink of the winds their chill small-beer," based on the second stanza of Villon's "Lais" (*P* 10). In his review of Yeats' *Responsibilities* in *Poetry* IX (December 1916), EP refers to "The Coat" as "the wild wolf-dog that will not praise his fleas" (150), while the so-called aboriginal number of *Poetry* IX (February 1917) containing ACH's Indian poems, prints an entire page of verse by Constance Skinner dealing with wolves (243).

The lute reference may be drawn from the Fenollosa/Pound Noh drama *Genjo*, mailed to ACH in 1915. The story is of a lute player who interrupts his journey to China to perfect his art by spending a night at Suma on the coast with a salt laborer, performing in his low hut and discovering that his host (actually a god in the disguise of a laborer) is, in fact, an extraordinary player. This convinces Moronaga, the lute master, not to continue to China. He also learns that on this spot the great Genji played, mixing "the shore wind . . . with the sound of his longing and carry[ing] it back to the city, to the margin of his desire" [5].

17. '*Noh*', *or Accomplishment, A Study of the Classical Stage of Japan* by Ernest Fenollosa and Ezra Pound was published by Macmillan in London on 12 January 1917.

18. Wallace Irwin (1875-1959), English poet, translator of the *Rubaiyat* (1909). His comic opera *The Dove of Peace* (1908) had music by Walter Damrosch. Irwin's *Love Sonnets of a Car Conductor* (1908) and *Letters of a Japanese Schoolboy* (1909) were semi-popular.

64

5, Holland Place Chambers, London W.8

<8-3-17> <note new postal address, or emendation. Kensington W.
is now London _W.8_>

Dear Alice

I am glad you like the poem. It seems very difficult to
get any CRITICISM.[1] Padre José brings back his copy with "Muy
bien, son muy bien". He hadn't understood 'em all "pero los padres
han compreso y dicen que son muy bien". I said the padre couldn't
possibly have approved of Valla's "Nec bonus etc." at which the
good father looked depressed and went on to say the part about
Corpus Christi was very enjoyable and that the dances in Cathedral
at Seville on Corpus <day> etc. etc.[2]

Eliot said it was worth doing and after standing over him
with a club I got some very valuable objections to various details. I
can't remember whether I've included the emendations in the mss. I
sent you. Don't delay publication in trying to find out, the changes
were all very minute and dont matter for a first publication.[3]

Your metric outburst i[s] encouraging and I'm glad you want more.[4]
I can't, however, Amy it out by the barrel or Fletcherize at 200 pages
per annum. The form of the bloody whole has got to begin to
commence to inchoho sometime or other. Also there is a great deal
to be left out.

I hope Harriet _will_ print it in April.[5] If I see the first lot in
type I may feel it more "cleared up" and better able to get on to the
next swot. At present I've only chunks and stray incidents.

/////

A.A. Knopf 220 W. 42nd St. New York is importing "Noh" and
bringing out my collected poems. I.E. a book called "Lustra etc."

containing that classic and as much of my earlier stuff as seems
worth reprinting. That is most of *Ripostes* and a selection from the
three earlier books.

I trust he will be prevented from making too hideous a "production". The actual appearance of some American volumes is distressing. Why the devil he cant peacibly copy Mathews "Lustra" I don't
know. However it will be a convenience to have the stuff in one vol.
and one can get the sheets rebound if he does anything too
appallingly horrible.[6]

I should like to see your "selection" all the same, though it is
too late for it to have any effect on present opus. Bill Williams sent
me his list, with which I fairly well agreed. I should still like to see
yours.

/////

About your book. I think it is rather soon for you to amalgamate
from the "Spinning Woman", especially as your style has very
considerabl<y> changed, and a selection from the *S.W.* would
probably bust the unity. I should make it an all new book now. And
reprint a selection from the *S.W.* in some later compilation.

////

Re/ H.M. and Bodenheim. He wrote me a silly letter about H's
favoring people who were "known". I wrote telling him he was
talking through his hat, and have not written since. At least I don't
think I have. I have a vague recollection that he wrote again saying
that part of his letter HAD been written through his hat. I also told
him a few.

I am a bit fed up with various sub-contemporarie<s>, some
have caused me more personal annoyance than seems worth my
personal while to put up with, and others have bored me, not *coram*
in person <but> by the arid expanse of their <printed> flaccidities. It
seems to me, at the moment, unlikely that Amy, or Fletcher or
Lawrence should by any new production convey to me any emotion
that I have not already received ad ennuiundam from what parts of
their verse I have already and in passato perused.

I am afraid H.D. is flowing in weaker repititions of her
charming self. I dont think I have said so, to many people. I don't
want it repeated.

I cant possibly write criticism of any of the people with

whom I have been closely connected, and whom I now see seldom
or not at all. If their present work caused me any enthusiasm it
would be easy enough to praise <it>. BUT as the whole lot seem to
me to be merely repeating at greater and greater length, there is
nothing for me to do but keep quiet <about them.>

I think Richard [Aldington] stupid, but every now and again
I find a line or a hint which makes me think he might be the best of
the lot. ma che ....

Rodker is silly and unballanced, *but* he has just done a story
with something to it. And I am not sure but he may go further than
any of them.

Joyce, Eliot and Lewis are the only men I at the moment
believe in. For Rodker I have hopes.

Sandburg, is as you say the best in Chicago. He is laggard
at letter writing but the "Chicago Poems" were harder in spots than
Masters.

Masters seems to me to be declining. I doubt if he will do
anything better than *Spoon River*.

???????????????

Remember I haven't the living personalities of these men near me to
stir up belief when the printed page does not.

As for writing reviews. Harriet still has a lot of short prose things of
mine, WHICH she has been keeping burried since forever. It is no
fun sending stuff that dont get printed within the memory of the
oldest living inhabitant.

What you say about 60% of the guarantors is encouraging.
How long do they guarant for?

Does 60% guarant mean general reduction in rates and
corresponding depression and reduction in quality?

I will look up Hen. Fuller's book. Are the 60% the just, or
the "conservative"? Would they stand for free speech and an
occasional lapse from Christianity?

An article on what the literati are doing at the front would probably
stop with the censor. Besides what can one say. William Roberts the
painter left his hole "to clean himself". His hole was an observation
post. He is still unrepentent. We dont know whether the whole
British Front fell in on account of Bobbie. Other communiques lead

us to suppose that it didn't but Bobby has no brilliant military future before him.

Ford has been in hospital. All we know for certain is that his false teeth fell out. ?? ague or shell shock. ???
Wadsworth's last words before leaving for Somewhere in X. were "What I believe is that ANYTHING connected with this war is going to be so bloody god damn dull that ...."

In his case it hasn't been. His occasional letters are occasionally amusing.

But an article on literati at the front would be little more than a bulletin of names.

None of the books you mention seems to me worth reviewing.

I did an article on Davies, but H.M. has suppressed it. She had a row with him once. As he has since told me.

I shall review Eliot as soon as I can get him published. I sent in a rev. of a rumm little anthology "Wheels".[7] Christo! I have reviewed several other books that weren't worth it, in my zeal to "correspond".

I still dont quite know why J.G.F. reviewed H.D. in preference to the For<eign> Cor<respondent> being axed for copy or an opinion.[8] But it is no matter. I had told H.M. once <before> that I didn't want to review Hilda myself which may easily account for it.

Fletcher[']s stock review with George Washington, Minerva, St Simon Stylites, Ste Beuve, Goethe, Sir Walter Scott, Sir Walter Besant, Michaelangelo and Hokusai all run in in a bunch at the end of each paragraph <to display his egregious kultur> is beginning to get monotonous.

Eliot is beginning to get articles taken in the weeklies here. I doubt if he will be much longer available for the prose part of poetry.

For the rest, things are damn dull. The *Mercure de France* has gone to pot. Vildrac is ill. H.M. wont or dont print the things by DeBosschère I sent her.

He <De Bos.> has had various things accepted here. Now has three books to illustrate for Heineman, and Lane bringing out a bad translation of his poems by Flint, with introd. by May Sinclair.

The war has turned a lot of not-poets into writers of

"poetry". The results are NOT interesting. There have been wars before and the ammount of war poetry that is literature is damn small. There is narrative, perfectly calm narrative poetry recording past deeds. There are a few laments, a few songs of incitation. With the exception of the last category, war poetry that endure<s> has been written by detatched persons writing after the event.

The one poem of the Napoleonic wars was written by a German,

Im franchreich zogen zwei grenadier, or something of that sort.

"Mein Kaiser, mein Kaiser verfangen" naturally the Hohenzollern wont forgive the man who wrote this way of a Corsican having no connection with their own Allerhochste familie.

The other great lyric of Napoleon is the prose beginning of *La Chartreuse de Parma*.

As yet .... etc.....

/////

Your letter: reexamination for points missed.

I.

Grotesques.[9] Chere enfante, there are times when the eye simply refuses to penetrate the page; when perusal is unwashedly impossible. Non possumus. . . .

WHY should I read

that bloody playlet?

It is printed. past tense. My reading it now will not prevent its having been printed. It will not feed the starving author.

WHY was it?

And being, why was it illustrated thatly? AND altogether too Cannellish as to the germanicogreekism of its decor !!!

/////

Doughty's prose "Arabia Deserta" is a classic. Yeats and I read it one winter, and on the strength of it we had the <">Dawn in Britain<"> shipped down to Stone Cottage, and we stuck. He stuck. I stuck.

And Cranmer Byng is no good, though he was the first man to buy a copy of "Personae" in the first year of my era.

And "nothing is happening France" in the monde poetique. They are all fighting.

And the "Seven Arts" is undergraduate, as you say. And there IS nothing but "Poetry", but there might become something. I should like to print a little creative prose, and have a place for other creative prose. A better "Egoist" or reinforced "Little Review." One wants a regular stand.

/////

Yrs. questions re/ metre. Yes, I think my "music" is too discon-nected, and that I must [put?] more resonance into the poema lunga as it procedes.

////

Reedy is not good. He probably printed "Spoon River" mostly for the wrong reasons. Judging from the rest of his performances it looks as if the righteous act was fluke.

///

MacDonagh's poems aren't in the same street with his criticism. I had them at the same time, and thought it better to confine myself to what I could praise.[10] Colum might do the poems.

///

I will tell Macmillan here to send you the English edtn. of "Noh".

That'll be about all for this evening.

March 9

About your volume: I should begin with "One City Only" then follow with most of the other <new> poems, then use the second sort of house atmosphere longish poem from the last lot you sent me. I forget what you call it, but it is the one about all the houses ["Old Houses"].

Then the remaining poems, probably the satires would go well in this section, and end with the epilogues (naturally, epilogues at the end.).

I dont see where the *Spinning W.* poems would fit in, BUT then I haven't the whole mss. before me and can only make rather vague suggestions.

The AMURkhn pote <in the mass> still suffers from appalling lacunae in his mental furnishings and from an utter lack of ideals, that is to say ideals of other than purely social and political natures. Those who have heard of literature, style etc, are too uneducated or else emotionally and intellectually impotent. Utter lack of any desire to do a good job. Still, and after five years of preaching.

There are a lot of belated aesthetes who talk about "finish" etc. but they are less than useless. Loose immitation of 1912, wont be any better than ditto. of the Celtic Movement . . I dare say it may be even worse. etc. etc. we have said all this so often before.

     Y basta.

                <Yours ever

                      E.P.>

<Ezra Pound>

<9-3- '17>

1. "Three Cantos." See Letter 63.

2. On Padre José, see Letter 61, note 4. *"Nec bonus"* refers to a passage in Canto III/242 (*P*).

3. This cavalier attitude of EP's toward textual accuracy persisted through-out the publication of *The Cantos*—see *SL* 306, 324—and has led to numerous confusions and complexities. Among many who address these issues are Richard Taylor, "Introduction" and "Annals," *Variorum Edition of Three Cantos* (Bayreuth: Boomerang Press, 1991), 1-22, and his "Reconstructing Ezra Pound's *Cantos*," in *Ezra Pound and America*, ed. Jacqueline Kaye (London: Macmillan, 1992), 132-148; also helpful is Peter Stoicheff, "Whose Poem is it Anyway? The Interwoven Authority of A *Drafts and Fragments* Text," unpublished paper delivered at the "Pound and History" conference, Yale University, October 1989.

4. See Letter 63.

5. The first of the "Three Cantos" did not appear until June. See "Three Cantos. I," *Poetry* X (June 1917): 113-121; the poem was the opening work of the issue and, buried in the "Notes" section, EP provided the following comment:

> As POETRY circulates among people definitely interested in the art, I do not feel apologetic about presenting the opening cantos of an exceedingly long poem. Most of the long poems that one can read were written before printing was invented, and circulated in fragments. More recent precedent may be found in the publication of separate cantos of *Don Juan*.
>
> It has been one of POETRY's chief services to make possible the current publication of work that otherwise would have been available only upon the issue of a complete volume of an individual's work. The harm which other magazines have done to poetry is largely in that they have fostered a habit among poets of setting forth only so much of their work as may be intelligible and acceptable in bits, only a page or so at a time. (167)

6. *Lustra of Ezra Pound, with Earlier Poems* (New York: Knopf, 1917). Published on 16 October 1917, although preceded by a printing of 60 copies for private circulation.

7. EP would review *Prufrock and Other Observations* (London: Egoist Press, 1917) in *Poetry* X (August 1917): 264-271, offering this comment—"Art does not avoid universals, it strikes at them all the harder in that it strikes through particulars"—in his praise of Eliot (267).

"A Flock from Oxford," *Poetry* X (April 1917): 41-44. EP opens his review by noting that the cover of *Wheels: An Anthology of Verse* is in "bright yellow [with] a scraggy nursemaid and a make-shift perambulator. It is the proper sort of ink-pot to hurl itself in the face of senile pomposity" (41). In the collection he favors Nancy Cunard and Sacheverell and Edith Sitwell, as well as prose translations of Rimbaud by H. Rootham.

8. John Gould Fletcher's review of H. D.'s *Sea-garden*, entitled "H. D.'s Vision," appeared in *Poetry* IX (February 1917): 266-269.

9. "Grotesques," the verse tragedy which opened *Poetry* IX (October 1916): 1-30. See Letter 63, note 6.

10. EP, "Thomas MacDonagh as Critic," *Poetry* VIII (September 1916): 309-312.

65

EP to ACH and HM   TLS 13 April 1917 5 ll. In the left-hand
corner of this letter in the fine handwriting of HM is the comment
"Dear Alice — Please return this, & I will file it for further
reference[.] I have answered it. All about the anthology." EP here
criticizes the appearance of his work in *The New Poetry* edited by
Monroe and Henderson, and comments on various introductory
statements.

5, Holland Place Chambers, London W.8

<13/4/'17>
Dear H.M. and A.C.H.

Rec'd just now your "NEW POETRY". On the whole a
good job for which you are to be congratulated.[1]

I shall never accept the statement that "poetry, new or
otherwise" looks outward rather than inward. Impressionism, hardly
even impressionism does that. Imagism (before it went to hell with
Amy's gush and Fletcher's squibbs, fluid diarrhoea in the first case
and a diarrhoea of bent nails and carpet tacks in the second).

Imagism of the first book "Des Imagistes" NEVER. never
looking out rather than in.

No, no, no, bad sentence. <yours>. Emotion "conveyed by
depiction of exterior objects", or even by "mention" of exterior
objects. That is the right way to phrase it.

The passion is the whole thing. Given enough
of it almost any other defects can be overcome.

//////////

It is unpleasant of you to include the mush of my "Piccadilly", and
also "The Choice" and ALSO "The Ballad for Gloom".

And it is unkind of you to follow the
earlier versions of "The Psychological Hour" and "Near Perigord",
instead of the improved versions in "Lustra".

I wish you could cut out the first three poems mentioned. With all
your talk of anglo-saxon influence, it would have been more apt to
have used "The Seafarer", which is the only decent piece of ang-sax
metre in modern English.

I also note the following mistakes in Bibliography.[2]

Exultations, first pub. 1909 (Autumn),
      (Personae had been pub. that spring)
Canzoni. pub. by Mathews. 1911
Provença, 1910
Guido Cavalcanti. Small Maynard 1912
   (That is much the better edition. The
      Swift publication need not be mentioned.
        S.M. was first any how.)
Two vol edit. Personae,-Exultations; Canzoni-Ripostes
        Mathews 1913
Cathay, 1915
Edited "Des Imagistes", pub. Feb. 1914
      Catholic Anth.   1915
???
Noh or Accomplishment, with Fenollosa. 1916
       <Macmillan. London
        Knopf. N.Y.>

I should be glad to have stated in note on "Des Imagistes".
      "No connection with any Imagist publication since that
date."

//////////

Blast the Biblical tradition. It has been rotting English poetry for
long enough. Stow it. Ecclesiastes, and the Song of Songs. yes/ But
the rest is mostly slush and bad rhetoric, together with a very
debased conception of the deity. God the papa is a rotter all through
and a megalomaniac and a bad tempered bigot.

      Besides its a bad thing to drag in. The Victorian era,
seeing they wo<u>ld have to throw it over as authentic religion, got
up this bluff about its being second to Shakespear as literature, pure
<hoar> of cheating clergy afraid they would loose their soft jobs if
the general fraud were found out too quickly.

   Read the bloody thing daily until one day I discovered that even
Swinburne wrote better than Eze<k>iel. Since then I have tried to
read the jews with my sense of criticism *awake* and not merely
woozing along thinking "yes, its great, I can go on without worrying

to think". Which is the way the "general reader" reads litterchure.

////

you've done a useful thing in bringing out *New Poetry*. It is the first thing in American or English to serve the purpose which van Bever and Leautaud['s] *Mercure de France* anthology serves in France.[3]

It ought to be worth correcting, and emmending, and possibly revising and reissuing in five years time, amplified.

I think Colum's "Drover" and "Woman Shapely as a Swan" ought to go in.

I think you tried to get Hueffer's "Heaven" ?.???

He has other things better than Antwerp.

Perhaps Manning's "Korè". Still think it the best thing he has done.

////

Another minute point. Poetry on the title page of anthology ought to be in "" marks.

       Editors of "Poetry".

otherwise how do you expect the furriner to know what it means.

       <Pass this on to A.C.H. as *per*salutation in heading>

                <Yours

                   Ezra Pound>

    <13-4-'17>

---

1. *The New Poetry*, ed. HM and ACH (New York: Macmillan, 1917), intended partly to oppose and correct Amy Lowell's series, *Some Imagist Poets* (1916, 1917, 1918). ACH intended to help HM but her illness in 1916 limited her role. Her name does appear as co-editor, however. Twenty pages of EP's verse are in the anthology, the largest block by one poet in the volume, although he was critical of their choices as this letter shows.

2. HM commented to EP on 3 July 1917 that "the bibliography . . . I assure you, was the meanest job I ever undertook. No more Anthologies for me" (Williams 189).

3. *Poetes d'aujourd'hui, 1880-1900: morceaux choisis accompagnes de notices biographiques et d'un essai de bibliographie*, ed. Adolphe van Bever and Paul Leautaud (Paris: Mercure de France, 1900). By 1917 the volume was in its 28th edition.

66

5, Holland Place Chambers, London W.8

Dear A.C.H.

Have at last had a letter from Harriet, consenting to print the Divina Commedia, in three sections during the silly season.[1]

It will lose a good deal of its force being split up, but I am past struggling with these things.

I wrote a few days ago re/ your anthology, saying it was on the whole as good a job as could be done with the material, and the conditions.

<Wrote> two days ago on receipt of cheque for $3.69 dollars, pointing out that two such cheques during six months did not show very high estimate of cash value of a foreign correspondent.

She had better get Fletcher if she wants him. He is more voluble, and more enthusiastic about the prospects of your country. If she prints the poem, even in fragments and sends me the £24 we will be able to part amiably. I shall for the moment be free of pressing necessity.

That is perhaps better than a row and rage.

She says you are reported to be better. I hope it is so, and that we can both be in Paris in the spring. Some spring or other, one need not specify which. Or perhaps I shall be dragged back to New Mexico to drill. as a conscript. I have already sent my name to the Embassy, but still America dont want volunteers, she wants conscripts. However let us be thankful that we shall at least pay a few bills for civilization.

<More anon. I've a long complicated business letter to answer>
<yours ever
Ezra>
<Ezra Pound
24 April 1917>

1. "Three Cantos" appeared in the June, July, and August 1917 issues of *Poetry*. See Letter 63 and notes.

67

5, Holland Place Chambers, London W.8

<14 June 1917>
Dear A.C.H.

Don't despair so over the L[ittle].R[eview]. . They promise an increase in format, and the company in the May number, and for the three numbers following is about as good as there is to be found.

Eliot's poems are just out, or at least advance copies of them.[1] The past does not engulph everything.

You must admit that two cheques of 3.75 dollars during six months are hardly enough to support me, and <">Poetry<"> never answers a letter; never takes any notice of any proposition for waking itself up, never sends back mss. that it is going to submerge, altogether too exasperating to depend on. I can't be expected to wait at the door indefinitely and with my cap in my hand. The steady stipend on the L.R. will be a comfort, though it is not large enough to live on, still it will pay the rent and the assurance of having stuff regularly and promptly printed, both mine and stuff selected by me, will also make it more interesting for me, than having interminably to argue every time I find an Eliot.

And if Harriet is away, why can't she leave an able bodied person in charge. Say Sandburg? At least someone who would try to do something and who would answer one<'>s letters, and in general try to think of "Poetry" as an active magazine with something to do.

The L.R. hasn't a permanent mania like the *Egoist* with D. Marsden burbling over its front. Their discontent is healthy.

I cant enthuse over Morris Ward, but he is no worse than the average stuff in *Poetry*.

As you yourself said long since, you and I should have been assured of a certain number of pages a month in the back of *Poetry*.

As it is I haven't even got an answer to my proposition re/ a series of essays by Eliot, DeBosschère, myself, on french poets.

The long poem is to be split up into sections. Good or bad it should have been lumped into one issue.

As for the L.R., I couldn't have gone into it before; not before they'd got disgusted with Ficke, and various others who were once affiliated.

Your not liking Joyce is the most serious critical error you have made. You once did lose your head over that ass Masefield, but this is worse, being a negation.

And you must be a long way off if Coomara pleases by much save his Stevensonian phiz.[2]

At any rate "Poetry" has become too feeble a crutch to me for me to trust my whole weight to it, and the May L.R. is for the most part pleasurable reading, and the schedule for the next few months is also dotted with excellent matter. Also it is a pleasure to have a little cash to distribute among contributors.

Whether it will help to wake up *Poetry*, I dont know. I hope so. I am not feeling the least elegiac over the prospects at the moment.

If Harriet isn't running *Poetry*, whatever my mental deficiencies, it would have been at least as sensible to ask me to run it for a few months as to turn it over to the Tietjens flapper. really!

Masters, Sandburg, someone might have been given a chance of expressing themselves and waking things up a bit.

///

On the otherhand it is my conclusion that Harriet would rather like me out the thing, and that it is, was, high time that I was looking for some other "situation". The *Little Review* wont "keep me" i.e. financially maintain me completely, but it will do more than *Poetry* has done for some time.

AND, which is more enjoyable, I am assured of a certain amount of space and a certain amount of good company in each number. And a free hand to say what I like, which is also a comfort.

I see nothing much against our chance of succeeding. It is inconvenient that Joyce has chosen this particular time to go into hospital, and that Lewis is in the firing line, and that Hueffer is engaged in military affairs. And, naturally, that I can't count on anything from Paris until the end of the war. But still there are about six numbers planned. Each of them with something of lasting value in it.

I am not giving *Poetry* the go by, the L.R. is a prose affair. Eliot[']s poem *y compris* as Harriet so objects to printing 'em. and Yeats' when *Poetry* offers him ridiculously small prices as £7 for the magnificent series on a dying lady.[3] Certainly as fine as anything he has ever done, and more vivid than the early *Wind Among the Reeds* stuff.

Still it will be a good thing for the Chicago plutocracy to know that the[y] must spend at least money if they want to be THE art centre.

Also it may relieve the congestion which H.M. is always complaining about.

AND we will certainly be a worse thorn in the side of the ungodly than *Poetry* with its policy of moderation, tolerance and politeness, and civility to W.D. Howells has been.

Also the brace up of the *Egoist* by putting Eliot aboard is going to give us two hands to punch with.

YOU GET WELL AND COME OVER HERE. And also if *Poetry* dont print you promptly, AND if it dont print your little poems about American poets, you send 'em in to M.C.A. <31 W. 14th St. New York.>[4]

She may be enthusiastic about Mary Garden, an enthusiasm which I have no means of judging; but she ain't dead, burried, embalmed, petrified and cremated.[5]

I started the union when she printed her half number blank with the remark that if she couldn't get something fit to print she would print nothing at all. That's the origin of our present alliance.

I think also that she is capable of getting an international view point. She is keen on getting french contributions.

//////

About Quinn's knowing art. People who have seen him selecting drawings out of a pile, say that he *has an eye.*

///

Re/ L.R. at any rate we shall soon print everyone of any distinction save Shaw, Kipling, and Anatole, who are too expensive, and too blasted exceeding old.

Lady Gregory is sending in a play which Yeats says is one of her best. I can't tell till I see it, and it may be too long for present format, but we are going up to 64 pages soon.[6]

////

I am of course please[d] that my stuff is being published in N.Y. (i.e. books) under favorable conditions. And the arrival of May L.R. and Eliot's poems within a few hours of each other, gives me the feeling that things are beginning again. speranze fallce?[7]

I wish Lewis weren't at the front. Richard is back after six months, with recommendation for commission.

///

I imagine there will be a new and rather severer grouping into a new anthology before long. I shan't be doing it, but I want them to use your "Love me at Last", as well as "One City Only". I think it excellent. One could slip into R.B.'s collected without anyone knowing it was an alien.[8]

Of course I am /pleased by Joyce's sweep of the tables after having fought the matter for so long.[9]

<yours ever>
<Ezra>

    <Ezra Pound>
  <14-6. 1917>

---

1. T. S. Eliot, *Prufrock and Other Observations* (London: Egoist Press, 1917).

2. This may allude to ACH's praise of Padraic Colum's *Wild Earth and Other Poems* in her review entitled "That Wilder Earth," *Poetry* X (May 1917): 105-108.

3. A reference to the 1916 debacle when HM censored T.S. Eliot's "Mr. Apollinax" resulting in TSE's decision never to publish any other poetry in the journal. See Letter 62, note 2.

Symptomatic of the problem, however, of EP's being Foreign Correspondent for both the *Little Review* and *Poetry* (see the angry letters from ACH to HM over EP's actions in Williams 207-208, and compare with EP's remark to Margaret Anderson of 11 June 1917, "common decency, [and cash reasons], but even more common decency demand that I should not throw over Poetry until there are worse rows and disagreements than any that have yet happened" [*EP/ LR* 67]) was Yeats' decision to publish "Upon a Dying Lady" in the August 1917 *Little Review* rather than *Poetry* because their rate was higher. HM offered Yeats $11.00 per page rather than her standard $8.00; however, the *Little Review*

offered more. HM clearly implicated EP in Yeats' decision (HM to EP, 3 July
1917, Williams 209-210); EP naturally took umbrage at HM's claims and noted
that Yeats gave his poems to the *Little Review* because he did not think *Poetry*
could publish them in time to synchronize with their English publication (EP to
HM, 23 July 1917 cited in Williams 211-212). EP's letter of 23 July 1917
effectively ended his role as Foreign Correspondent for *Poetry*, although the
official break did not occur until 1919.

4. Margaret Anderson, editor of the *Little Review*.

5. Mary Garden (1877-1931?), Scottish operatic soprano who debuted in
America in *Thais* in New York on 25 November 1907 and later joined the
Chicago Grand Opera Company where she performed from 1910-1931. A
favorite of Margaret Anderson's. See *EP/LR* 241.

6. Lady Gregory's "Hanrahan's Oath," *Little Review* (November 1917):
6-16.

7. *Prufrock and Other Observations* (1917); "false hope?"

8. Most likely the poet laureate Robert Bridges' anthology, *The Spirit of
Man* (London: Longmans, Green & Co., 1916).

9. EP may be referring not only to the paiseworthy reviews of *A Portrait of
the Artist as a Young Man* by H. G. Wells, the *Times Literary Supplement*, and the
Little Review, but also to its sold-out status. Published in 750 copies on 12
February 1917 by the Egoist, the first edition of *A Portrait* was out of print by
early June, although its publication was a struggle. As Joyce explained to the
literary agent J. B. Pinker, after the Egoist press accepted the novel, nearly
twenty printers in England and Scotland refused to print it. Consequently, the
Egoist had to import printed sheets of the American first edition from the
publisher Ben Huebsch in New York and bind them in England. For the second
edition of 1,000 copies, proposed for September 1917 but not published until
March 1918, Harriet Shaw Weaver located a printer willing to set the text, a
necessity since new regulations prevented the importation of printed sheets from
the US to England. See Richard Ellman, *James Joyce*, rev. ed. (New York: Oxford
University Press, 1982) 415.

Another possible cause for EP's celebration of Joyce was a letter from him
of 5 June 1917 reporting his completion of the "Lotus Eaters" and "Hades"
sections of what would become *Ulysses*.

68

5, Holland Place Chambers, London W.8

<8/9/'17>

Taciturn Female:

I trust by the time this reaches you, you will be beginning to see WHY I took up with the *Little Review*.[1] Or that at least by the time we begin the Hueffer mss. and the novel Joyce says he will finish by the first of next year, you will begin to notice some raison d'etre, apart from my rest, which it is a comfort to have guaranteed for two years.[2] (Rent, not food and clothing, but still a steady screw however minute is not to be scornéd.[)]

I wish I could find out what's become of your pomes on potes. Is H.M. printing them?[3]

DeBosschère's poem with Flint's translation, are out. In a handsome wollum.[4]

H.M. has sent me £5. since the £20 for the long pome.[5] The Aug. number however, has not arrived YET. She might try sending only two copies, and sending the rest in a separate packet.

I am having a long run in the *New Age*. and getting some fun out of it. Began July 12. and seven more weeks to run. Possibly will make it a booklet. Fontenelle is set up. American "Lustra etc" has been finally corrected.[6]

Knopf in N.Y. is also considering a vol. of selected prose.

And, I believe, a small bibliography.[7]

<Hope you are at least beginning to get well. = End this ere it be lost.>

<yours ever

Ezra Pound>

1. EP began his association with the *Little Review* in April 1916 with the appearance of "A Letter from London" criticizing the tariff on books. In November 1916 a second article on the same subject appeared. By 26 January 1917 EP outlined, in a letter to Margaret Anderson, the conditions of his collaboration with the *Little Review* (see *EP/LR* 6-12) which included the regular publication of Eliot, Joyce, Lewis, and himself.

In April 1917 the journal announced EP's affiliation with the *LR* as Foreign Editor and the May 1917 issue printed EP's editorial which explained his reasons for joining the magazine while summarizing his problems with *Poetry*. However, he explained that his "connection with the *Little Review* does not imply a severance of my relations with *Poetry*. . . . But [*Poetry*] has never been 'the instrument of my radicalism'" (*LR* May 1917). EP maintained his association with the *Little Review* from 1917 until the spring of 1919 and again from 1921 until the spring of 1923. His efforts as Foreign Editor resulted in the serial publication of *Ulysses* from March 1918 to September/December 1920.

2. EP most likely refers to Ford Madox Hueffer's (later Ford) *Women and Men* which appeared in six installments in the *Little Review* in 1918, although Hueffer began the work in 1911.

Ulysses is the novel by Joyce EP mentions which began to appear in the *Little Review* in March 1918 with "Telemachus" and ended in September/December 1920 with "Oxen of the Sun."

EP's financial arrangement regarding the *Little Review* involved a grant from John Quinn of $750 for two years to finance his part of the magazine, $300 to be kept by him in return for editorial duties, the balance for contributors.

3. The set of eleven satiric poems by ACH dealing with types of American poets. See Letter 60. The poems include portraits of the "debonair poet" whose work on his dead mistress "may be read between tango and tea" and a female "poetic Tammany" who is "the boss, the delegates, and the whole works." *Poetry* never published the poems.

4. F. S. Flint's translation of Jean de Bosschère's poem *The Closed Door* was published in London by John Lane in 1917. May Sinclair introduced the bilingual edition of twelve poems.

5. "Three Cantos." Williams says payment for "Three Cantos" was £21 (208). On "Three Cantos," sent first to ACH in Santa Fe, see Letters 62 and 63.

6. The four-part series "Provincialism the Enemy" ran in *The New Age* XXI (12 July 1917): 244-245, XXI (19 July 1917): 268-269, XXI (26 July 1917): 288-289, and XXI (2 August 1917): 308-309.

EP's translation of Fontenelle first appeared as a twelve-part series in *The Egoist* between 1 May 1916 and June 1917. It was published in book form in October 1917 as *Dialogues of Fontenelle*, tr. Ezra Pound (London: The Egoist Ltd., 1917).

Lustra was printed for Private Circulation in New York, October 1917 (sixty copies) and was distributed *gratis* by John Quinn. Knopf, however, published a trade edition that same month.

7. This became *Ezra Pound: His Metric and Poetry*, anonymously written by T. S. Eliot (New York: Knopf, 1917) and published in conjunction with *Lustra*. Pound reviewed the ms. making corrections and changes and contributed the bibliography on pp. 29-31. See G B17.

69

EP to HM   TLS [27–30 February 1918?] 1 1 + 4 Enclosures, including a letter to ACH from Homer L. Pound dated 21 September 1917. This letter from EP to HM and the enclosures were forwarded to ACH in Santa Fe with a volume of poems by Lawrence Atkinson entitled *Aura*.

5 Holland Place Chambers, London W.8

Dear H.M.

I promised to send this book (AURA by L. Atkinson) under separate cover. to *Poetry* for review, but I find it such a bare-faced imitation of the Imagist Anthology, cadence, words etc. that I think it would be best to put it merely in the column of books received. However give it to A.C.H. my notes may amuse her.[1]

His sole contribution to original literature is the adjective "flowery-arrowed". For the rest the body of his aura is the Anthology, and, saving some modesty, my *Ripostes.*

I dont want the poor man bush-whacked or held up as an example, so I think the best plan will be to pass him in silence. It isnt so much that he is positively bad, as that he lacks the hardness, passion (of H.D. in particular) and concentration which make the anthology worth while. He is far below Fletcher or Cannell. However I promised to send the book over, so I do so.

We shall soon be as tired of, orange coloured ochre rose leaves as we now are of dove-greys and dim hair.

<Yr

E.P.>

[Enclosure 1:] Printed invitation addressed in ms. to "Mr & Mrs Henderson" reading: "Mr & Mrs. Hope Shakespear / At Home. / on the occasion of / the marriage of their daughter, / Dorothy, / to / Ezra Pound, / on Saturday, April 18th, 3:30 - 6:30. / 12 Brunswick Gardens, / Kensington, W. R.S.V.P. [The wedding was held on the morning of 20 April 1914.]

[Enclosure 2:] TS carbon of opening of letter from ACH to EP dated 17 February 1917. See Letter 63 for complete text.

[Enclosure 3]: Clipping from *Times of London* of 20 January 1914 headlined "Mr. W. S. Blunt," reporting visit on 18 January 1914 of committee of poets consisting of Yeats, Pound, John Masefield, Richard Aldington, Sturge Moore, Victor Plarr, Frederic Manning, and F. S. Flint to Wilfrid Scawen Blunt in "token of homage for his poetry." Presented to him was "a carved reliquary of Pentelican marble, the work of the sculptor Gaudier Brzeska." In response to the congratulatory poem, Blunt said of himself that "he was to some extent an impostor. He had been all sorts of other things, but never a poet. . . . He had written a certain amount of verse, but only when he was rather down on his luck and had made mistakes either in love or politics or some branch of active life. He found that it relieved his feelings." For a visual record of the visit see the well-known photograph reproduced in Carpenter, 370-371.

[Enclosure 4:] Homer L. Pound to ACH   ALS Sept. 21, 1917 1 1. With ms. addition in Pound's hand: *"found Feb. 27, 1918."*

Sept.21 — 1917

A.C.H. =

    Poetry - Chicago, Ill.

    That was a great *find* for Poetry = Aug. No. = "High C*h*in Bob."= It grip[ped] one = and I have read it to several of my friends & Hope the magazine will find us more like it.² Folks can understand that sort.=

    I am wondering if as the magazine starts out for another year, whether it will be short of one. *E.P.* or is the "Giantess" = willing to keep him on the staff = ? I know that *E.P.* - thinks A-*C-H* = about his *fir*mest friend. But, as I once had an exciting experience in Idaho with "Mountain Lions" (it was exciting for me, do not think the lions minded it very much) - when I read High Chin Bob, of course I enjoyed it more than most folks.

Yours sincerely,

US Mint Phil. Pa.   Homer L. Pound

---

    1. Lawrence Atkinson, *Aura* (London: Elkin Mathews, 1915). Five hundred copies of these pseudo-imagist poems were printed in March 1915, the first book of poetry printed that year by Mathews. In a letter to Quinn of 24 January 1917, EP cites Atkinson as a poor imitator of the Vorticists, especially Wyndham Lewis and Edward Wadsworth (*SL* 105).

    2. "High Chin Bob," *Poetry* X (August 1917): 225-227 is identified as a *"Cowboy Song - Author Unknown."*

Between February 1918 and January 1921, the date of the next letter, EP was active in London reporting on new developments for *Poetry*, the *Little Review*, and the *New Age*, while also writing music reviews as William Atheling and art reviews as B. H. Dias. He continued to translate Arnaut Daniel and other French writers, and fitfully reworked the early sections of *The Cantos*. In February 1918 he published a sixty-page essay, "A Study in French Poets," in the *Little Review* IV (1918): [3]–61; and in August, the first of three installments appeared in *The Egoist* entitled "Early Translators of Homer" (V [August 1918]: 95–97), including an essay on Andreas Divus. In April of that year his friendship with Marianne Moore began, while in June *Pavannes and Divisions* appeared in New York. In late 1918, through A. R. Orage and the *New Age*, an influential association started for EP, that with Major C. H. Douglas and his Social Credit program which was to dominate many of the poet's economic ideas. Joyce at this time had sections of *Ulysses* published in the *Little Review* (March 1918–December 1920) under EP's direction, while Yeats presented a disillusioned world in "Nineteen Hundred and Nineteen," and a disheartened Eliot awkwardly negotiated through John Quinn to get a volume published in the U.S., with *Poems by T. S. Eliot* finally appearing in February 1920.

In March 1919 sections of EP's "Propertius" appeared in *Poetry* XIII: 291–299, while in April he and Dorothy began an important walking tour of southern France, not returning to London until September when "The Chinese Written Character" began to appear in the first of four installments in the *Little Review* VI (September 1919): 62–64. In October of that year John Rodker at the Ovid Press published *The Fourth Canto*, while the Egoist Ltd. printed EP's *Quia*

Pauper Amavi in London. The year 1920 saw continued periodical publications for EP and the appearance of *Instigations* in April (NY: Boni and Liveright, 1920), as well as *Mauberley* (London: Ovid Press, 1920) in June. That same month Elkin Mathews published *Umbra: The Early Poems of Ezra Pound.* Also in June EP met Joyce for the first time at Sirmione on Lago di Garda. By early July EP was in Paris settling the Joyce family and after spending the fall in London, he and Dorothy left England permanently for France in January 1921, spending the first few months of the year in the south from where the postcard—Letter 70— was sent (Letter 70). In mid-April, however, they would move to Paris, their home for the next four years until they relocated to Rapallo.

During the 1918–1921 period ACH established her New Mexico life, studying Indian art and culture and writing new poems which appeared in *Red Earth: Poems of New Mexico* (1920). She also enlarged her Santa Fe literary circle and continued to contribute important essays and reviews to *Poetry*. Two of her most valuable are her analysis of Imagism, entitled "Imagism: Secular and Esoteric," *Poetry* XI (March 1918): 339–343, and one of the earliest and most important studies of American Indian poetry and its influence on American poets, "The Folk Poetry of These States," *Poetry* XVI (August 1920): 264–273.

70

EP to ACH   APC 25 January 1921 I I. Postcard from "Var" with photo of "Plage de Cavalière près LaVandou, Ligne du Sud de la France."

                    1921

Jan. 25. Palm leaf hut on the beach — even though
sun not at the moment blazing   =
Dare say even Santa Fe
has "*nothing* on me" for
climate.
                    aristoes,
                        E.P.

71

<12 Mars.> [1922]
70 bis, rue Notre Dame des Champs
Paris VI e.

Dear Alice:

In reply to your letters of the past decade or so and with thanks for pixtures of the Indian dances.

I dont know that there is much to say, save my communiques via books (which I can with difficulty procure in this city[)]..... you ought to wangle review copies ....

and my *Dial* letter, supposed to appear in Alternate months.[1]

La[st] winter on the Riviera. Wrote an opera, i.e. the music during the summer; at least I had the aria for half of done when I left England, and did the rest of the job here last summer.[2]

It wd. displease everyone, presumably, as it does not follow in the path of Debussy, or accord with 'Les Six' or in short please anyone save myself. However as it will never be performed, that can't be held against it. It is probably the best thing I have done. At any rate the only opera with great verse as a libretto.[3]

Have found this atelier, and hope the landlord will respect the terms of the lease . .

"Ulysses", is as you probably know "out" triumphantly and the edition probably sold by now ... without the necessity of accepting American orders ... with risk of the book being seized and the subscribers wanting their money back. Record sale for one day was 136 on last Tuesday. So thaaats that.

///

Have you a tame millionaire; or rather do you know anyone with
sense and a couple of thousand dollars a year that they care to invest
in the future of American literature. It is the half-rich who do these
things. (Thayer excepted)

The case is this[.] Eliot wd. rather work in a bank than write punk.
<H>e is NOT an object of charity.

It is also an impertinence for patrons to think they are indulging in
charity when the[y] support an artist.

They are merely doing with a little or much spare cash what the
artist does with the whole of his energy;

or with all of it he dont expend on bare living.

Eliot works in a bank, but the poems do not get written and the
world is thereby the poorer.

He broke down completely this winter. HAD to have three months
off, in which he did very possibly the most interesting 19 page poem
in the language. ~~Certainly~~ the most important poem or poem
sequence of that length in American. with ~~nothing but~~ Whitman's
Lilacs as a possible peer.[4]

He then went back to his bank, and has since got steadily
worse. *It is the greatest WASTE in contemporary letters.*
Joyce has now a permanent subsidy, not a luxurious fund,
but enough. It wd. be ample if he had not two offspring. Eliot ought
to have the same. sort of thing.
Frost who is of one tenth Eliot's importance has been given
some kind of sinecure.[5]
If Eliot were English he wd. be provided for.
As my income is about 1200 dollars a year, with luck, I can not offer
him a permanent basis of freedom[.]

Thayer is dropping $40,000 a year on the *Dial* and feels that his
offers to Eliot (space monthly ... also another EXTREMELY

generous proposition to some fourflushers who wanted to make
Eliot an editor of a magazine, but didn't come up to scratch ...)
                    anyhow Thayer is doing his bit; and there
OUGHT to be some other honest man in America. Eliot was born
in St. Louis. I dare say the culture belt ends at Chicago ?????

His family ought to be flayed and burnt in oil. However that is
impractical and the results wd probably not sell for a high figure.

Is Harriet any use ?   IS anyone any use ? They appear to pay
enormous prices for bunk <art> in Chicago ??

I suppose Harriet wd. rather go on printing poussins than be of real
use to literature ? She might of course do both.

Oh well, O hell. Its immortality for some patron if the patron exists.
And its the usual eternal shame for the country if the patron cant be
found.
                    They will
go on weeping over Poe .... oh yes, free weeps ...
Flowers on Longfellow's grave. etc.

I will do anything I can, ta<lk>, write etc...
only I am universally execrated .. and cant be of any use unless you
or someone can "put me through" to some one or some several.

                    Next Morning.
Pas de blague. Something has got to be done. I pro<po>se turning
Eliot into a limited liability company. With his poor healt<h> and
wife, the minimum necessary is £300 per year (1500 bones). I
propose to divide this into 30 guarantees of 50 dollars.[6]

Aldington and I start the show with one share each, the pledge is
annual for life, or for as long as Eliot needs it.

I can see about 20 shares. God knows where the remaining ten are
to come from.

No one to take more than two shares (100 dollars a year) Unless
some one really intelligent plute is foun[d] who will take ten shares
(500 dollars).

Please be serious. Put this up to Harriet. and to the MacWilliams,
and to Mrs. Moody, and any other possibilities.

Disgrace to America if all this cash has to be raised in bankrupt
Europe.

<yours for the heave
civilization must be
restarted>   <and r.s.v.p.>
<Ezra>

---

1. EP began to publish his "Paris Letter" in *The Dial* LXXII (January 1922);
the series continued until March 1923.

2. While staying on the Riviera during the winter of 1921-1922, EP
reworked what became *Le Testament de Villon* based on the poetry of the 15th-
century troubadour, François Villon. Set mostly in a brothel next to a cathedral,
the opera was to last an hour. On Villon see *SR* Ch.VIII.

3. The group of French composers known as Les Six included Milhaud,
Poulenc, and Auric. Cocteau became their promoter and spokesperson, Satie
their overseer. See *SL* 167.

Le Testament de Villon was performed on 29 June 1926 at the Salle Pleyel
with EP playing percussion. Joyce, Hemingway, Eliot, McAlmon, Djuna Barnes,
and Virgil Thomson were present (Carpenter 451).

4. Eliot's poem was "The Waste Land" which appeared in *Criterion* in
October 1922, *The Dial* in November 1922, and was published by Boni &
Liveright in December 1922.

EP read and edited parts of "The Waste Land" manuscript on two
occasions: in the middle of November 1921 when Eliot visited him in Paris on his
way to Lausanne for treatment with Dr. Roger Vittoz, and in January 1922
during his return trip to London. In addition to the final 19-page typescript, the
surviving manuscript contains a mixture of holograph drafts, fair copies, and
typescripts totalling 54 leaves and approximately 1000 lines of poetry. Pound
reduced this to 434 lines, Eliot himself discarding lines 1-54 of the original
opening, "He Do the Police in Different Voices: Part I. The Burial of the Dead."
Notably, EP cut 70 lines of Popian couplets plus other passages from "Part 3.
The Fire Sermon," totalling some 130 lines; he also deleted some 80 lines in part
4, "Death by Water." In all, EP altered or removed some 350-400 lines of the
poem.

By February 1922 EP was celebrating the poem to Quinn in New York:
"about enough, Eliot's poem, to make the rest of us shut up shop," characteristi-
cally adding, however, that "I haven't done so; have in fact knocked out another
Canto (not in the least *à la Eliot*, or connected with 'modern life') . . ." (*EP/JQ*

206). *The Waste Land: A Facsimile and Transcript*, ed. Valerie Eliot (New York: Harcourt Brace Jovanovich, 1971) is a vivid record of EP's editorial commentary and excisions.

Whitman's "When Lilacs Last in the Dooryard Bloom'd," written in response to the assassination of President Lincoln, first appeared in *Drum Taps and Sequel* (October 1865) and was later added to *Leaves of Grass*. EP admired Whitman for forging an American poetic voice and expressing the "American keynote . . . a certain generosity; a certain carelessness or looseness . . . a desire for largeness, a willingness to stand exposed" (*Selected Prose* 123). EP's 1909 essay, "What I Feel about Walt Whitman" (*Selected Prose* 145-146) and his poem "A Pact," in which he writes, "It was you that broke the new wood, / Now is a time for carving" (*P* 90) confirm Whitman's importance for EP.

5. In October 1921 Frost was offered a $5000 fellowship from the University of Michigan to be poet-in-residence. He accepted and stayed on for a second year.

6. EP's concern over the recurrence of Eliot's breakdown following his treatment in Lausanne led to his "Bel Esprit" project of 1922 (named by Natalie Barney) to generate funds to permit Eliot to quit his position at Lloyds Bank. "Not charity" but the "release of energy for invention and design," EP stated to Agnes Bedford (*SL* 173; Carpenter 409). Circulars were prepared and retracted because Eliot objected to the mention of his employer. EP obtained 21 of the 33 required subscribers but the plan eventually faltered for lack of funds and the emergence of a rival program, Lady Ottoline Morrell's Eliot Fellowship Trust. In 1923, however, EP sent Eliot £120, the total collected. On "Bel Esprit," see EP, "Credit and the Fine Arts," *New Age* XXX (30 March 1922): 284-285 and "Paris Letter," *Dial* LXXIII (September 1922): [322]-337; also *G* E2e.

Correspondence between EP and ACH from March 1922 to January 1931 has not been located. During those years, however, EP frequently visited Italy, settling permanently in Rapallo in February 1925, the year Mussolini established his dictatorship. He also developed new interests in Confucius, Thomas Jefferson, and Frobenius, edited and published four issues of *Exile* and continued to draft his *Cantos*, publishing *A Draft of XVI Cantos* (1925), *A Draft of the Cantos 17-27* (1928), and *A Draft of XXX Cantos* (1930), as well as *Personae* (1926). He also began his relationship with Olga Rudge whom he met at the beginning of 1923 and who moved to Venice in 1929 and later to Sant'Ambrogio above Rapallo.

Alice Corbin Henderson during this time extended her Santa Fe literary circle, beginning a friendship with D. H. Lawrence who visited in the fall of 1922, collected important poetry from Southwest writers which she edited in *The Turquoise Trail: An Anthology of New Mexico Poetry* (Boston & NY: Houghton Mifflin, 1928), and wrote new poetry which appeared in *The Sun Turns West* (Santa Fe: Writers Editions, 1933). She also continued to contribute to *Poetry* and correspond with Harriet Monroe.

7 2

via Marsala, 12 int.5, Rapallo

24 Jan. 1931   <Italy>

Dear Alice

I have been asked to do a SMALL anthology, for Italian use. That is very limited 200 copies, no pay for anyone, can't be. Scheiwiller stands a loss on every book he prints but they are usually very nice books (neat, not de luxe).

What I propose to do is to tell the story (as I have seen it) in poems that I still remember.

<Book may orient a few of the younger wops not startin to read American>

I want to use that "One House only" or whatever its title was, that I had in the Cat. Anth. in B.C. whenever it was.[1]

My introd. says that the list of contents has been made out from memory and without opening a book, that ought to give one sort of test, one dimension at least, without getting into academic solemnity, pretending to ascribe merit and pass grades :: and without the strain and hypocracy of putting in a lot of rot from a sense of gorsloppum duty or justice or whatever.

Heaven knows where you are // and equally WHY you never come east.

Benedictions

<E.P.>

1. EP means "One City Only," which he included on pages 20-21 of *Catholic Anthology, 1914-1915* (1915).

EP's project became the 142-page *Profile: An Anthology Collected in MCMXXXI*, ed. Ezra Pound (Milan: Giovanni Scheiwiller, 1932). 250 numbered copies were printed with the following note by EP: "A collection of poems which have stuck in my memory and which may possibly define their epoch, or at least rectify current ideas of it in respect to at least one contour."

In addition to six poems by EP, one by Joyce, four by Williams, three by Eliot, and five by Marianne Moore, it contained one poem by each of the following: Hemingway, Yeats, Zukofsky, Bunting, and ACH.

73

ACH to EP   TLS 8 February 1931 1 1 + 1 Enclosure. Beinecke.
ACH's response to EP's letter of 24 January 1931 (Letter 72) asking
permission to use her poem "One City Only" in a new anthology
proposed by Scheiwiller.

Santa Fe, New Mexico

Sunday, Feb, 8. '31

Dear Ezra: —
   "One City Only" is yours —
I enclose also "Love Me At Last" which you mentioned as liking, I
think it was in "Instigations." Send me your book for the "Wops." I
may be out of touch, but I am still among the quick, and not the
dead, in more senses than one.
   More anon — and I am glad to have your personal address. . . .

   Yours ever,

      <Alice Corbin>

Alice Corbin Henderson
Box 444, Santa Fe.
New Mexico, U.S.A.

▬▬▬ [Enclosure 1:]

LOVE ME AT LAST

Love me at last, or if you will not,
   Leave me;
Hard words could never, as these half-words,
   Grieve me:
Love me at last — or leave me.

Love me at last, or let the last word uttered
    Be but your own;
Love me, or leave me — as a cloud, a vapor,
    Or a bird flown.
Love me at last — I am but sliding water
    Over a stone.

                Alice Corbin

74

EP to ACH   Typed postcard 10 October 1933 + 1 Enclosure. Addressed to "Mrs W.P. Henderson, Writers Edtns /, P/O/ Box 822, Sante Fe, New Mex, U.S. AMerica."

via Marsala, 12 int.5, Rapallo

<10 Oct> [1933]

Dear ACH

your're a bit chary of news. And postag stamps now cost 7 cents. / Why dont youze guys HOOK up / various associations for unpopular books ought to join each other for mutual boost. ref / Bill Williams and Zuk's new project. OUGHT to unite. I dont spose Writer's edtns / WANTS any outside material??[1] There is an excellent trans / of Cocteau's *Mystere Laic* that ought to be brought out.[2] John's took to sending rubber chqs / and I dont want to get Cocteau into another fizzle.

Have at last an English pubr / who seems to function but America STILL 20 years behind the world.[3] Wot do you do with all yr / time. What about the OLD OLDE effort to edderkate Harriet ??

[Typed up left margin:]
or is there ANY other object more likely to advance?

[Typed on left front:]
where do you print what you writ or what you dont? And who zoo in murka ? . Active Anth. due out in Eng / day after tomorrow.[4] U.S. still following Louie Untermeyer, or wottell ? Sent you local bulletin. The Chilesotti stuff exceptionally fine[5] / Pier della Francesca quality.

yrs E.P. <E.P.>

[Enclosure 1:]
                Printed program in Italian of a concert series offered at the "Gran Sala del Municipio di Rapallo" during the 1933-1934 season

(10 October 1933 to March 1934) performed by Olga Rudge, violin; Gerhart Münch, piano; Luigi Sansoni, violin; and Marco Ottone, cello. The program includes a printed statement by EP dated 6-9-XI [1933], reprinted from *Il Mare*, on *Settimana Mozartiana* and the transcriptions of Oscar Chilesotti. Typewritten across the top of page I is "via Marsala 12/5."

1. The Objectivist Press, started in June 1932, was financed by George Oppen and had as one of its first but uncompleted projects the publication of EP's collected prose. On its advisory board were EP, Williams, and Zukofsky. The press was best known for publishing *An 'Objectivists' Anthology*, ed. Louis Zukofsky (Le Beausset, Var, France & New York, New York: Objectivist Press, 1932). Maurice Darantière in Dijon, who printed Joyce's *Ulysses*, also printed this volume.

Writers Editions was the publishing company ACH established in Santa Fe organized "to publish books of unusual quality at a moderate price," stressing limited editions of "living poets and writers." Each copy of the 250-500 print run was numbered and signed by the author (advt. circular, Writers Editions).

2. Jean Cocteau, *Le Mystère laïc, essai d'etude indirecte, avec cinq dessins de Giorgio de Chirico* (Paris: Editions des Quatre Chemins, 1928).

3. Faber & Faber, earlier Faber & Gwyer when EP began to publish with them in November 1928, the month *Selected Poems*, edited and introduced by Eliot, appeared.

4. *Active Anthology*, published 12 October 1933 by Faber & Faber contained work by poets "in whose verse a development appears . . . to be taking place," Pound announced [5]. Included in the collection is work by William Carlos Williams, Basil Bunting, Louis Aragon, Louis Zukofsky, e.e. cummings, Ernest Hemingway, Marianne Moore, George Oppen, D. G. Bridson, T. S. Eliot, and EP.

5. EP refers to the six-part concert series devoted to work by Corelli, Purcell, Ravel, Scriabine, and others based on transcriptions by the Italian musicologist Oscar Chilesotti (1848-1916), best known for his study of the lute. The series took place at the Gran Sala del Municipio di Rapallo from October 1933 to March 1934 and was performed by Olga Rudge, Gerhart Münch, Luigi Sansoni, and Marco Ottone. See description of Enclosure 1, this letter.

75

ACH to EP   ALS 2 January 1934 I 1. Beinecke.

Box 444, Santa Fe, N.M.
January 2 — 1934.

Dear Ezra Pound: —

I sent you my book today — by registered mail —[1]

If you feel like saying anything about the book, you might say it for Orage.[2]

We're friends — he spent a month in Santa Fe several years ago — His copy & other review copies won't go out for a week or two — as my part of the editions got bound before Xmas.

A Happy New Year to you & best wishes from

Yours as ever

Alice Corbin

---

1. *The Sun Turns West* (Santa Fe: Writers Editions, 1933).

2. A. R. Orage (1873-1934), editor of *The New Age* from 1907-1922 and in many ways mentor to EP in England between 1911 and 1920. Between 1928-1930 Orage lived in the United States.

76

EP to ACH   TLS 17 March 1939 1 l. Stationery printed with Gaudier-Brzeska profile of EP.

Via Marsala 12-5, Rapallo

17 March <'39>

Dear A/C/H

Do you ever get as far east as Chicago?
I dont see that [I] can git as far inland as Noo Mex
even supposing I emigrate[.]¹

I send this via *Poetry*/ as last address of yrs/ in my ad/ bk/
seems so very antient.

<Yours EP>

1. On 13 April 1939 EP sailed from Genoa to the United States, arriving on the 21st—his first trip back since 1911. He visited New York, Washington, Cambridge, MA, New Haven, CT, and Clinton, NY, but not Chicago nor certainly New Mexico.

EP's life between 1939 (Letter 76) and 1948/49 (Letters 77, 78) was as eventful as it was turbulent. Following his return to Italy in July 1939 from his four-month trip to America, Pound found that the impending world conflict—Britain and France declared war on Germany only two and a half months later—seriously altered his personal life. As Italy's involvement with the war increased, EP shifted between the safety of Rapallo, with occasional visits to Siena (where Olga Rudge assisted with Count Chigi's annual Accademia Musicale) and the turmoil of Rome. At one point, in early September 1943, with the Allies landing at Salerno and daily expected in German-occupied Rome, EP undertook a dangerous 450-mile journey—a good part of it on foot from Rome to the Tyrol to visit his daughter Mary.

EP's radio broadcasts for the Fascist Ministry of Popular Culture began in January 1941 and continued until July 1943. He recorded these broadcasts in a Rome studio on the Via Veneto and would frequently spend several weeks a month taping a series of talks. Usually aired twice a week on a short-wave program beamed to Europe, England, North America, and the Pacific entitled "The American Hour," the inflammatory broadcasts frequently accused the U.S. government and its leaders of immoral behavior while defending Pound's own position as a loyal American. Following the downfall of Mussolini in July 1943, EP continued to contribute scripts for Mussolini's short-lived Salò Republic from the autumn of 1943 until the government collapsed in the spring of 1945.

Despite the war, Pound continued to publish, concentrating on prose, notably journalism, a translation of Confucius, and political and economic pamphlets. Social thought, not poetry, absorbed him. *What is Money For?* (1939), *Carta da Visita* (1943), *L'America, Roosevelt e le Cause Della Guerra Presente* (1944), and *Testamento di Confucio* (1944) are four representative titles. Faber, however, published *Cantos LII–LXXI* (completed in 1939) in 1940, as well as *A Selection of Poems* (1940). EP's journalism appeared largely in *Meridiano di Roma, Giornale di Genova,* and *Il Popolo di Alessandria.* His two Italian cantos, numbered LXXII and LXXIII, were published in 1945 in the Venetian paper *Marina Repubblicana,* although they were not included with *The Cantos* until Mary de Rachewiltz's dual language edition published by Mondadori appeared in 1985.

On 26 July 1943, the day after Mussolini resigned, a grand jury in Washington, DC, indicted EP for treason because his radio broadcasts were declared to freely give "the enemies of the United States aid and comfort." News of the indictment did not deter EP who continued to submit scripts to the reconstituted Mussolini government. However, on 3 May 1945, approximately a week after Mussolini was killed, EP was arrested by partisans at Casa 60 in Sant'Ambrogio, Olga Rudge's apartment above Rapallo, and taken to Genoa where, after several weeks of confusion and cables to Washington, he was taken to the Disciplinary Training Center at Pisa on 24 May 1945. He spent the first three weeks of what was nearly a six-month imprisonment in an exposed, reinforced steel cage. While at the DTC, EP translated Confucius and composed what would become *The Pisan Cantos* until his sudden removal to Washington on 16 November 1945.

Following arraignment on 19 November 1945, EP was recommended for an extended psychiatric examination which concluded with a jury hearing on 13 February 1946 which determined that EP was of unsound mind and not fit to stand trial for treason. Judge Bolitha Laws, presiding, then declared that EP be permanently committed to St. Elizabeths Hospital in southeast Washington, DC, where he had earlier been sent for examination. While at St. Elizabeths in 1948 and 1949, EP achieved notoriety if not fame with the publication of *The Pisan Cantos* and the first collected edition of *The Cantos,* both appearing in July 1948. In February 1949, he was awarded the first Bollingen Prize for Poetry for *The Pisan Cantos,* given amid controversy by the Library of Congress.

EP remained at St. Elizabeths, writing, translating, and instructing disciples and visitors, until his release, facilitated by Robert Frost and Archibald MacLeish, at age seventy-two in April 1958. He returned to Italy on July 9th, first to Brunnenburg in Alta Adige to live with his daughter Mary and then, restless and in poor health, to Rapallo, Rome, and, finally, Venice where he died at age eighty-seven on 1 November 1972; his grave is on the island of San Michele in the Venetian lagoon.

In the decade between 1939 and 1949, Alice Corbin Henderson continued to participate in the cultural activities of Santa Fe, although she published no more material after 1937. Her husband died in 1943, and Henderson's own health gradually began to deteriorate; she died at the age of sixty-eight in July 1949.

77

ACH to EP ALS 24 August 1948 | l. Lilly Library.

Sun Mount, Santa Fe, New Mexico.

Saturday Night.
August 24-48

Dear Ezra -

Hal Bynner & I are sitting together at a Fiesta party, with guitars & voices going, but talking of you.[1] He brought me news of seeing you in Washington & I am remembering old days when we wrote so constantly — although we never met. I have always cherished our real friendship — this is just a little gesture of our continuing affection — in spite of the hub-bub —

affectionately,

Alice Corbin -

1. In 1908 as poetry editor of *McClure's*, Bynner briefly met EP before his departure for Europe. EP revisited him on his 1910-1911 trip to the U.S. and Bynner helped him place his first book published in the states, *Provença*, printed in Boston by Small Maynard and Company in November 1910. In November-December 1947 Bynner (who had been sending books to EP) visited the poet at St. Elizabeths. (See Bynner 193-194, *SL* 15-16, and *EP/JQ* 72 for EP's early and unflattering views of Bynner.) Bynner moved to Santa Fe in the summer of 1922 and quickly became friends with ACH with whom he had corresponded as early as 1912 when a group of his poems appeared in *Poetry* I (February 1913): 150-159.

78

EP to ACH   ALS 11 April 1949 1 l. Addressed to "Alice Corbin Henderson / El Cuervo Ranch / RFD Tesuque / Santa Fe, N.Mex " by EP who wrote from St. Elizabeths Hospital, Washington, DC. Stationery has large half circle printed with the following at the top: "J'AYME DONC JE SUIS."

---

11 Ap [49]
S. Liz
D.C.

Yaas 'm'
    Thank you —
can't read names of
yr witnesses but
wd be glad know
who are.[1]

Sar *asa*ti? which
gd' son or wot.
if you d print 'em
like yr address.

         Happy Daze
           Yrz
             EZ

---

1. It appears that EP wrote this concluding letter upon receiving a copy of "Alice Corbin: An Appreciation," a special issue of the *New Mexico Quarterly Review* 19 (Spring 1949): 33-79, published in her honor shortly before her death in July 1949. Edited by Witter Bynner and Oliver La Farge, the section blends biographical accounts of her life and her contributions to Santa Fe culture with analyses of her poetry, notably *Red Earth* (1920), and her prose narrative, *Brothers of Light, the Penitentes of the Southwest* (1937). The participants were Witter Bynner, George Dillon, John Gould Fletcher, Carl Sandburg, Padraic Colum,

Ruth Laughlin, Haniel Long, Spud Johnson, and Oliver La Farge. Three previously unpublished poems by ACH also appear.

EP's reference to Sarasate in the next paragraph appears to be a response to ACH's poem "Music" cited by Padraic Colum (ibid., 57). EP, however, misunderstands the allusion to the Spanish violinist and composer (see Letter 44, note 1, and Canto 80/517). In the poem, which appeared in *Poetry* VII (January 1916): 166, Henderson describes how old songs and musicians are forgotten, concluding with the lines:

> The old songs
> Die—
> And the lips that sang them.
> Wreaths, withered and dusty,
> Cuff-buttons with royal insignia,
> These, in a musty museum,
> Are all that is left of Sarasate.

Thirty-three years earlier, from Coleman's Hatch with Yeats, EP told HM that two poems by ACH in the January number of *Poetry* were the "best," adding that although he favored "One City Only," "the Sarasate poem, with its memory of Spanish metre, is also good" (*SL* 67).

Selected Bibliography

Bynner, Witter. *The Selected Letters of Witter Bynner*. Edited by
　　　　James Kraft. New York: Farrar Straus Giroux, 1981.
Carpenter, Humphrey. *A Serious Character: The Life of Ezra Pound*.
　　　　London: Faber and Faber, 1988.
Ellmann, Richard. *James Joyce*. Rev. ed. New York: Oxford University Press, 1982.
Hoffman, Frederick J., et al. *The Little Magazine: A History and
　　　　Bibliography*. Princeton: Princeton University Press,
　　　　1947.
Homberger, Eric, ed. *Ezra Pound: The Critical Heritage*. London:
　　　　Routledge and Kegan Paul, 1972.
Joost, Nicholas. *Years of Transition: The Dial 1912-1920*. Barre, MA:
　　　　Barre Publishers, 1967.
Kenner, Hugh. *The Pound Era*. Berkeley: University of California
　　　　Press, 1971.
Longenbach, James. *Stone Cottage, Pound, Yeats, and Modernism*. New
　　　　York: Oxford University Press, 1988.
Monroe, Harriet. *A Poet's Life*. New York: Macmillan, 1938.
Nelson, James G. *Elkin Mathews*. Madison: University of Wisconsin
　　　　Press, 1989.
Pound, Ezra. *The Cantos*. 11th printing. New York: New Directions,
　　　　1989.
———. *Guide to Kulchur*. 1938. New York: New Directions, 1968.
Pound/Joyce: The Letters of Ezra Pound to James Joyce. Edited by
　　　　Forrest Read. New York: New Directions, 1970.
———. *Selected Prose, 1909-1915*. Edited by William Cookson. New
　　　　York: New Directions, 1973.

Reid, B. L. *The Man from New York: John Quinn and His Friends.*
New York: Oxford University Press, 1968.

Stock, Noel. *The Life of Ezra Pound.* Rev. ed. San Francisco: North
Point Press, 1982.

Terrell, Carroll F. *A Companion to the Cantos of Ezra Pound.* 2 vols.
Berkeley: University of California Press, 1980.

Thompson, Lawrence. *Robert Frost.* 3 vols. New York: Holt,
Rinehart & Winston, 1970, 1976.

Wilhelm, J. J. *Ezra Pound in London and Paris 1908-1925.* University
Park: Pennsylvania State University Press, 1990.

Williams, Ellen. *Harriet Monroe and The Poetry Renaissance: The First
Ten Years of Poetry, 1912-1922.* Urbana: University of
Illinois Press, 1977.

Index